SILVER BONANZA

How to Profit from the Coming Bull Market in Silver

JAMES U. BLANCHARD III

SIMON & SCHUSTER

New York London Toronto Sydney Tokyo Singapore

SIMON & SCHUSTER
Rockefeller Center
1230 Avenue of the Americas
New York, New York 10020

Designed by Irving Perkins Associates, Inc.

Manufactured in the United States of America

10   9   8   7   6   5   4   3   2   1

Library of Congress Cataloging-in-Publication Data
Blanchard, James U.
    Silver bonanza : how to profit from the coming bull market in silver / James U.
Blanchard III.—Rev. ed.
        p.   cm.
    Includes bibliographical references (p.   ).
    1. Silver—United States.   2. Silver—Prices—United States.   3. Futures.
4. Options.   5. Speculation.   I. Title.
HG307.U5B55   1995
332.63—dc20   94-38861
                                                                                        CIP

ISBN: 0-671-50297-2

Silver Bonanza™ is a trademark of Jefferson Financial, Inc.

Acknowledgments

In my college days back in the 1960s, my primary areas of study were economics and history. At the same time, my main form of savings consisted of keeping all the silver change I received. So it was natural that silver, and its history as a form of money, began to interest me on an academic level.

Consequently, I began to read all the books I could find on silver, and soon became convinced that the metal was, indeed, an excellent investment. (At about the same time, Lyndon Baines Johnson saw things differently and replaced the last circulating hard money of the world with our present copper nickel tokens.)

Over the coming years, as inflation and the prices of precious metals steadily rose, I had a persistent urge to write a book on silver and its value as an investment. But I was young and there were so many things I wanted to do; so the book was pushed aside, although never forgotten. Then silver went to $50 an ounce in 1980, and I didn't think I would ever have a chance to write my book.

Now silver has returned to multidecade lows, and the long-term outlook for the metal as an investment is even more exciting than it had been in the late 1960s. In fact, there is now a great case for a private re-monetization of silver, which would add to the metal's coming bull market.

So, in March 1993, up in my Blue Ridge Mountain retreat, I pulled out several boxes of collected material and began what I thought would be a twelve-page special report on silver. To make a long story short, that twelve-page report turned into a fifty-page analysis of silver as an investment.

But that just whetted my appetite. In the thirty years that I have been following the precious metals, there has never before been a really well-done, comprehensive book on silver, from its earliest historical role as money to its role as an investment today.

I realized the time had come for the quintessential guide to silver investing, a book that would cover thousands of years of history as well as explain the new factors in silver's supply/demand dynamic and countless other factors that investors have to consider before they can realize the full potential of this most versatile metal.

I realized that this book had to be written and that I had to be the one to do it.

But it was a big job, and I needed a partner and collaborator in the project. My longtime friend Bob Meier suggested that the perfect person for the job was Franklin Sanders, one of today's most eloquent advocates of sound money.

I couldn't have been happier with the result of our collaboration. In my opinion (and with all modesty in regard to my contributions), the book you see before you is the most comprehensive, detailed, and useful research work on silver ever created, and it could not have been possible without the tireless efforts, extraordinary dedication, and unique talents of Franklin Sanders. I owe him a debt of deep gratitude for his help in creating this remarkable work.

In addition to Franklin, I would like specifically to thank Jerome Smith, who first introduced me to silver as an investment in 1967. I would also like to acknowledge the late Verne Myers for his early guidance on silver in the 1960s. Thanks also go to the other early, hard-money investment writers from the late '60s and early '70s, including Harry Schultz, Richard Russell, and Franz Pick.

As to the wider question of money and its role in a free society, my greatest debt is to Ludwig Von Mises. In particular, I would like to acknowledge F. A. Hayek, the Nobel laureate whose 1975 speech on money privatization at my investment conference in Switzerland spawned his various writings on free market competition in money and the whole issue of legal tender.

Within my own company, many thanks to Lisa Herring for her unflagging efforts in the various stages of this book's production, to Rick Thayne and Dave Tomsick for their herculean efforts in getting this book to press, and to Brien Lundin, my friend and editor of much of my writing.

If many, many friends had not extended their hands, lent books and documents, and discussed perplexing aspects of silver's story, this book would never have seen the light of day. I want to thank especially Robert

Meier, without whose unflagging encouragement and open-handed help I would never have dared to undertake a project this big; Elizabeth Currier, who has made possible so much education for so many; John Lutley of the Silver Institute, who was always ready to help; Don Daisley, who has brought so much to my attention; Dick Solyom, who kindly loaned me out-of-print Del Mar books; Ellice MacDonald, who made available Elgin Groseclose's invaluable work; Paul Ward of Kodak, for his clear, patient explanations; Glenn Dobbs, William Green, and Berry Huelsman, who provided so much material on mining stocks; Steve Puetz and James Turk, who always made time for my questions; Lowell H. Becraft, Jr., and Dr. Edwin Vieira, Jr., who patiently explained the intricacies of monetary law and history; Michael Buettner at Elliot Wave International; Timothy Green, for points about silver use in China; Art Brown of Hecla Mining and Dennis Wheeler of Coeur d'Alene Mines, for patient and informative interviews; Shantilal Sonawala, for his thorough information about silver use in India; and Susan Sanders, who helped in a thousand ways.

All my own efforts and those of this outstanding roster of contributors would not, however, have achieved so splendid a forum as this Simon & Schuster book had it not been for the encouragement and representation of my literary agent, Michael Baybak, to whom I owe a special thanks.

Last, but not least, I would like to thank my wife, Lesia, for her advice and counsel.

—James U. Blanchard III

Contents

Chapter 3   DEMAND EXPLODES IN ASIA   62

Chapter 4   THE GOLD–SILVER RATIO   80

Chapter 5   THE TECHNICAL EDGE   87

Chapter 6   INVESTING IN SILVER: AN INTRODUCTION   102

Chapter 7   INVESTING IN PHYSICAL SILVER   111

Chapter 8   COLLECTIBLES, NUMISMATICS, AND THE MATHEMATICS OF SILVER   128

Introduction

A Once-in-a-Lifetime Opportunity

This book could literally change your life. Why? Because only once, maybe twice in a lifetime are you given the opportunity to participate in an investment bull market of such magnitude that you cannot only realize huge profits, but actually become independently wealthy. I believe silver will be *the* investment for the rest of the 1990s, and in the following pages I will explain exactly how you can profit from the coming boom in silver prices.

The quote that begins this book, *"The major monetary metal in history is silver, not gold,"* was told to me by the world's greatest living economist, Nobel laureate Milton Friedman. This statement is significant not only because it comes from one of the great minds of the twentieth century, but also because it offers the prime reason why the roaring bull market now beginning in silver is not just a short-term phenomenon.

It is not a bull market that will last for only a few months or even a year or two. It is a bull market with the power of history behind it— one of truly epic proportions that promises to last well into the next century. We are already in the very early stages of a massive sea change in monetary, economic, and investment trends, all of which are converging to propel silver prices to levels that even I may be unable to imagine.

All around us, we see evidence of new megatrends that are changing the world as we know it: the collapse of the Soviet Union, the worldwide rush toward free-market economic systems, the shift of economic power and wealth from Europe and North America to Asia, and a technological revolution destined to carry far more impact than even the industrial revolution of the nineteenth century. Investment analysts have talked endlessly of how these megatrends will affect world stock, bond, currency, real estate, and commodity markets. But there is one little-known investment that will be the *prime beneficiary* of this great transition during the rest of the '90s and into the next century.

That investment is silver.

In the past thirty-two years, I have been involved in many successful business ventures. I began a company with $50, built it into a $115 million-a-year industry leader, and sold it to the third largest corporation in America. I started a mutual fund group long before mutual funds were as popular as they are today: The Blanchard Group of Mutual Funds has since invested *billions* of dollars. I have published an investment magazine and many investment newsletters, including *Gold Newsletter,* the world's largest precious metals newsletter, now in its twenty-fifth year of continuous publication. I am cofounder and copublisher of the largest circulation investment newsletter in financial publishing history, *Louis Rukeyser's Wall Street,* with four hundred thousand subscribers. My business interests include a small oil and gas firm, heavy involvement in the gold and silver mining industry, and a seemingly endless variety of other ventures. Over the years, I have made millions of dollars as a private investor, the vast majority of which have come from the precious metals sector of the markets.

I say these things not to pat myself on the back. I owe this success (and all the adventure and fun that have gone with it) to the marvelous American free-market system, to some luck, and to a lot of hard work. Rather, I mention these various business investment successes to assure you that I am not some Johnny-come-lately investment analyst pushing a new investment fad, like the latest tip from your stockbroker.

My interest in silver began many years ago. In fact, my earliest business success came from buying silver and silver coins to pay my way through college. Since then, I have been a big winner in each bull market in silver, managing to ride the tide of all these very exciting and profitable waves.

But I can tell you now that in all my thirty-two years of involvement in many different investments and businesses, I have *never* seen a more extraordinary investment opportunity than silver offers today. It compares to such once-in-a-lifetime opportunities as buying into the stock market at the lows of the 1930s, buying computer stocks in the late 1960s, and buying prime agricultural land at $10 to $25 per acre.

It is impossible for an investment analyst to tell you precisely how high any investment will go. But the very *minimum* price I expect for silver during the rest of the 1990s is $30 per ounce. And there are many powerful factors that could send it to $50 or even $75 per ounce between now and the end of this century.

WHY THIS BOOK?

This book is designed to give you everything you need to know to be among the smart, foresighted investors who will make fortunes in silver during the rest of the 1990s. In putting this book together, I have combined my extensive knowledge of silver and the silver markets into a concise "why-to, how-to, and where-to" guide that will help you to profit in one of the most extraordinary bull markets in history. Once I get involved in a major new investment trend, not just a simple market trade, it becomes a passion for me, a total commitment not to let *anything* sidetrack me from my long-term investment goal. This book is designed to give you the same knowledge, commitment, and courage to make the basic decision to be a long-term silver bull. And once you are committed, this book will give you the specifics on how and where to invest in silver, including bullion, coins, options, futures, and silver mining stocks.

By the late 1990s, thousands of investors will wonder in hindsight why they didn't have the foresight to participate in the great silver bull market of the 1990s—why they missed the opportunity of a lifetime. The reason is simple: Silver is the best-kept secret in the investment world today. Amazingly, with very few exceptions, the hundreds of thousands of money managers around the world have ignored the powerful potential of silver. The major financial media have completely disregarded the metal, and nearly every investment advisory newsletter in the United States has failed even to mention it.

When you thoroughly understand how the markets behave and how market opportunities are created, this is not surprising. When an investment is grossly undervalued and trading is at historical lows, most investors—both institutions and individuals—are blinded by the pessimism associated with bear market bottoms and the early stages of bull markets. But when an investment is *overvalued* and soaring toward its peak, most money managers are fully committed, and individual investors tend to jump in with both feet. That is when the major financial media are full of bullish headlines about an investment that in reality should be *sold,* not bought.

That is the way markets have always been and will always be. So in the final analysis, this book is designed to put you among the few investors who are bold enough to go against the crowd. If you follow the advice in these pages, you will be *selling* your silver at tomorrow's peak to the vast majority of investors who are not interested in silver today.

HOW MUCH MONEY COULD YOU *REALLY* MAKE FROM SILVER?

To answer that question, let's look at some recent history. Silver prices soared from $1.32 per ounce in 1971 to $52.50 in 1980—a leap of more than 3,800 percent. It's not often that you have the chance to muliply your money thirty-nine times over. Yet, as this book will show you, silver offers *even greater potential today than it did in 1971,* due to a better supply/demand picture and more sophisticated methods of investing.

But perhaps a better way to look at the upside potential of silver is to illustrate how grossly undervalued the metal truly is. Some of history's most successful investors, such as Bernard Baruch, J. Paul Getty, and Warren Buffet, became not just millionaires, but billionaires, by learning an important lesson: Buy an investment when it is out of favor with 99.9 percent of all other investors. Buy real value and have the courage to stick with it over the long term. *Buy an investment that is at historical lows.*

That is a perfect picture of today's technical and fundamental outlook for silver. In fact, from its high of $52.50 in 1980 to its low of $3.50 in 1993, silver experienced one of the deepest bear markets ever recorded. The three greatest commodity bear markets in this century have been the 97 percent decline in sugar between 1920 and 1932; the 94 percent decline in sugar in from 1980 to 1986; and the 93 percent decline in silver between 1980 and 1993. Because the 1980–93 bear market in silver has been one of epic proportions, it is perfectly understandable why investors have turned against the commodity. But a careful study of these rare and extreme market collapses that leave unprecedented real value in their wake leads to an important investment conclusion: *The bull market that follows such collapses is powerful and unstoppable.* For this and literally dozens of other technical and fundamental reasons, thoroughly explained in this book, now is the time to buy silver.

TIME TO LEARN, TIME TO ACT

The bull market in silver is just beginning. That's why this book is so important to you. It gives you the chance to be light-years ahead of not only the average investor but the world's superrich as well. The billions of dollars *not* interested in silver as an investment today will rush into silver as the 1990s unfold.

Finally, there is one more reason why this book is so important: It provides everything you need to know to participate in an investment of unprecedented promise, one that can give you the chance to change your life completely and fulfill personal goals and dreams. Whether it is your dream house, a sailboat, world travel, a second home in the country, more leisure time with your family, or the chance to be your own boss— all these things can be yours—if you follow the advice in this book step by step and have the boldness to *act now.*

It is well known that the advice in most investment books, once read, is not seriously followed. But if you have a real determination to get involved as a major silver investor, implement the goals and strategies in these pages, and *stick with the long-term trend,* you will succeed when most others will fail. Many millionaires and multimillionaires will be made in the coming boom in silver prices, but it is up to you whether to participate. And that is the ultimate purpose of this book—to encourage you to seize this opportunity to secure your financial future and make all of your dreams come true.

The major monetary metal in history is silver, not gold.
—Nobel laureate MILTON FRIEDMAN
In an interview with James U. Blanchard III for the
20th Anniversary New Orleans Investment
Conference, November 7, 1993

Chapter 1

SILVER:
THE USEFUL METAL

Imagine for a moment that we are watching a typical American, John Q. Public. At six o'clock, his electric alarm clock buzzes to awaken him. He reaches for the wall switch beside his head to flick on the light, and peers sleepily at his watch.

John stretches, then shuffles into the bathroom, where he flicks on another light and gazes at his image in the mirror. Once he finishes his shower, he walks into the kitchen. John fills his coffee cup with water from the tap and sticks the cup in the microwave. He selects the time on the number pad and pushes "Start" to heat the water for his morning coffee. Whoops—he notices that Mrs. Public forgot to turn on the dishwasher last night, so he closes it and flips the switch.

From the refrigerator he pulls out bacon, places several strips in a frying pan, and turns on the stove. John notices that the picture of his family from last year's summer vacation is hanging crooked on the wall, so while he waits for his bacon to fry, he straightens it. Just as he is removing the bacon from the skillet, grease pops up on his hand, leaving a nasty burn. He opens the cabinet door where his wife keeps the burn ointment and places a dab of soothing cream on his hand.

After breakfast, John dresses in his wool and polyester blend suit, then runs into his study to work just a minute on his personal computer. He flips it on and types in a few notes. Minutes later, he hurries from the kitchen door to his car. He inserts the key and turns it, releasing the door locks. He hops in and starts the car. Mrs. Public left the seat too far forward. He reaches for the power switch, scoots the seat back, then lowers the electric window just a crack. The air is brisk. There is a trace of frost on his back window, so he turns on the rear window defroster.

What is unusual about this morning in the life of a typical American before he even leaves his home? Why, nothing at all—but every move we have described *required the help of silver*.

John's clock uses a reliable, long-life silver battery, as does his watch. The electric wall switches in his house all use silver, because it resists pitting caused by spark gaps when electrical contacts are interrupted. His mirror gets its perfect reflectiveness from silver, and his drinking water filter uses silver to prevent bacteria growth in the filter medium. John's microwave is controlled by a membrane switch panel with silver contacts. The same reliable silver device is used in his personal computer keyboard.

The photograph of Mr. Public's family would be impossible without the sensitivity to light of silver-halide compounds. The tubing in the cooling system of John's refrigerator is joined with reliable silver brazing. His dishwasher and stove employ silver contacts in relays and switches. When John burns himself, he uses an ointment made of silver-sulfadiazine that both promotes healing and prevents infection—and is *fifty times* more powerful than sulfadiazine alone. The polyester in Mr. Public's wool blend suit would be impossible to make without silver catalysts. John's car relies on silver in almost every relay, whether locking the doors, scooting back the seat, lowering the electric windows, or defrosting the rear window. Amazingly, these are only a *few* of silver's indispensable applications.

NATURE OF SILVER

Silver's rare chemical and physical properties make it virtually irreplaceable in most industrial uses. We all know the value of shimmering white silver in jewelry, the warm glow of sterling silver tableware, or its arresting beauty in art. Sculptors particularly treasure silver's agreeable, cooperative nature. The metal seems to come alive under their hands.

But the chemical and physical properties of silver give it a unique usefulness beyond its simple beauty. We borrow silver's chemical symbol (Ag) from the Latin word for silver, *argentum* (from an Indo-European root word that means "brilliant" or "shining"). Silver is extremely dense —that is, very heavy per unit of volume: 6.25 troy ounces per cubic inch with a specific gravity 10.5 times water's. It resists all sorts of corrosive agents and dissolves only in nitric or concentrated sulfuric acid.

Silver melts at 1,762 degrees Fahrenheit. When the first International Temperature Scale was adopted in 1927, it was based in part on the accepted melting point of silver, 960.5 degrees Celsius, the "silver point." Silver boils at 2,212 degrees Celsius. Its atomic weight is 107.868 and its atomic number is 47.

One of the most useful metals known to mankind, silver is applied over a bewildering range of uses, an average of two hundred new ones every year. We know we are overusing the word "unique," but nothing else acts like silver, so we're stuck with it. Here are some of silver's unique properties:

- Silver is relatively inert chemically, but its compounds formed with halides (chlorine and bromine) offer a unique sensitivity to light that makes them irreplaceable in photography.
- Silver has unique bacteriostatic properties. It not only kills bacteria on contact but also activates oxygen to kill bacteria. Relatively inert in the human body, silver compounds protect wounds and heal burns.
- Silver conducts heat and electricity better than any other metal, making it indispensable in electronic applications.
- Silver resists oxidation, corrosion, and the electric sparking that devours nonsilver contacts. Corrosion resistance also makes silver useful as a catalyst.
- Silver is the whitest of all metals and is the most reflective, throwing back almost all of the light that strikes its surface. That's why the backs of mirrors are "silvered" instead of "molybdenumized."
- Silver is the most malleable metal except for gold. Silver can be beaten into leaves 0.00025 mm thick.
- Silver is the most ductile of all metals except gold. One gram can be drawn into a wire 120 meters long.
- Silver is very stable chemically .
- Silver has a sweeter resonance than any other metal and makes incomparable bells and musical instruments.

SILVER AND LIGHT

Light disturbs the structure of silver halide crystals. This enables the crystals to be reduced selectively to metallic silver by a reducing agent ("developer"). *Silver halides provide greater sensitivity to light than any known chemical.* A tiny silver salt crystal could detect the light falling onto the Earth from a candle on the Moon, if the moon reflected no sunlight on its own. Even in the tiniest quantities, silver compounds can amplify light one billion times.

Two factors make silver practically irreplaceable in photography. First, no other element can imitate or equal its performance. (Well, if you want some *very* expensive photos, certain salts of *platinum* can *approach* silver's performance.) Second, no other element can deliver silver's performance at the same low cost and consumption. One ounce of silver can be used to take five thousand color photographs. If silver rises $1, the cost per photo rises two one-hundredths of a cent; *who cares?*

For more than twenty years, rumors about a replacement for silver in photography have periodically sent rigors and chills across the silver market, but upon closer inspection they all evaporate. Face it: A $1,500 electronic camera with a $300 television set that produces photos of questionable resolution ("Is that you, Maude, or the cat? I can't tell") just isn't a substitute for a $35 camera and a $3 roll of film. Silver-halide images contain two hundred times as many pixels as electronic images. High silver prices in the 1970s and early 1980s forced photographic concerns to economize on silver use, but *as a practical matter, there is no replacement for silver in photography.*

Why is that so important? *Because, on average, from 1977 through 1993, 34 percent of world silver fabrication demand came from photography.* In most developed countries it's even higher. For example, in the United States, the world's largest consumer of silver, photography claimed 54 percent of the silver consumed in 1992 (1977–92 average, 47 percent). Photographic demand is such an important component of silver demand that we have treated it in a separate section below.

ELECTRICAL AND ELECTRONIC APPLICATIONS

Silver's electrical conductivity, the highest of all metals, makes it perfect for electrical and electronic applications. From printed circuit boards to electric contact points, silver quietly serves mankind everywhere. Silver is used (and consumed) in household appliances, communications equipment, gauges, switches, membrane switch panels, thermostats, computers, and automobile relays and switches. Because silver resists the corrosion and pitting caused by sparking when electrical connections are broken, nothing can match silver in contact points. Responding to high silver prices, silver use in electronic and electrical applications was reduced in the 1980s. However, in this and every application, there is a lower limit to which the amount of silver can be reduced, and *much of this reduction has already taken place.* Certainly in the short term, industrial silver usage cannot be easily or greatly reduced.

BATTERIES

Silver batteries provide high voltage and power levels over extended time periods. They are light and compact, yield a high energy output, resist high temperatures, and have a very long shelf life. These characteristics make silver batteries ideal for critical applications as diverse as portable surgical tools, TV cameras, and the space shuttle.

When combined with cadmium or zinc, silver batteries are rechargeable—but other replacements for silver won't do the same job. Because they have a high ratio of energy delivered to weight, silver batteries are indispensable in some applications. They have fifteen to twenty times the electrical capacity of comparable dry cells and twice that of lead acid batteries. In the five years from 1987 through 1991, demand for silver in the battery sector increased 30 percent.

MEDICAL USES

Because it does not react readily in the human body, silver can be used in human surgery without side effects. Silver wire immobilizes bone frac-

25

tures or sews up large wounds, and silver electrodes have even been inserted to promote healing. Because tiny concentrations of silver or silver salts kill bacteria, the eyes of all newborns in the Western world are washed with silver nitrate eyedrops to prevent blindness from venereal diseases. Best of all, bacteria do not develop resistance to silver, as they do to some antibiotics.

Any parent who has ever experienced the tragedy of a burned child has thanked God for silver sulphadiazine and its improved form, Silvadene. It has become the standard treatment for difficult burns worldwide. These silver compounds are painless and can be used to treat or prevent infections in second- and third-degree burns. Burns take a long time to heal, and bacteria frequently develop a resistance to topical antibiotics. Because microbes do not become resistant to silver's bactericidal action, silver compounds have been especially useful in treating burns.

Silver exhibits this same bactericidal action when electrically generated silver ions are introduced into hard-to-heal wounds, *and* it promotes healing even in very stubborn cases. In some tests with difficult fractures, healing occurred twice as fast when treated with silver ions. Treatment with silver anodes seems to produce fast-growing embryonic-type cells that cause wounds to heal more quickly.

DENTAL USES

Since early in the nineteenth century, an amalgam of mercury and silver has been used to fill tooth cavities. This is still the most commonly used dental filling material.

WATER PURIFICATION

Silver effectively kills bacteria even when present in minute amounts— the so-called *oligodynamic effect*. In simple terms, *a little goes a long way*. This silver property is especially useful in treating drinking water. Silver is bonded to efficient carbon in water filters to purify the water and to prevent bacterial growth in the filter medium. Some filters release minute amounts of elemental silver into the filtrate. This inhibits bacterial growth for hours after filtration. Pure silver is also used in ceramic water filters.

In water, silver activates oxygen to destroy bacteria and viruses instantly. In 1992, Fountainhead Technologies of Providence, Rhode Island, introduced a silver-alumina system that does not depend on chemicals or filtration. Rather, it uses a catalytic process by which silver first destabilizes oxygen molecules, which then break apart and attach to bacteria. Tests show a 99.9 percent kill rate and removal of *E. coli* bacteria within 2.5 seconds. In the second stage, silver atoms are released into the water stream to keep on sanitizing.[1]

Using silver to purify water is certainly not new. The ancient Greeks and Phoenicians knew that silver vessels kept water from fouling on long voyages. Settlers in the American West put silver dollars in their water barrels to keep the water wholesome. As concern about the harmful health effects of chlorination increase, silver water purification systems will look more and more attractive. In normal use and concentrations, silver is not toxic to humans.

RAINMAKING

Silver iodide crystals seed clouds for rainfall.

WINDOW COATINGS

Silver coating increases the insulating and reflecting characteristics of glass, and protects heat-reflecting gold layers in window glass. Fine silver wires are embedded into auto glass to make rear-window glass defrosters.

LUBRICATION

Silver-coated ball bearings deliver superior lubrication qualities. Silver electroplating gives steel transmission gears much longer life. Silver's resistance in metal-to-metal wear far surpasses that of all other commonly

27

used bearing faces, so silver is extremely valuable in applications where petroleum-based lubricants cannot be used.

BRAZING AND SOLDERING

Joining disparate metals requires alloys that melt at temperatures below the melting points of the metals being joined. Silver-rich alloys fit the bill. Certain changes in the composition of the brazing alloy can even make it flow before it melts. Silver brazing alloys are used in air conditioning and refrigeration, plumbing, automobiles, motors, and electrical appliances. These uses of silver are generally nonrecoverable.

CATALYSTS

Silver catalysts are used in oxidation reactions. They are essential in producing formaldehyde, antifreeze, and man-made fibers such as polyester.

SILVER-COATED TEXTILES

Silver can be deposited as a fine coating on textile fibers for antistatic carpeting in hospitals, hotels, and other public places. Silver-coated fibers are also used in antistatic filters to eliminate dust particles.

COINAGE

Although silver has been politically demonetized around the world, coinage continues to be a notable consumer of silver. Silver consumption in United States coinage increased dramatically in the 1980s, largely as a result of the American Silver Eagle coin issued in 1986. From 1983 through 1992, the United States minted 68.7 million ounces of silver coins. Since 1986, the United States has averaged coining about 9.1 million ounces every year.

World coin usage decreased as nation after nation removed silver from its coinage, but since its 1981 low at 9.5 million ounces, silver coinage has steadily increased. Despite violent ups and downs until 1986, silver coinage grew an average of 4 percent yearly from 1977 to 1993. Silver coinage in 1993 of 38.0 million ounces represented a 29 percent increase over 1992.

Mexico has released new "plugged" bimetallic silver coins that will vastly increase silver usage. These new coins represent, in effect, a revolutionary *remonetization* of silver. The 10-peso and 20-peso pieces are not to be issued as collector's items or even as an investment form of silver (like the Mexican *Libertad* or the American Silver Eagle). Rather, the bimetallic coins are part of a new coinage system and currency reform establishing a new monetary unit called the *nuevo peso*. The 10-peso coins contain about 0.17 ounce of silver, the 20-peso coins about 0.25 ounce.

Production of these coins will consume about 7 million ounces a year out of Mexico's 70-million-ounce production. Mexico is the world's leading silver producer, followed closely by the United States, Peru, and, more distantly, Canada.

With silver at $5 an ounce, a 10-peso coin contains about 80 cents' worth of silver (the silver in a 20-peso coin is worth about $1.25). With the *nuevo peso* trading at about 31 U.S. cents, the coin is worth a little over $3.10 (or for the 20-peso coin, $6.20). At this low silver price, the coins have a very low intrinsic value. Silver would have to rise above $19 to make their silver content equal to their current paper exchange value. *Nevertheless,* authorities expect the Mexican public to hoard the coins, so another 7 *million ounces a year* will be effectively removed from world supply. Even with the tiny silver content, this effective remonetization of silver has revolutionary implications. The very idea that circulating currency should have *any intrinsic value at all* contradicts the world of central bank *fiat* money where, since 1971, no national currency or coin in the world has possessed any intrinsic value whatever.

In 1987, Mexico also announced another remonetization of silver with its Banco de Mexico silver certificates (CEPLATAs), each backed by 100 troy ounces of 99.9 percent pure silver stored in a Mexican depository. More than 7 million ounces have been used in this program since it began.

PHOTOGRAPHY: NOTHING BUT BULLISH DEVELOPMENTS

Everlasting silver bears sing one tired old song: Don't buy silver because some new technology will replace silver in photography any day now. That, they tell us, is a major reason for not owning silver. Indeed, rumors periodically sweep the silver market that this "revolutionary" technology has been discovered, sending tremors from top to bottom. Inevitably, the closer one examines these mighty "replacements," the punier they appear. In fact, the whole silver-will-become-obsolete-in-photography argument has more holes than a dime-store sieve, and we will explain why.

The latest of these revolutionary silver "replacements" (the word begs for quotation marks) has been electronic imaging. But after more than a decade of huffing and puffing, silver is still safe on its photographic throne. The revolution has failed to revolt. Manufacturers are even down-grading these efforts because of "consumer resistance to their expense, bulkiness, technical difficulty, and most of all, poor resolution."[2]

Unless you're a member of the Saudi royal family, a $500 to $900

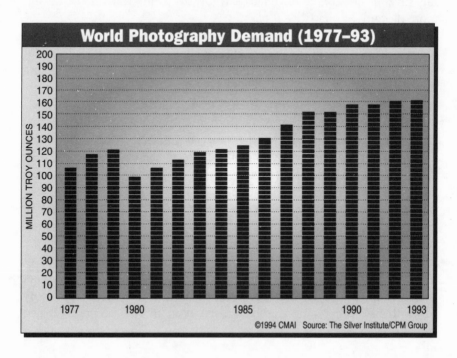

©1994 CMAI   Source: The Silver Institute/CPM Group

electronic imaging rig simply won't replace a $30 camera and a $3 roll of film, certainly not when the resolution of the inexpensive, high-quality silver halide technology is 100 percent to 9,000 percent clearer than electronic images. Silver bears ought to face the facts: No other technology produces such sharp, clear photographic images for anywhere near the cost. (Well, if you want to spend $20,000 for an electronic camera you can *approach* the resolution of silver technology.) The truth is, electronic imaging really offers no threat to silver in photography. In fact, *hybrid* electronic systems may actually *increase* photographic use of silver.

Knowledgeable analysts pointed out years ago that electronic imaging's hard copy printing was unlikely to provide the image quality necessary to challenge silver-halide technology. At the Gold and Silver Institute's 1993 annual meeting, Paul Ward, laboratory manager of the Imaging Division for the photography giant Eastman Kodak Company, said that *silver will never be replaced as the material of choice for high-quality photographic images.* In fact, Ward pointed out, electronic imaging will actually increase the use of silver in photography.

Mr. Ward is not the only photographic expert who shares this opinion. Thomas J. Dufficy, executive vice president of the National Association of Photographic Manufacturers (NAPM), says, "The photographic industry has long sought an alternative to silver in the photographic process. We have not found a substitute that works as well. . . . There really are no alternative sources to meet the quality/value ratio of silver imaging at this time."[3]

Photographic expert and executive Peter Krause writes in the *World Silver Survey 1992,* "[S]ilver halide photography will continue to be the main imaging system in the amateur and professional sector for the next five years, but hybrid and pure electronic systems will have a growing share of an expanding market."[4]

It's not hard to understand why electronic systems face such a hard row to hoe against silver. Still video systems are silver's main competitor in amateur and professional still photography. In the United States during 1990, about 3,000 still video cameras were sold, versus more than *11 million conventional cameras.* Krause blames poor image quality and high price for this lackluster performance. Consider the Canon XAP Shot camera (it costs about $500) equipped with a 200,000-pixel CCD sensor and an effective exposure index of ISO 100. An ordinary point-and-shoot 35 mm camera sells for about $100, and with ISO 200 color negative film provides about *18 million* pixels per frame, a *9,000 percent advantage at one fifth the cost!*[5]

SILVER-HALIDE PHOTOGRAPHIC TECHNOLOGY

No other physical substances react quite like the halide salts of silver in the presence of light. Light disturbs their crystalline arrangement so that exposed film can be chemically reduced to produce a negative for transferring an image onto photographic paper.

This basic process was invented by Daguerre in 1839. Researchers have been seeking a replacement for silver, without significant success, since Daguerre opened his first shop. This technology has been applied in hundreds of ways, not only in still and movie photography but also in industrial and medical X rays, graphic arts, microfilm, and other fields.

In the past fifty years, understanding of how silver halides work has made significant progress. This understanding, especially in the past fifteen years, has made it possible to reduce the silver content of films and papers by 50 percent to 60 percent. *Still, the use of silver in photography continues to climb year after year.* From a 1991 worldwide use of 194.6 million ounces, photographic expert Peter Krause projects world use of silver in films and papers to increase to 222.6 million ounces by 1996.[6]

But there is a lower limit to the reduction of silver in film: *diminishing returns.* After the reductions of recent years in photographic and X-ray films (30 percent since 1960), it is unlikely that major new reductions will be brought to market any time soon.

BULLISH INNOVATIONS

Expensive, hard-to-use electronic imaging systems have not yet offered any serious threat to silver. In fact, along with other innovations, the use of silver in photography is more likely to *skyrocket* in the next ten years.

WHAT HAPPENS WHEN THE CHINESE . . .

There is no accurate head count for the Chinese population, but one thing is certain: There are a lot of them. Estimates range from 1.1 billion to 1.7 billion people. In our chapter on the growing Asian demand for silver, we discuss the astonishing economic growth rates in China, rates approaching 20 percent a year. Economic growth means rising incomes, and rising incomes mean more consumer dollars to be spent on photography. In Japan, the amateur photography market progressed in lockstep with the huge economic growth there in the 1950s and 1960s. As incomes rise, consumers are able as never before to record all the important and memorable events of their lives *on film*.

"Astounding" is the only word to describe the long-term potential for photographic demand in China. By the end of the decade it could reach half of U.S. photographic demand. A typical three-by-five photograph uses about 0.003 ounce of silver. That doesn't seem like much silver, but in 1991, American amateur photographers made *16.2 billion camera exposures and ordered 22 billion prints.*[7] Photography in America alone consumed 64.4 million ounces of silver in 1992, for approximately 250 million people. Compare this with China's 1.1 billion to 1.7 billion population, and the growth potential for silver demand is stunning. If photography in China approached just 50 percent of American usage by the year 2000, Chinese silver demand for *photography alone* would range from 141 million to almost 220 million ounces per year, just about the entire *world* demand for photographic silver in 1992.

Although it is unlikely, even assuming the continuation of China's rapid economic growth, that Chinese use of photographic silver would reach these levels that quickly, this calculation does illustrate the astonishing depth of the potential demand for silver *just in photography,* not to mention the other irreplaceable uses of silver in a developing economy.

SILVER IN PHOTOGRAPHY'S FUTURE

Contrary to the conventional assumptions about "revolutionary" technologies replacing silver in photography, silver's place in photography is quite secure for the foreseeable future. Moreover, competing technologies

PERCENTAGE OF WORLD SILVER FABRICATION DEMAND
COMPOSED OF PHOTOGRAPHY
(millions of troy ounces)

	World				United States		
	Photo	**Total**	**%**		**Photo**	**Total**	**%**
1977	129.6	494.4	.26		53.7	153.6	.35
1978	142.9	491.9	.29		64.3	160.2	.40
1979	146.1	479.2	.30		66.0	157.3	.42
1980	123.8	379.3	.33		49.8	124.8	.40
1981	128.1	364.9	.35		51.0	116.7	.44
1982	136.5	373.3	.37		51.8	119.0	.44
1983	140.3	366.7	.38		51.8	116.3	.45
1984	147.3	389.9	.38		55.3	114.9	.48
1985	152.7	400.9	.38		57.9	118.6	.49
1986	157.8	436.4	.36		55.4	118.9	.47
1987	172.1	461.0	.37		60.2	115.3	.52
1988	185.1	476.0	.39		62.5	112.0	.56
1989	185.9	508.4	.37		65.2	120.0	.54
1990	193.2	544.2	.35		68.0	125.3	.54
1991	193.0	576.2	.33		66.0	118.7	.56
1992	195.3	593.4	.33		64.4	118.9	.54
1993	195.9	678.7	.29		65.0	121.1	.54
Averages	160.3	471.4	.34		59.3	125.4	.47

Source: Data from The Silver Institute World Silver Survey, 1994

will probably have *a positive impact* on global silver use, while increasing incomes in the Far East will increase overall silver use in photography and other areas of demand.

Let's summarize these and other positive developments for silver:

- The photography industry seems committed to the long-term use of silver-halide technologies in all areas of photography, well into the twenty-first century.

- Kodak, the world's leading producer of photographic products, has assured the future growth of silver-halide film with a remarkable list of new products, including new color negative and color reversal films, a new underwater film, eight new camera products, and a series of new photo products for children. This development is typical of other photographic concerns throughout the world.
- Even in the microfilming industry, where silver is slugging it out nose to nose with digital technologies, *after fifteen years,* silver retains 70 percent of the market. Microfilm volume will increase 17 percent by 1996, and with it comes an 11 percent increase in silver use.
- Polaroid, the world's leader in instant photography, has introduced a new product line that will *increase* the use of silver-halide film. Instant photography *permanently* consumes much more silver than conventional photography.
- Emerging free markets in formerly controlled economies are opening up massive new demand for silver-halide film. In China alone, demand could approach 100 million ounces by the end of the century. Demand there will almost certainly be much greater than most analysts have predicted.

The important thing for investors in silver to realize is that the rumors about "revolutionary" photographic technologies eliminating silver simply have not proved true. In fact, the future for silver-halide film seems secure. Much more important, growth in photographic silver use could be extraordinary. Both imply a *powerful* rise for the price of silver.

ARE WE RUNNING OUT OF SILVER?

Many years ago, metal market analysts forecast that silver would be the first strategic metal to disappear. In 1977, a World Bank Research report stated that the only significant minerals with assuredly tight geological reserves are silver and tin.

Silver is one of the rarest metals on earth, composing only 73 *parts per billion* of the earth's crust. It is estimated that there is only eleven times as much silver in the mantle of our planet as there is gold (a fact consistent with the monetary gold–silver ratio of 10–1 to 12–1 that prevailed for several millennia). With silver at its lowest price in real terms since 1968, most of this is not economical to mine. After thirteen years of falling silver prices, very few *primary* silver mines are still open. About two thirds of all the new silver mined comes as a byproduct of base metal mining—copper, lead, or zinc.

INCREASING SILVER USAGE

Every year, new uses of silver are reported. In the vast majority of its existing industrial usages, there is no ready, economical replacement for silver. For the past twenty years, industrial users have been squeezing down silver usage wherever possible.

The 1980 silver bull market peak brought a silver supply glut that kept the market stuffed with silver for almost a decade. That all changed in 1990; the balance of silver fabrication demand against supply went into deficit by 41.9 million ounces. Economic slowdown didn't affect the growing silver shortfall. In 1991, the deficit grew to 85.8 million ounces; in 1992, to 88.6 million. The Silver Institute's prestigious *World Silver Survey 1993* projects record silver usage in 1993: 625 million ounces, resulting in a 143.2 million ounce *shortfall*. Meanwhile, silver demand continues to grow every year. *Lights! Action! Prices!* The fundamental stage is set for the next silver bull market.

Chapter 2

SILVER SUPPLY AND DEMAND

As we take up *fundamental* analysis of supply and demand for silver, we have to remember three great shortcomings. First, the data we deal with are all *past* data, while markets are as dynamic as a living body. Your doctor can sample your blood after you've fasted for twenty-four hours, and the blood sugar level will show a certain figure. But no sooner do you leave the doctor's office and pop a hard candy in your mouth than your *entire body* (not to mention your blood chemistry) begins to react to that new input. First, the enzymes in your mouth begin to break down the sugar, and as you suck in satisfaction on the candy (carefully avoiding that silver filling that a hard candy can snatch right out of your tooth), the sugar goes down into your stomach, after which it is absorbed into your bloodstream, changing your blood chemistry as it strives to maintain balance.

In exactly the same way, markets are vast organisms, communicating all of the innumerable decisions, perceptions, and emotions of every buyer and seller through the *price mechanism*. They respond *immediately* to perceived or real changes. Because markets are composed of *human* participants, these changes are not grounded in physical supply and demand alone, but also in the countless inscrutable and infinitely mutable desires and insights of all those people. And people, let's face it, don't always react *rationally*. Much of the time they *overreact*. This human factor can make fundamental or technical analysis, in the end, something far less than a science—an art at best, and, at worst, an attempt to forecast the future as futile as reading the entrails of goats.

Second, with all due deference and respect to those faithful number gatherers who assemble the data for fundamental supply/demand analysis, *some of the numbers just aren't there*. Who really can know how many mines will be producing silver next year, how many earthquakes or floods or explosions will shut some down completely? But where boxes must be filled, what's an analyst to do? *He makes an educated guess*. These may be good guesses, but they are guesses still.

The respected *World Silver Survey of 1993* is a case in point. This is probably the best respected supply/demand analysis of silver published in the world, and with good cause. It's thorough and careful, but in the section "World Mine Silver Survey 1992–1996," they illustrate that projecting supply is not an exact science. "The world mine production of silver in 1992 was *nearly the same* as projected one year ago; *8 percent less* than projected two years ago; and *12 percent less* than projected three years ago."[1]

Third, data analysts may not always understand their subject the way experienced market hands understand it. Errors can creep in. In the esteemed *Stocks of Silver Survey Around the World 1992* by Charles River Associates, the authors show the American Eagle Bullion Coin with a silver content of 0.7734 ounce—but it contains 1 full troy ounce of silver.[2] In another place, the study seems to indicate that sterling silver table knives and candelabra are solid sterling, when in fact they contain only a thin sterling silver foil wrapped around an epoxy resin or cement core. Although these discrepancies may only skew the study minutely, they still show the difficulties that even the most astute professional analysts face when investigating a field that requires day-to-day dealers and traders years to master.

Does this mean that fundamental analysis or these studies are worthless? Absolutely not. They are the very best available. It simply means that we must be very careful about the weight we accord their results. It also means that we must weigh fundamental analysis against other measures, such as technical analysis, to confirm our conclusions.

OUR RADICAL THEORY

Our years of studying and trading silver have led us to a radical theory about the price action of silver. One worrisome and almost inexplicable fact about silver is both a help and a caution to every trader: Silver and gold tend to move together. Experienced traders always look for the metals to move together to confirm any trend change.

But in theory, this tandem price action shouldn't exist! First, the demand for silver is so overwhelmingly industrial, and the demand for gold so overwhelmingly monetary, that it isn't hard to imagine a situation of severe economic panic or depression where everyone was running to gold (for safety), but silver was going nowhere (because nobody was producing anything that consumed silver). Shouldn't silver and gold move separately?

By 1880, every major nation in the world (except India and China) had politically demonetized silver. It was precisely because the major demand component for silver—monetary demand—was removed that silver entered a long price slide that lasted almost fifty years.

Just as the primary force powering the decades-long drop in silver's price in the late nineteenth century was demonetization, so the primary question underlying silver's price in the late twentieth century is: Will the public of its own accord remonetize silver?

Of course, governments and central banks around the world try to contend that even gold has been demonetized, too, but the facts (26 percent of world central bank reserves in gold) show how hollow this claim really is. Gold is the preeminent monetary asset, the ultimate asset that is not simultaneously someone else's liability.

But what about silver? Wasn't silver demonetized over a century ago? If so, why does its price move with gold? Isn't more than 90 percent of the demand for silver industrial demand? If that's so, then why do silver and gold prices still move together?

We believe that latent monetary (or investment) demand for silver is the key to the rapidly building boom in silver. In technical economic terms, silver benefits from a substitution effect in relation to gold; silver rides gold's coattails. The public (especially the American investing public) perceives silver as a substitute for gold for monetary purposes. Because in the short run industrial demand and supply for silver are relatively fixed, it is this monetary demand for silver at the margin of the market that actually drives the silver price in the short run.

Take the price of blue jeans as a comparison. Blue jeans are primarily a utilitarian garment. You want to wear them when you're under automobiles changing oil, riding through the brush herding cattle, working in a warehouse, and so forth. But what happened when the most consuming consumers, American teendom, suddenly decided that blue jeans were *de rigueur?* Demand at the margin skyrocketed, and it had nothing to do with any rational or quantifiable reason. It was simply a change in fashion, a change in human perception.

Oddly enough, government brought about the change in the investing public's perception of silver. In 1965, the U.S. government decreed that silver was "too expensive" to use for mere coinage, and removed it from American circulation. Those few nations around the world that had not already debased their coinage quickly followed suit. But the public's long memory and even longer distrust of government recognized the monetary danger signal. Following the wise French proverb that "nothing is officially confirmed until officially denied," the public began to hoard silver in earnest. It was pure monetary demand. Despite all the ups and downs of the silver market in the ensuing thirty years, one basic fact remained: The public had privately remonetized silver by again demanding it for monetary purposes. Call it a "hedge against inflation" or a "hedge against currency depreciation" or "investment demand," it is still the same thing: a demand for silver *as money.*

Where does the substitution effect come in? The perceived unit price for gold is vastly larger than for silver. Silver is perceived as "cheaper" than gold. That's the reason silver is called "poor man's gold"—even the poorest Indian or Chinese peasant can afford an ounce of silver by which he can store his hopes for the future.

But there's more. Silver offers more bang for the investment buck. You don't have to be an investment genius to see that silver is far more volatile than gold, and rises much faster than gold off bear market lows. In the initial move up from the bear market silver bottom in 1993, silver rose almost two and a half times faster than gold. If silver rises twice as fast as gold, then $400.00 invested in 80 ounces of silver (at $5.00 an ounce) offers a lot more leverage than 1 ounce of gold (at $400.00 an ounce). If gold rose 25 percent to $500.00, silver at the same time would rise 50 percent to $7.50 an ounce, or $600.00 for the 80 ounces.

This is not all pie in the sky. We well remember the 1982 lows in silver and gold on Midsummer Day, June 21, 1982. Silver touched down at less than $5.00 ($4.98), while gold dropped to $301.00. By February 18, 1983, eight months later, gold had risen to $505.70 (a 68 percent increase), while silver had soared to $14.71 (a 195 percent increase). Silver's increase was 286 percent of gold's, nearly three times as much as gold's.

The 1980 price action also shows how silver can outpower gold at the peak. On January 22, 1979, gold closed at $233.40, while silver closed at $6.39. One year later, at the peak of the market on January 21, 1980, gold closed at $825.00 while silver finished at $44.00. (These are closing prices and hence usually lower than peak prices.) In a year, gold had gained 253 percent; silver, 588 percent. Silver outperformed gold by 232 percent, an increase of nearly double.

The longer-term view also shows silver outperforming gold. For investors who squirreled away silver in 1965, the difference in performance between silver and gold was quite gratifying. In 1965, you could buy silver for $1.29 an ounce, but gold cost $35.00 an ounce. Taking the bull market peaks above, gold from 1965 to 1980 increased 23.5 times, while silver increased 34.1 times (145 percent as much).

The public also perceives a greater potential for increase with silver. It may not be factually pertinent or even necessarily logical, but anyone can see that silver at $5.00 an ounce can double to $10.00 an ounce before gold can double from $400.00 to $800.00.

Only a tiny fraction of 1 percent of American capital diverted into silver would generate an enormous price rise. At $5.00 an ounce, every bit of the silver stocks reported in exchange and dealer stocks at the end of 1992—319.1 million ounces—could have been bought for less than $1.6 billion. Charles River Associates, Inc. (CRA) of Boston estimates that throughout the entire world, at prices of $10 an ounce or less, only 541 million ounces of silver are potentially available to the market.[3] That's $5.4 billion, or about the amount the American government spends between the time you eat your breakfast and brush your teeth in the morning.

Just compare the value of the entire silver stock to a few large New York Stock Exchange companies. In August 1993, Exxon was tied with Wal-Mart for the top spot as America's largest market capitalization company. With 1.24 billion shares trading at $64 a share, Exxon has a market cap of $79.42 billion. In other words, *nearly fifteen times the value of all the silver in the world available at prices under $10.00!*

General Motors was number 16 on the S&P 500 list when we last

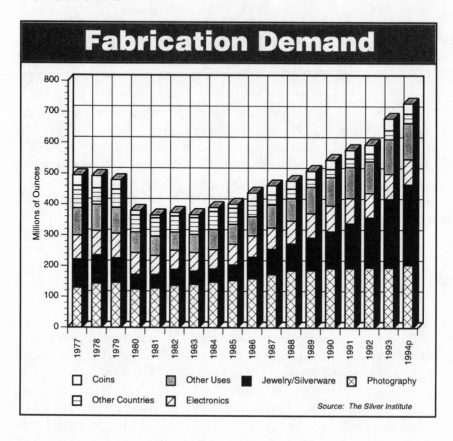

Fabrication Demand

Millions of Ounces

Legend: Coins, Other Uses, Jewelry/Silverware, Photography, Other Countries, Electronics

Source: The Silver Institute

checked. With 744.68 million shares trading at $51.75, GM had a market cap of $38.5 billion. Just this one NYSE company was worth *almost six and a quarter times as much as all the silver in the world available at prices under $10.00!* This says nothing of the minuscule value of the silver stock when compared to the gargantuan U.S. bond market, or the *$1 trillion-a-day* Eurodollar market, or the $5 trillion market capitalization of all U.S. exchange-listed and OTC stocks.

Finally, one reason that marginal monetary demand for silver can change total demand—and therefore price—so quickly is that it quickly becomes *panic demand*. People worrying about the safety of the currency or the liquidity of the government or the banking system are *looking* for confirmation of their fears. The slightest thing can touch them off, like sharks in a feeding frenzy. When they see the price of silver and gold edging up, especially in the absence of much inflation, the rising prices

42

themselves tend to fuel the public's panic level with the most powerful human motivator: greed.

All things considered very broadly (we know we're cramming a lot into this generalization), it was the decline of that monetary demand for silver at the margin that furnished the underlying basis for the silver bear market of the 1980s. Yes, *industrial* demand as well as supply proved far more elastic than most analysts predicted, but it was *monetary* demand for silver that reached a crisis blowoff top in 1980. During the 1980s, increased silver supply, changed perceptions about the monetary integrity of the U.S. government under Volcker and Reagan, and other more lucrative investment opportunities chipped away for thirteen long years at that monetary demand for silver. The general public perception that "things were all right" as well as the general feeling of economic well-being during the '80s undercut—indeed, almost annihilated—monetary demand for silver.

In the early 1990s, the supply/demand picture for silver began to change. Consumption increased over supply, and our old friend the "supply gap" returned as more silver was used every year than was produced. Then the Clinton administration arrived, and with it that old public monetary *uneasiness* began to climb back in the saddle. The "feel good" '80s, along with their economic optimism, have disappeared into the gloom of chronic recession. We believe that gold and silver markets are being fueled by this loss of confidence, not by any actual return of inflation—yet. The *fundamental* stage is set for silver to revenge its honor. The *technical* stage is set after thirteen years in the dungeon. We believe that imponderable *monetary demand for silver as a substitute for gold* will drive silver demand to frenzied heights that today seem ridiculously optimistic —but they're coming.

One last thing: CRA notes, "The high *velocity* and *volume* of 'paper silver' passing among dealers, traders, miners, refiners, users, fabricators, and investors swamps reality [and] creates the *wrong perception* that the *volume* of 'physical silver' traded is high."[4] (Emphasis in the original). On the Comex, for example, millions of ounces are traded in futures contracts (on an average day, etc.), but only a tiny percent of those contracts result in an actual exchange of physical silver. Moreover, CRA notes, it is very difficult to differentiate highly visible *business* stocks from equally visible *investor* stocks.[5]

This merely confirms our opinion: *Even sophisticated analysts and market participants believe that vast quantities of silver are available to the market at* *prices above $5, but the opposite is true.* CRA estimates that at prices of $20 or under, 1.07 billion ounces would be available to the market; at prices of $15 or under, 1.15 billion ounces; at prices of $10 or under, 541 million ounces.[6] We suspect (but cannot prove) that *at prices under $30 an ounce, far less silver will come out than most analysts believe.*

What does this false notion of huge overhanging available silver supply accomplish? It will keep most market participants *bearish* all the while silver is pushing through the first laborious stages of a *bull* market. When the error finally dawns on the market, a huge wave of bullish sentiment will wash over silver.

SILVER SUPPLY AND DEMAND

Just how much silver is there in the world? In 1992, the Silver Institute commissioned Charles River Associates to answer that question. CRA found that from 4000 B.C. through 1991, 37.5 billion troy ounces (1,165,132 metric tons) of silver have been produced.[7] Only about 25 percent of total world silver was produced before the American Revolution. The discovery and exploitation of the huge American deposits after 1492 flooded Europe with silver. Later, technical advances in silver extraction (including production as a byproduct of base metal mining) led to even greater silver production.

CRA estimated that of the 37.5 billion ounces of silver ever mined, only about 19.1 billion ounces still exist in the form of bullion, coins and medallions, and silverware and other art forms.[8] Bullion and coins plus medallions are conventionally defined as "total stocks"—that is, stocks readily available to the market.

However, the important question is not how much silver exists above ground. Rather, how much of this silver is available for sale, and at what price? The CRA study says, *"The common perception in the market that silver stocks are very large and thus readily available is wrong. The stocks are large, but are not all readily available."* (Emphasis in the original.)[9]

If large stocks are available, even at bear market bottoms, they aren't just floating up in the air. Somebody owns them. The presence of large stocks doesn't necessarily mean that nobody wants silver. Large stocks can mean that sophisticated investors are accumulating silver for the long term.

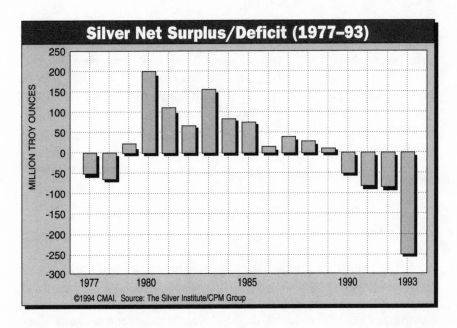

Silver Net Surplus/Deficit (1977–93)

©1994 CMAI. Source: The Silver Institute/CPM Group

Including bullion, coins and medallions, and silverware and other art forms, CRA places worldwide stocks of silver *available to the market at prices of $10 or less* at 541 million troy ounces. Some of this silver includes business stocks required for production. It might come onto the market at very high silver prices, but only temporarily. Silver will have to be rebought to carry on business. Most coins and medallions are held by families in small amounts, for sentimental or other reasons. This silver is not terribly responsive to small changes in price. Finally, under normal market conditions, very little silverware or other silver art forms will hit the market. They are spread out among small holders who have an emotional attachment to them, or they are held for their high value as art. No one will sell a Bernini salt cellar because the price of silver jumps from $5 an ounce to $20 an ounce. Likewise, churches around the world won't line up to hock their chalices, crucifixes, and decorations just because silver's price breaks through $30. At prices of $20 an ounce or less, CRA estimates that 16.85 billion ounces of silver are simply unavailable to the market, except in small increments over many years *if* high silver prices persisted.

One anecdote will serve to illustrate how much of this silver supply available at $20 an ounce or less has been exhausted. Anyone who participated in the Mad Silver Melt of 1979–80 can relate similar tales of price-less heirlooms sold for scrap. We remember particularly one visit to a scrap dealer about 1983 when we saw on the shelf some pieces he had pulled out of the melt pile. It was a silver tea service, engraved as a gift to the mayor of Augusta, Georgia, in 1854! If family heirlooms such as this are lured into the melting pot by high silver prices, we can speculate that not much heirloom silver is left to melt for market at prices under $30 an ounce, much less $20.

YEARLY FLOWS OF SILVER AND THE EMERGING SUPPLY GAP

More pertinent to the price of silver than the total estimated world supply is the yearly delivery and offtake of silver in the marketplace: How much silver is consumed and produced each year? In theory, when more silver is consumed than is produced, the price should rise to encourage production, and vice versa.

When we look at silver supply and demand since 1950, certain trends immediately emerge. From 1950 through 1959, there were deficits that averaged 59.5 million troy ounces a year. From 1960 through 1963, deficits and surpluses resulted in a 13.8 million ounce surplus. The next seven years (1964–70) brought huge surpluses to market, averaging 86 million ounces per year. The majority of the '70s, 1971–78, however, saw years of supply deficits, averaging 54.5 million ounces per year.[10]

The Hunt debacle of 1979–80, when silver soared to $50 an ounce, brought huge supplies to market and encouraged producers to cut silver consumption. When the price jumped to $6.40 in 1974, silver producers had already received their warning. Many took it, and began to reduce their silver usage. The 1980 bubble confirmed their vulnerability to a rise in silver's price. It's not surprising, then, that from 1979 through 1989, silver was in oversupply, averaging more than 76 million ounces a year.

But in 1990, the worm turned. For the first time in eleven years, the silver flow went into deficit. In 1990, the deficit was 41.9 million ounces; in 1991, 85.8 million; in 1992, 88.6 million, with a *143.2 million deficit* projected for 1993, the largest deficit in the forty-four-year period 1950–1993.[11]

What happened? For more than ten years, declining silver prices discouraged production from primary mines, let alone exploration for new silver sources. Furthermore, about two thirds of all silver produced by mining comes as a byproduct of refining lead, zinc, copper, or other base metals. By 1993, these metals were putting in multiyear lows, which further threatens to curtail silver production. Low silver prices curtailed scrap recovery and new scrap to the market—it dropped a dramatic 11.9 percent from 1989 to 1990.

Meanwhile, fabrication demand had been steadily increasing since 1984, at an average rate of 5.5 percent. Inevitably, demand increasing faster than supply will produce a supply deficit. Just as inevitably (so economic theory tells us), decreasing supply should raise the price of silver. After thirteen long years spent recovering from the unparalleled blowoff silver top in 1980, silver had reached bottom. In February 1993, silver touched off at $3.50. The stage was set for recovery.

QUIRKY SILVER

Both the supply of and demand for silver show a quirk economists call inelasticity. When supply or demand for a product responds greatly to changes in price, they are *elastic*. A product that doesn't respond greatly to those changes is *inelastic*. For numerous reasons, silver's supply and demand are relatively *inelastic* to price *in the short term*. That last qualifier is very important, because, given enough time, any market will finally respond to changes in price.

DEMAND INELASTICITY

Other than monetary demand, the demand for silver *as silver,* silver's unique physical properties make it relatively irreplaceable in most applications. Silver has the highest electrical and thermal conductivity of any metal, which makes it essential in certain critical applications. Only gold is more ductile and malleable. Silver salts react in the presence of light like no other metallic salts, so in spite of periodic announcements of substitutes, silver's position in photography is relatively secure. Silver's

47

bactericidal properties are unique. It also resists corrosion and oxidation exceptionally well.

Most silver applications have one thing in common: *The amount of silver required is relatively small compared to the total cost of the end product.* As long as the price does not soar into the outer atmosphere, this offers little incentive to reduce silver use, because small price increases can be absorbed or easily passed on to the end user. In addition, silver users have had the past two decades to squeeze out silver consumption. This does not mean that silver consumption cannot be reduced, but simply that further reductions and substitutions become less and less economical without substantially higher silver prices. Further reductions offer only diminishing returns.

IRRECOVERABLE LOSS

Some silver is irrecoverably lost through fabrication demand, constantly decreasing the total pool of silver. Silver is forever consumed and lost through photography, electrical usage, dentistry, brazing and soldering, electroplating, mirrors, and medical usage. CRA estimates that in the seven decades from 1921 through 1990, a total of 10 billion ounces were irrecoverably lost in North America alone, and 12.6 billion ounces for the entire world.[12] About 1.4 billion ounces were lost in the past decade. Although this loss has declined in the past three decades, it nevertheless puts unrelenting pressure on the world's silver supply as year by year more silver is lost or tied up in new goods. That's not all. As the economies of China, India, the newly freed East European bloc, and the rest of the world grow, these irrecoverable losses can only grow.

NATURE'S OWN QUIRK

Newly mined silver must replenish supply, but a geological problem stands in the way: *Epithermal deposition* or condensation near the earth's surface. Simply put, the richest silver deposits are nearest the surface of the earth. The deeper mines go, the less silver they tend to produce. The deeper the mine, the more expensive the silver. This also means that almost all the *primary* silver mines in the world have already been discov-

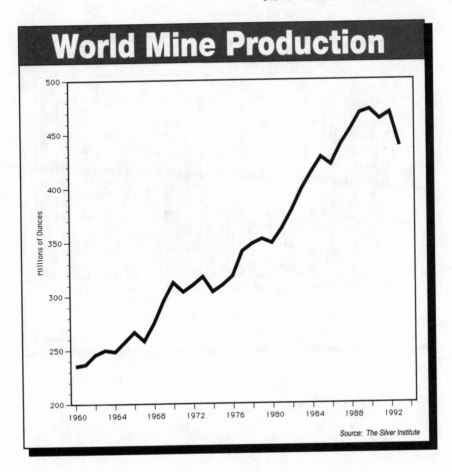

World Mine Production

Millions of Ounces

Source: *The Silver Institute*

ered. Remember that silver is so scarce that it forms only about 73 parts *per billion* of the earth's crust.

COINAGE

Obviously, *coinage demand* for silver is inelastic as well, as governments make decisions with all the speed of a slug with its transmission in "park." U.S. coinage demand has steadily risen since 1986, and now Mexico has announced new coinage that will consume about 7 million ounces a year. Nevertheless, coinage increased throughout the 1980s to an estimated 50 million ounces worldwide in 1993.

49

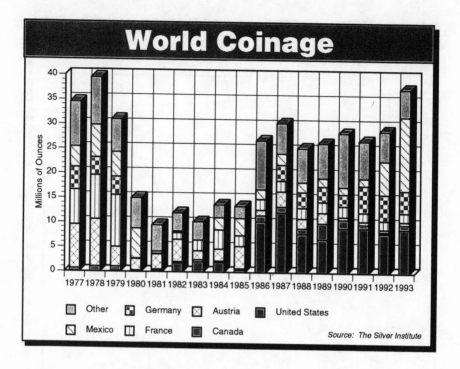

World Coinage

Legend: Other, Germany, Austria, United States, Mexico, France, Canada

Source: The Silver Institute

SUPPLY INELASTICITY

MINING

Most silver production from mining, about two thirds, comes not from primary silver mines but as a byproduct of base metal mining. Thus the bulk of all silver mined depends not on the price of silver, but on the price of these base metals. Even if many of these metals were not hovering around long-term lows, a rise in the silver price will not pull out more silver.

The prolonged bear market of the 1980s has devastated primary silver mining. In terms of 1950 dollars, the real price of silver in 1992 averaged $1.40, 8 cents lower than its real price in 1968! Mining companies have notoriously long lead times from decision to production, from five to seven years. Increasing environmental and land use regulations raise their costs and stretch out lead times. In a private interview during our research, the CEO of one of the biggest silver producers in North America,

Dennis Wheeler of Coeur d'Alene Mines, estimated that prices of at least $7.50 an ounce will be required to spur exploration and development. Once those decisions are made, *five more years will lapse before any new silver is brought to market.*

SCRAP RECOVERY

Scrap silver recovery has been fairly constant since the 1980 peak sucked 320 million ounces onto the market. Since 1981, recovery from secondary and other sources has averaged 144.6 million ounces yearly, declining slightly with silver prices. Although much more quickly responsive to price than mining, much scrap recovery is the price inelastic result of processing industrial scrap. It only increases as industrial usage increases, not as price increases.

An unpredictable new element has butted its head into the silver reclamation world: *environmental regulation.* Because of new ecoregulations, *all* scrap refining is becoming much more expensive. New regulations may stop *some* refining altogether. Varying national regulations, for example, mean that electronic scrap, such as printed circuit boards, which do not require special treatment in the United States (yet), is classed as "hazardous waste" when it reaches the Canadian border. When the value of the scrap is very low, these increased costs can mean that people cease recycling it altogether.

DEATH OF THE DEALER MARKET

Old silver scrap—the knives, forks, spoons, trays, and jewelry we saw pouring into scrap dealers in the Mad Melt—is not *momentarily* available to the market. First it must be bought from retail holders, then brought to market, and then refined. An extensive retail buyer network is needed to locate and buy the scrap and, unlike the late '70s and early '80s, that network simply *no longer exists.* It has completely disappeared.

While much higher silver prices would seem to stimulate that entrepreneurial buying, one relic of the Mad Melt stands in its way. The high price of silver was blamed for an increase in burglaries and other thefts, so many states and municipalities reacted with stiff regulations on precious metals buyers. Typically these require the buyer to obtain a thumb-

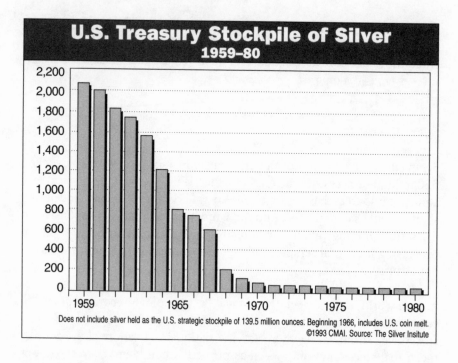

U.S. Treasury Stockpile of Silver
1959–80

Does not include silver held as the U.S. strategic stockpile of 139.5 million ounces. Beginning 1966, includes U.S. coin melt.
©1993 CMAI. Source: The Silver Insitute

print and even a photograph of the seller, as well as the items sold. Most regulations mandate holding periods, some as long as thirty days!

These regulations are burdensome enough in themselves, but to the entrepreneur they pose two mountainous hurdles. First, the risk of having to hold unhedged inventories of silver thirty days when the price is very volatile makes the entire project much less attractive.

Second, the capital requirements imposed by a holding period multiply the cash required many times. During the Mad Melt, it was not unusual for an *average* buyer to spend *$500,000 a week* buying silver. (We know several dealers who were buying *a cool $1 million worth of silver every day.*) While the refineries were open, the dealer could turn this inventory the day he delivered it for melting. If, however, he was required to hold his inventory for a month before he could sell it, he would need *$2.15 million in capital* just to carry one month's inventory. These staggering capital requirements, which directly result from legally mandated holding periods, will keep most entrepreneurs out of the silver scrap buying business.

Furthermore, that was all cash and carry business in 1980. Present federal regulations concerning cash, not to mention the government's capricious, arbitrary, and spiteful administration of these money laundering laws, leave most entrepreneurs terrified. This is another significant bar to entering the business.

Last but not least, we suspect that much of the available old silver already went into the furnace in 1980. Much, much higher silver prices will be required to lure the remaining old silver out in anything like the quantities we saw during the Mad Melt.

Hoards Have Disappeared

The huge hoards that overhung the silver market in the 1970s—threatening every moment to drop into the market and disrupt the supply-demand equation—no longer exist. Since 1986, the United States has consumed more than 66 million ounces of silver in coinage. The Silver Institute estimates that at the present rate of usage, the U.S. national defense silver stockpile will disappear completely by 1998 through coin-

Ounces of Silver Needed to Buy a Median Single-Family U.S. Home (1890–1993)

Thousands of Ounces

Freemarket Gold
& Money Report
P.O. Box 4634,
Greenwich, CT 06830

Data Courtesy of Paul Montgomery, Legg Mason Wood Walker, 600 Thimble Shoals, Newport News, VA 23606

age alone. India, which fed silver onto the market from 1968 through 1984, has dissipated its hoard and become a silver importer on a rising scale. Today no major hoard threatens the market with an instantly available supply.

SILVER VS. THE PRICE OF HOMES

In 1968 the median price of U.S. single-family homes was $20,283. Today the same home costs *five times* that much. Clearly, it's the same house today as it was in 1968. The number of homes versus the number of families hasn't changed. The house still provides the same shelter it provided all those years ago.

The house hasn't changed, *but the dollar in which it is priced has dropped drastically.* A dollar today purchases far less than a 1968 dollar, *75 percent less,* in fact. All sorts of distortions arise when you express prices in paper "dollars." To compare prices over time we have to account for these distortions. After adjusting for the dollar's debasement, the price of the median single-family home today remains essentially *unchanged* from 1968.

Ounces of silver can also be used to express prices, and this will show very, very clearly how cheap silver is compared to history. The accompanying chart presents the price of a home in the United States measured in ounces of silver.

In 1968 that home cost 3,760 ounces. As of August 1993 the same home cost nearly 26,000 ounces, *nearly seven times as much!* (Home price of $105,100 / $4.05 silver = 25,935 ounces.) Recognizing that the usefulness of this home has remained unchanged for the more than one hundred years depicted on the chart on page 53, we can make a very important observation about the purchasing power of silver.

Since 1890 there have been three periods when the median single-family home cost more than 20,000 ounces: 1931–32, 1961, and 1991 to the present. With the benefit of hindsight we know that silver was very cheap in 1931–32 because of the Great Depression. In the early 1960s the U.S. Treasury was trying to control silver's price. From its colossal silver hoard it flooded the market with more than *193 million ounces* in fewer than two years.

Now that the median home once again costs more than 20,000 ounces of silver, we can conclude that silver is cheap once again—in fact, *too cheap*. Ever wish you could buy silver when it was 24.5 cents an ounce, or 90.5 cents? Well, here's your chance. Measured against the median home, silver is as cheap now as it was in 1931–32 and 1961.

The conclusion? *Silver is a good value today,* worth accumulating and holding until the median single-family home again costs fewer than 5,000 ounces to purchase. When that happens, says our chart, the purchasing power of silver is near its maximum. At that point silver will be expensive and no longer a good value.

But today, measured by the median single-family home, the price of silver looks astonishingly cheap. Never before in history has it taken so much silver to purchase a home, and it probably never will again.

SUPPLY AND DEMAND: THE BOTTOM LINE

When we add it all up, the fundamentals of silver supply and demand depict a market vulnerable to vast, volatile price gyrations *with an upward bias.*

- Silver use in most products is irreplaceable, has already been reduced to economic limits, or is not economically feasible until substantially higher silver prices emerge. *Inelastic demand.*
- The cost of silver relative to end products is usually minor, offering little incentive to reduce consumption without much higher prices. *Inelastic demand.*
- Higher silver prices cannot quickly bring out newly mined silver because of long lead times. *Inelastic supply.*
- Two thirds of the silver produced comes as a byproduct of base metal mining, which will not be increased just to mine more silver. *Inelastic supply.*
- Silver recovered from industry depends on the industrial pool of silver already in process, which is not responsive to silver price. *Inelastic supply.*
- Scrap from old silver was fairly well depleted at prices under $30 an ounce in 1980. The dealer network necessary to bring this silver to market has disappeared, and new dealers face substantial regulatory barriers. *Inelastic supply.*

- Silver hoards overhanging the market in the 1970s and 1980s have disappeared. *Inelastic supply.*
- For the first time since 1979, silver entered a deficit of supply over demand in 1990. This supply gap has continued and increased since then: 41.9 million ounces in 1990, 85.8 million ounces in 1991, 88.6 million ounces in 1992, 207.5 million ounces in 1993, and 248.4 million ounces projected for 1994. The 1994 deficit will be the largest in the forty-five years from 1950 through 1994. *Inelastic supply meets inelastic demand.*

When a limited, inelastic supply meets inelastic demand, there is only one way to clear the market: *The silver price must rise.*

A CHANGE OF ENVIRONMENT

One strict cautionary note is needed. In the 1960s and 1970s, *government intervention was driving the precious metals markets.* For long decades, governments (especially the U.S. government) had tried to hold the price of gold and silver low (to cover their tracks) while they were inflating their paper currencies wildly.

Prices act like safety valves on pressure boilers: *They prevent explosions.* The longer governments wired the safety valves shut trying to suppress gold and silver prices, the greater the inevitable upside explosion when governments eventually lost control. The exaggerated peak of January 1980 resulted largely from government price controls.

The government intervention picture is different now. For more than twenty years we have lived under a regime of floating currency exchange rates. The official fiction holds that these are determined by free markets. Nonetheless, central banks, acting alone or in concert, actively intervene to manipulate currency exchange rates for purely political goals. Because gold forms a large part of central bank reserves and is the currency of last resort, it can benefit or suffer from this intervention. To the extent that silver is a surrogate for gold, it gains or loses along with gold. But the direct government price controls that held silver down for thirty years are not now a factor in the silver market. Therefore the outcome of this bull market may take quite a different turn than in 1980.

However, we should remember that government intervention may be able to accelerate an underlying market trend, or even temporarily reverse it. In the long run, however, market trends will override even the gargantuan resources of governments. Government intervention only exaggerates the eventual price adjustment *in exactly the opposite direction government desires.*

THE SWING FACTOR: MONETARY DEMAND

We have seen that silver's supply is, over the short run, price-inelastic. Similarly, demand for silver is, over the short run, price-inelastic. Both tend to increase slowly over time, *other things being equal.* Barring massive new discoveries of silver or the sudden discovery of economically feasible substitutes, there is only one remaining component of demand that can affect price: *monetary or investment demand.* Unlike industrial demand, monetary demand is purely the product of human psychology, infinitely and instantaneously changeable. When it appears, as it did in the 1960s and 1970s, it can divert gigantic amounts of silver from the market and put titanic upward pressure on the price. Like the mysterious intuition that wheels a flock of birds together in flight, its causes are hidden: fear of world events, fear of inflation, bull market greed, or even a change of fashion.

While industrial supply and demand are relatively constant, monetary demand enters the silver market at the margin, like an elephant at a tea party. Its appearance can drive silver from $7 an ounce to $50 an ounce. Its disappearance can leave the market in a thirteen-year coma. The places at the tea party are now set. The slow forces of supply and demand have turned in silver's favor. The vast oversupply of the Mad Melt has been worked off. India has again become a silver sink instead of a silver fountain. Fabrication demand is exceeding supply. Silver has begun to push up out of the mud of a bear market bottom. Around the world, distrust of government's ability to cope with intractable economic and political problems is growing. A sense of unease and malaise, and a loss of confidence in the fecklessness of politicians have gripped the Western world. Newly liberated economies in China and India (and soon the East European bloc) are prospering, and their citizens need a storehouse for new wealth. In short, in the face of tight supplies and rising industrial demand, *monetary demand for silver East and West* is set to explode.

SILVER DEMAND GROWTH
Total World Fabrication Demand (including coinage)
(millions of troy ounces)

Year	Ounces	% Increase/Decrease
1980	379.3	-20.85
1981	364.9	-3.80
1982	373.3	2.33
1983	366.7	-1.79
1984	389.9	6.33
1985	400.9	2.82
1986	436.5	8.88
1987	461.0	5.61
1988	476.1	3.28
1989	508.4	6.35
1990	544.1	7.02
1991	576.2	5.90
1992	593.4	2.98
1993	678.7	14.37

Source: Data from The Silver Institute, World Silver Survey, 1994

WORLD SCRAP SUPPLY

(millions of troy ounces)

(actually shows all nonmine supply)

Year	Secondary	Other	Total	% Increase/Decrease
1980	302.0	18.0	320.0	37.33
1981	184.0	12.0	196.0	-38.75
1982	155.0	1.00	156.0	-20.41
1983	197.5	18.0	215.5	38.14
1984	165.6	-14.0	151.6	-29.65
1985	140.9	12.0	152.9	0.86
1986	129.3	-4.4	124.9	-18.31
1987	137.9	26.1	164.0	31.31
1988	143.9	14.2	158.1	-3.60
1989	136.2	17.0	153.2	-3.10
1990	118.0	17.0	135.0	-11.88
1991	117.6	17.3	134.9	.07
1992	125.2	13.7	138.9	2.97
1993	126.8	13.8	140.6	1.22
	2,180.8		2,342.5	
1980–93 average,155.7			167.3	

Source: Data from The Silver Institute

WORLD SILVER COINAGE

(millions of troy ounces)

Year	Ounces	% Increase/Decrease
1977	34.5	n/a
1978	39.5	14.49
1979	31.0	-21.52
1980	15.0	-51.61
1981	9.5	-36.67
1982	12.0	26.32
1983	10.2	-15.00
1984	13.7	34.31
1985	13.4	-2.19
1986	26.8	100.00
1987	30.4	13.43
1988	25.3	-16.78
1989	26.3	3.95
1990	29.8	13.31
1991	27.7	-7.05
1992	29.4	6.14
1993	38.0	29.25
Average	24.3	5.64

Source: Data from The Silver Institute

U.S. SILVER COINAGE

(millions of troy ounces)

The American Silver Eagle bullion coin was first minted in 1986. Note how the annual production of U.S. silver coinage has increased since this coin's production.

Year	Ounces	Ounces Since Am. Eagle Coin
1983	2.1	n/a
1984	2.0	n/a
1985	0.4	n/a
1986	10.3	10.3
1987	12.2	22.2
1988	7.9	30.4
1989	6.8	37.2
1990	9.1	46.3
1991	9.1	55.4
1992	8.1	63.5
1993	8.9	72.4
1994*	9.3	81.7
Average:	**7.2**	

* Projections. Sources: Gold Newsletter, data from The Silver Institute

Chapter 3

DEMAND EXPLODES IN ASIA

The economies of Asia are booming, and that means booming new demand for silver. Because silver is indispensable in thousands of consumer applications, from photography to electronics, rising Asian consumer demand will pull silver consumption right along with it. "Consumer demand" also includes the vast array of silver applications in the electronic, telecommunications, and electrical infrastructure. As these economies grow, their infrastructures—highways, ports, airports, telecommunications, electrical distribution—must grow in tandem. *The Economist* recently had quite a bit to say about Asia.[1]

How big will the market be? In the next ten years, Asia—India, China, and points east—will increase its share of world population to about 60 percent. More important than that, Asia has a baby boom all its own, and these boomers will be moving into their twenties and thirties, the years of greatest consumption.

How big will the consumption be? Incomes are rapidly rising. In developing countries, the worldwide pattern of consumption has been to increase purchases *abruptly* after income passes a certain level. Thus a 10 percent rise in average income might increase the number of households that can afford to buy motorcycles *sevenfold*. Demand, as they say, *explodes*.

How fast will it grow? In the past twenty years, Asia has raced ahead of

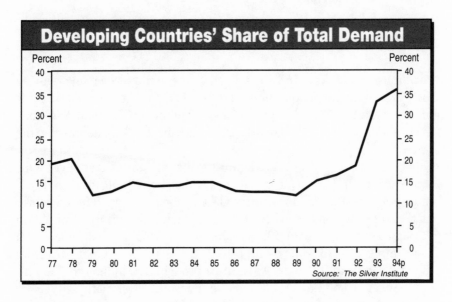

Developing Countries' Share of Total Demand

Percent / Percent

Source: The Silver Institute

the rest of the world in economic growth, chalking up a robust real 7 percent growth every year, compared with an anemic 2.5 percent for the industrialized countries. Even India has grown almost 5 percent per year over the past twenty years. The World Bank estimates that Asia will continue to outpace the rest of the world in growth by at least 2 to 1, while India outruns the world by only 1.5 to 1. This prolonged growth has produced an Asian middle class with tremendous demand for consumer goods.

But consumer demand is not alone. By the year 2000, Asia outside Japan will have to spend an estimated $1 trillion on infrastructure—telecommunications, distribution, and electronics—*all of which use indispensable silver.*

In an exclusive interview with *Gold Newsletter,* Robert Lloyd George of the Hong Kong-based investment management firm Lloyd George Management pointed out that the increasing demand for precious metals in China and the rest of Asia results from the *secular* trend of growing wealth, economic power, and income. In the past ten years, per capita income in Hong Kong has soared from $5,432 to $16,382. Don't stop there: The savings rate is an incredible *31.4 percent of income.* The same pattern appears in Singapore, Malaysia, Thailand, Indonesia, and South Korea, where incomes have tripled in the past ten years.

63

INDIA: THE GREAT SILVER SINK

For thousands of years India has acted as the world's silver sink. During the 1970s, the greatest question mark overhanging the silver market was India's enormous silver hoard. Rising silver prices threatened to coax that Indian silver out of hoards and onto the market, depressing the price.

It's difficult to get an *exact* figure for the amount of that silver. Our source in the Indian silver industry says that from 1968 through 1984, India poured 546.6 million ounces (17,000 tons) of silver onto the world market. Precious metals expert Timothy Green estimates that from 1965 through 1985, more than 500 million ounces (15,552 tons) came out of India in response to rising world prices.[2] Let us simply estimate that from the mid-1960s to the mid-1980s, India brought 500 million to 550 million ounces (15,552 to 17,000 tons) to the world silver market.

From the mid-1960s through the mid-1980s, silver flowed out of India. *That flow has now reversed, and India is siphoning silver out of the world market.* Timothy Green estimates that silver amounting to nearly 60 million ounces (1,866 tons) was smuggled into India in 1990, and nearly 48 million ounces (1,500 tons) in 1991—a total of nearly 108 million ounces.

Little wonder that silver is smuggled into India, since in India it carries a large premium over the world silver price. As long as the price of silver in India carries a premium to the world price, how much silver will come out? Who will risk confiscation and arrest to smuggle silver *out* of India for the privilege of selling it $1 to $2 *lower* than the Indian silver price? Right—exactly nobody.

Estimates of the total Indian silver stock vary from 3.2 billion ounces (100,000 tons) to 3.8 billion ounces (117,884 tons). CRA estimates that the total of all silver in India, plus the recoverable pool in use, amounts to 3.63 billion ounces (112,908 tons).[3] India's share amounts to about 12 percent of the world stock of silver. North America, by comparison, has 24.7 percent of the world stock; Western Europe, 27.6 percent; the Middle East, China, and the rest of Asia and Oceania, 12.5 percent.

Statistics from India, though not terribly reliable, show that for the period 1953–64, India fabrication demand amounted to 66.8 million ounces, an average of 5.57 million ounces per year. From 1965 through 1977, fabrication demand was virtually stable, totaling 199.6 million ounces and averaging 15.35 million ounces per year. In 1978, however, fabrication demand jumped to 21 million ounces and remained stable at that level through 1988, consuming a total of 241.8 million ounces, an average of 22 million ounces annually.

Another watershed year in India was 1989. In that year, fabrication demand jumped to 27.1 million ounces (840 tons). That began a series of years in which demand *more than quadrupled.* The next year, 1990, fabrication demand *leaped 54 percent,* to 41.8 million ounces (1,300 tons). In 1991, demand jumped 6.5 percent, to 44.5 million ounces (1,384 tons); in 1992 it leaped again, 29.9 percent, to 57.8 million ounces (about 1,800 tons); and 1993 saw the greatest increase of all, to an astonishing 119.0 million ounces—more than double the previous year's demand. The sheer schizophrenia of these figures makes them appear doubtful, but the increases are genuine, according to our sources.

THE INDIAN SWING FACTOR

The swing factor in Indian silver demand is the success of those who depend on agriculture for their living: 60 percent of the Indian population of 866 million, or about 520 million people. When crops are good, they have money. They save it in the form of silver. They save, in fact, about *25 percent of their incomes.* For Indian peasants, the economic situation has reversed from the period 1968–84. With incomes increasing, they now have savings with which to buy silver.

This class of people had for years lived on abysmally poor incomes. Suddenly they found themselves in comfortable economic conditions, which enabled them to increase their savings on a large scale. Farm and agricultural production increased substantially, and this income is exempt from all taxes. For these people, silver is their traditional savings account, whether they buy it as silver utensils, ornaments, or simply silver bars.

But peasants on the land are not the only Indians with rising incomes. Indeed, as incomes improve, industrial wage earners, the lower middle class, and peasants are all buying silver as well.

First, there is no alternative Indian investment as safe and as liquid as silver. In 1992, some Indians thought that the stock exchange would be that alternative investment, but so many people got their fingers burned there that they have turned back to gold and silver. The very rich are

65

INDIAN SILVER FABRICATION DEMAND
(million troy ounces)

Industrial Uses	1988	1989	1990	1991	1992	1993
Photography	4.8	4.8	5.6	2.6	2.6	2.3
Electroplating	3.2	3.2	4.8	6.4	6.4	6.4
Electrical/electronics	3.2	3.2	4.0	4.2	4.2	4.2
Brazing alloys	2.4	2.4	2.4	3.2	3.2	3.2
Jari	1.6	1.6	3.2	5.1	6.4	6.4
Foils	—	—	1.0	1.6	2.3	8.0
Other	0.8	0.8	1.4	2.6	2.3	1.6
Subtotal	16.0	16.1	22.5	25.7	27.3	32.2
% Change year ago	*15.9*	*.5*	*40.0*	*14.3*	*16.3*	*17.7*
Jewelry and Silverware						
Jewelry	—	—	—	9.6	16.1	41.3
Silverware	—	—	—	9.2	14.4	45.5
Subtotal	6.4	10.9	19.3	18.8	30.5	86.8
% Change year ago	*1.6*	*70.3*	*77.1*	*-2.6*	*62.2*	*184.6*
Total	22.4	27.0	41.8	44.5	57.8	119.0
% Change year ago	*11.4*	*20.4*	*55.0*	*6.5*	*29.9*	*105.7*

Source: The Silver Institute

buying diamonds. Gold is more in demand in the cities among the higher-income groups, who use it to dodge taxes. Silver is the *permanent savings account* for the bulk of the Indian population.

Second, why silver rather than gold? For the lower middle class, wage earners and farmers, the high ratio of gold to silver makes silver far preferable, even though gold is more available. In fact, our source says that as long as the gold–silver ratio remains above 40 to 1, Indian buyers will continue to buy silver. At about $10 to $12 an ounce, they may stop buying silver or won't buy quite as much. However, that slowdown in demand might also come at about a gold–silver ratio of 40 to 1, rather than at a certain silver price.

At what price will Indians sell silver? That's not the right question. Because silver is their savings account, they won't sell until the economy turns down or crops fail. They're not looking for a target price to sell, but an occasion of need.

Indian Silver Demand

When you look at the accompanying table of Indian silver usage, remember that the figures involve some estimation. Remember also that in 1991, official imports through the State Bank of India amounted to 1.24 million ounces, but "unofficial imports," smuggled silver, were estimated to be *42 million ounces!* Our table does not include investment demand, the swing factor in the calculation. In 1992, Timothy Green estimated coin and investment demand at 9.4 million ounces for 1990 and 6.9 million ounces for 1992. Green also estimated official seizures from smugglers as 6.9 million ounces in 1990 and 6.4 million ounces in 1991.[4] This seized silver went into government stocks. Silver production from India itself is not significant. In the past it has hovered at about one million ounces— that is, 1.75 percent to 2.4 percent of annual usage in the past three years.

LEGAL CHANGES IN INDIA

Most of the silver entering India has been imported by smugglers operating out of Dubai or Singapore because the government permits only meager imports, basically just tit for tat against exports of jewelry. Reports of legalization of imports have been exaggerated. The legal change of February 1993 will enhance imports by 600 to 700 tons, but so far that policy change has only *trimmed,* not eliminated, the premium on silver's price in India. Dubai traders estimate that 118.4 million ounces (3,700 tons) passed through in 1993, versus 1,600 tons in 1992, and that European dealers report declining stocks. Once again, India is becoming the world silver sink.

The legal change applied only in a few cases. Resident and nonresident Indians (NRIs, those who have lived out of India for more than six months) can bring into India 100 kilograms (about 3,215 troy ounces) of silver upon payment of a duty of 500 rupees per kilogram (about 50 cents an ounce), but they can *only* bring in 100 kilograms *once every six months.*

Indian Fabrication Demand

Millions of Ounces

1987 1988 1989 1990 1991 1992 1993

■ Silverware   ▣ Foils   ▨ Electrical/Electronics

⊠ Jewelry   ☐ Jari   ▦ Electoplating

■ Others   ▥ Brazing Alloys   ☐ Photography

Source: The Silver Institute

This is a great improvement over previous restrictions, but hardly a rollicking free market.

Actually, the Indian government is doing silver a favor by maintaining barriers to its free flow into and out of India. As smugglers must risk life, limb, and capital to sneak into India half or two thirds of the silver Indians desire every year, then silver's price in India *must* continue to carry a large premium above the world price. That premium will include a risk premium for smugglers as well as the 50-cents-per-ounce tax.

The change in the law has already substantially reduced the Indian silver premium, which had been 60 percent to 100 percent above the world price. The partial legalization sucked the wind out of the premium's sails so that in June the price of silver touched Rs.8,000 per kilogram (about $8.00 an ounce). In July 1993 the price drifted down to Rs.6,500 per kilogram (about $6.50 an ounce), while the world price was below $5.00. Despite this premium, there is still no *floating stock* of silver available in India. Increased demand can be met only by increased imports, smuggled or otherwise.

There is other evidence that Indian government silver sales may actually *raise* the price. As the Indian silver price is brought down into line with the world price, Indians will be getting more silver for their money. The medals and small bars given as gifts will probably show stronger sales as a result of any drop in price. Silver jewelry and silverware sales would also benefit. For all these reasons, we think that Indian government silver sales will have very little *long-term* effect on the world silver market and may actually stimulate Indian silver consumption.

In summary, Indian silver demand is improving hand in hand with the economy. Indian demand for silver has less to do with inflation or the price of silver than with rising industrial and consumer demand. These higher incomes channel savings into silver, the traditional form of savings. The silver outflow of the 1960s, 1970s, and early 1980s has been reversed, and India is now draining new silver supplies off the market. Barring severe crop failures and economic downturn, both fabrication and monetary components of silver demand will increase in the near to medium term.

CHINA: THE SMOKING DRAGON

In 1992, China emerged as the biggest source of demand in the world gold market. How in the world did that happen?

Since the 1989 unrest in Tienanmen Square, the Chinese regime has "mellowed." However, unlike the Soviet regime, this mellowing has been primarily economic, not political. There is vast new economic activity as the long-chained entrepreneurial genius of the Chinese people is liberated, and this activity will continue to grow.

But this story is not new. Since 1978, the Chinese GDP has been increasing an average 10 percent a year. Although the Chinese economy varies greatly from province to province, Guangdong Province, the pacesetter for economic reform, grew by 19.5 percent in 1992! Since 1978, Chinese per capita GDP has multiplied more than fourfold.

China is fast becoming a global superpower. According to the Asian Development Bank's latest annual assessment of Asian economies, China's 1992 GDP grew an estimated 12.8 percent. Despite serious drought, agricultural output grew by 1.7 percent, while industrial sector growth in 1992 accelerated to an estimated 20.4 percent. Everywhere the nonstate sector was the prime mover behind this remarkable growth. Nor is the government likely to use authoritarian measures to stifle this economic growth. Rather, in the opinion of Robert Lloyd George, their tenuous hold on power depends on the economic boom continuing.

Peasants comprise about two thirds of China's 1.2 billion population. The summer of 1993 saw major peasant unrest brought on by unfair taxes and oppressive, corrupt local officials. In Sichuan Province, 10,000 peasants went on a rampage, and 200 similar rural disturbances were reported in the first half of 1993. To protect themselves, peasants are joining rural secret societies and political groups. Totalitarian government is losing total control.

CHINESE COINS THROUGH 1935

In 1935, China was the last major power to leave the silver standard. Before 1889, the Chinese imperial government issued only brass cash coins. Silver was used for larger payments, but it was silver in *sycee*— boat- or shoe-shaped ingots. (*Sycee* is a corruption of the Chinese *hsi ssu*, "fine silk," or *sai ssu*, "fine silver.") These ingots passed by weight, usually by the *tael*, a Chinese weight varying from 1.125 troy ounces to 1.22 troy ounces.[5]

For several centuries, Mexican and Spanish American pieces of eight were standard in the Chinese trade. Today many of these survive, complete with "chop marks," the counterstamps of Chinese merchants certifying their genuineness. From 1907 through 1911, the imperial government, and from 1912, the republican government issued "dollar" or *yuan* silver coins. The fineness and silver content of these coins varied from 0.7554 troy ounce to 0.7899 troy ounce, and at the end of the period there was even one coin minted in 72 percent silver that contained only 0.463 troy ounce (by comparison, the U.S. silver dollar is 0.7734 troy ounce fine silver).

CHINESE SILVER COINAGE, 1911–49

(millions of troy ounces)

Year	Ounces	Year	Ounces
1911	59	1926	72
1912	63	1927	50
1913	29	1928	93
1914	78	1929	9
1915	109	1930	14
1916	80	1931	1
1917	38	1932	5
1918	0	1933	3
1919	0	1934	19
1920	109	1935	41
1921	35		
1922	59		
1923	90	1938	4
1924	12	1949	33
1925	70		

Source: Charles River Associates, Stocks of Silver Around the World

Between 1911 and 1949, 1.2 billion troy ounces of silver were struck into Chinese coinage. It is very difficult to get any idea of how much of this remains in China. However, the October 1992 CRA *Stocks of Silver Around the World* estimates that in the five years after the Chinese demonetization of silver in 1935, China melted its coinage and sold about 1 billion ounces on the world market. Of the remaining 450 million ounces of silver in China, other Asian countries, and Oceania, CRA estimates that about 45 million troy ounces survive. Remember, this last figure includes not only China but other countries as well.[6]

WHERE DID ALL THE CHINESE COINS GO?

In 1981, *The Wall Street Journal* reported that silver coins were financing consumer goods being smuggled into China.[7] Rising incomes from improvements in the Chinese economy had sent demand for consumer goods soaring. Around Hong Kong, there was a boom in smuggling so great that restaurant owners were complaining that the price of fresh seafood had doubled—crewmen and boat owners could make much more money smuggling than fishing. One trip could earn a crew member the equivalent of two years' income from fishing.

This smuggling was financed by silver coins coming *out* of China. Over many years, they had been squirreled away as an emergency reserve, like a savings account. As these coins existed in China, most of them were melted. The Red Chinese government was so worried about the "drain of silver" that it banned fishing in a twenty-three-mile belt along the coast of Guangxi and Guangdong provinces. No one knows how much silver has left China to finance smuggling since 1980, but there was very little silver to begin with. CRA estimates that the Middle East, China, and all other Asian countries (excluding Japan and India) and Oceania held 19.5 percent of all the world's available and unavailable silver stocks at the end of 1991. Estimated coin in China then was 45 million ounces. By comparison, 1992 U.S. use of silver in photography alone was 64.4 million ounces.

According to a private communication from respected precious metals analyst Timothy Green, there is in fact virtually no silver business with China. Chinese hoarding and investment is all channeled into pure gold jewelry (24-karat) or small gold bars. In several visits to China from 1991 to 1993, Mr. Green had seen almost no silver jewelry on display. The only silver in evidence is in the form of old silver coins, which people in China occasionally try to sell to foreigners for dollars.

Most of the silver entering China would have to pass through Hong Kong, and much of the 4.6 million ounces of silver officially and unofficially imported into Hong Kong no doubt finds its way into China, but no one knows the specific amounts.

Chinese Silver Demand

There is at present little identifiable monetary demand for silver in China. However, as the benefits of the economic boom filter down to China's 800 million peasants and rural dwellers, we suspect that monetary demand for gold will find a ready substitute in cheaper silver. Regardless of Chinese monetary demand, an economic growth rate approaching 20 percent a year will demand huge quantities of silver in consumer and infrastructure applications.

Although there aren't any precise statistics available for present Chinese silver consumption, let's extrapolate some figures based on Chinese population and U.S. silver consumption. We quickly admit that the U.S. is the world's largest consumer of silver. Chinese silver demand won't look like U.S. demand for another forty years, but guesswork can give us some idea of how deep and broad Chinese demand might be. Remember, there are three broad categories of demand: monetary, consumer, and infrastructure or industrial.

The United States now consumes about 0.25 ounce of silver per capita *in photographic uses alone*. China has 1.2 billion people, so at the present level of American photographic use the Chinese would need *300 million ounces of silver for photography alone*. America now uses about 0.08 ounce per capita for electrical contacts and conductors. In China that would mean about 100 million ounces of silver annually.

In the next four to five decades, China will be installing an infrastructure, both in industry and communications. How many telephones, telephone switches, distribution devices, relays, fax machines, and on and on and on will be required? Silver is also indispensable in building an electrical distribution network, which China must have on an unheard-of scale. *Every one of these applications must have silver.* Based solely on a static population of 1.2 billion, the Chinese at the present level of American silver use would need about 0.5 ounce of silver per person per year, or almost *610 million ounces!*

SOUTH KOREA

Before 1990, South Korean fabrication demand hovered at about 5 million to 6 million ounces yearly, but that year it rose dramatically. After 1991, new capacity to produce silver-milled products and chemicals for electronics uses began to eat up even more silver as production of silver items was shifted to Korea. In 1992, recession temporarily cut back growth in silver demand. More than half of the South Korean silver demand goes for consumer items such as silver spoons and chopsticks, and this area suffered along with recession-pinched incomes.

SOUTH KOREAN SILVER FABRICATION DEMAND
(millions of troy ounces)

	1989	*1990*	*1991*	*1992*	*1993*
Decorative/sterling	4.3	4.5	5.1	4.8	5.0
Electronics	0.0	0.0	0.6	0.5	0.8
Chemicals	0.0	2.2	3.2	3.2	3.7
Mirrors	0.0	0.0	0.0	0.0	0.0
Brazing alloys	1.0	0.1	0.2	0.3	0.5
Jewelry	0.0	0.0	0.2	0.2	0.5
Total:	5.4	6.8	9.4	9.1	10.5
% Change year ago	—	*27.4*	*36.7*	*-3.1*	*15.8*

Source: The Silver Institute

TAIWAN

In Taiwan, too, silver consumption has increased sharply in recent years. Traditionally there was never much jewelry or sterlingware demand for silver in China, but this seems to be changing. From 1990 to 1992 silver use in jewelry leapfrogged from 128,600 ounces (1990) to 643,000 ounces (1991) to 964,500 ounces (1992). Silver primarily goes into electronics in Taiwan, and this is expected to increase as well.

TAIWANESE SILVER FABRICATION DEMAND

(millions of troy ounces)

	1990	*1991*	*1992*	*1993*
Photography	0.1	0.1	0.1	0.1
Electronics	0.3	0.3	0.4	0.4
Electroplating for Electronics and Decorative	1.6	1.9	2.3	2.5
Chemicals	0.3	0.5	0.6	0.6
Mirrors	0.3	0.4	0.5	0.5
Brazing alloys	0.5	0.6	0.7	0.7
Jewelry	0.1	0.6	1.0	0.9
Total:	3.2	4.5	5.5	5.6
% Change year ago	—	*40.5*	*23.0*	*2.2*

Source: The Silver Institute

HONG KONG

Hong Kong serves the silver market both as an *entrepôt* and as a fabrication center. In 1992, official and unofficial imports for fabrication demand totaled 4.6 million ounces. Ninety percent of this was reexported. Another 4.6 million ounces enters over and under the table but is simply exported without any further treatment.

The Asian pattern of growing silver use also appears in Hong Kong. Net silver use rose 24 percent in 1992, up from 3.7 million ounces in 1991. Electronics (in Hong Kong, mostly batteries) takes the lion's share, with jewelry growing strongly. The accompanying chart tells the tale. Investment demand, however, has declined since the 1980s. Hong Kong investors buy fewer than 25,000 ounces of silver per year.

HONG KONG SILVER FABRICATION DEMAND
(does not include silver not worked in Hong Kong,
transshipped silver roughly doubles the 1992 total)
(millions of troy ounces)

	1985	1986	1987	1988	1989
Jewelry	0.9	0.9	0.9	0.8	0.9
Silverplate/decorative	0.2	0.2	0.2	0.2	0.2
Electronics	1.9	1.9	1.9	1.8	1.8
Mirrors/other	0.2	0.2	0.2	0.1	0.2
Total:	3.2	3.1	3.1	3.0	3.1
% Change year ago	—	-3.0	-1.0	-4.2	3.3

	1990	1991	1992	1993
Jewelry	0.9	1.0	1.3	1.4
Silverplate/decorative	0.2	0.3	0.3	0.4
Electronics	1.9	2.2	2.8	2.9
Mirrors/other	0.2	0.2	0.2	0.3
Total:	3.2	3.7	4.6	4.9
% Change year ago	5.3	15.0	24.4	7.5

Source: The Silver Institute

THAILAND

Here's another success story for government import duties and restrictions. The Thai government charges a 25 percent duty on fabricated silver imports and a 10 percent duty on unwrought silver. As a result, enterprising "unofficial alternative market supply facilitators" (a.k.a. smugglers) import about three-fourths of the Thai silver supply. Back-handed government regulations actually encourage Thai corporations to use black market silver to duck corporate income taxes. Companies must reveal actual revenues to qualify for reimbursement of duties on official imports, which makes smuggled silver just that much more attractive.

The electronics industry has not yet begun to grow in Thailand but probably will spurt in the later 1990s. All the silver fabricated in Thailand goes into silver jewelry (90 percent of demand), silverware, and other decorative items. The accompanying table illustrates the situation:

THAILAND SILVER FABRICATION DEMAND
(millions of troy ounces)

	1986	1987	1988	1989
Jewelry	5.3	6.6	7.4	10.1
Silverplate/decorative	0.6	0.7	0.8	1.1
Total:	5.9	7.4	8.2	11.2
% Change year ago	—	*25.0*	*11.1*	*36.7*
	1990	*1991*	*1992*	*1993*
Jewelry	9.9	27.3	31.0	37.3
Silverplate/decorative	1.1	3.0	3.4	4.1
Total:	11.0	30.4	34.5	41.1
% Change year ago	*-1.9*	*176.2*	*13.5*	*20.0*

Source: The Silver Institute

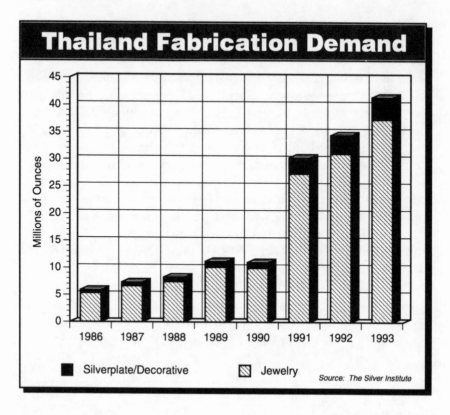

Thailand Fabrication Demand

Millions of Ounces

1986 1987 1988 1989 1990 1991 1992 1993

■ Silverplate/Decorative   ▨ Jewelry

Source: The Silver Institute

PROSPECTS FOR THE FUTURE

Rising fabrication demand for silver all over Asia is smashing all records. This silver demand is the partner of economic growth and development. While we can expect overheated growth rates to moderate, or even to dip from time to time, the overwhelming trend continues to push consumer and industrial demand for silver into the upper reaches of the Eastern sky. And only in India have we really considered the effects of monetary demand for silver.

In the *Gold Newsletter* interview cited above, Robert Lloyd George estimated that a maximum of 20 percent of the Chinese population would be able to participate in the gold market. Imagine what will happen if even a portion of the rest of that demand for a stable form of savings is channeled into silver. Imagine what will happen to monetary demand for silver when a few large countries experience severe inflation, as we already see in China and the former Soviet Union. Of course, monetary chaos breeds monetary demand for silver. Consider just these areas where severe monetary danger threatens:

- 851 million Indians
- 1.2 billion Chinese
- 300 million in the former USSR
- 2.35 billion people

And every one of these inflation-racked people has an overwhelmingly pressing reason to buy just a little silver. Suppose every one of them bought *just 0.5 ounce*. . . .

Chapter 4

THE GOLD–SILVER RATIO

Why would anyone buy gold when the ratio is 8 to 1 and dropping?

—An Old Trader

Not long ago we were talking to a special old friend of ours. You know the type—when they're soldiers they're called "battle-scarred veterans." Maybe with veteran commodity traders you call them "wise old traders" or "gnomes of Chicago." At any rate, our friend has been trading commodities for more than fifty years (he started with cotton). He knows markets. Occasionally he calls us to talk about the markets, but mostly we just ask a few questions and *listen*.

Lately he's wanted to talk about only one thing: *silver*. The last time he called, we asked him about gold and the gold–silver ratio. He said with a snort, "Gold! Why would anyone buy gold when the ratio is 8 to 1 and dropping?"

WHAT DOES THE GOLD–SILVER RATIO MEAN TO INVESTORS?

What is the "gold–silver ratio"? Nothing more than the market price of gold divided by the market price of silver. If gold is $400 an ounce and silver is $5, then the ratio is 400/5 or 80 to 1, also written as 80:1. The ratio is important to understanding silver for two reasons.

First, for thousands of years there were *statutory ratios* of gold to silver. These were laws or statutes (and sometimes custom with the force of law) that decreed a certain ratio of gold to silver—the price of gold in ounces of silver. When the ratio in the market diverged from the statutory ratio, then the opportunity arose for *arbitrageurs*, those watchful traders who take advantage of *arbitrage* (small price differences between markets). These watchful traders would buy one metal or the other in the countries where it was cheap, ship it to countries where it was dear, and pocket the difference.

Second, traders who study markets closely often notice that certain

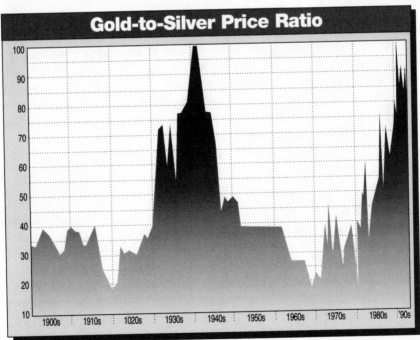

Source: U.S. Bureau of Mines, Handy and Harmon

relationships between commodities stubbornly return to certain levels. If you know these historical ranges, you can make a more informed and accurate decision about the price trend of one or more commodities—*and that means money in your pocket.*

For just a second let's think in very broad terms. First, glance at the accompanying table, "The Gold–Silver Ratio." Suppose you graphed the ratio of gold to silver for the past *six thousand years,* and you made the graph 60 feet long. Each foot represents a century in time. Almost all but the last sixteen inches of that graph would show the ratio between 8:1 and 16:1, and most of the graph would fall between 10:1 and 12:1. Only in the last *fifteen inches* (125 years) has the gold–silver ratio ever risen above 16 ounces of silver to one ounce of gold. Only twice in all of recorded history has the ratio reached 100:1—once in 1940, and it steadily slid from there to 16:1 (briefly) in 1980; and once again, in 1991, and it has been sinking from there ever since.

The Gold–Silver Ratio

The more ancient ratios are estimates for long periods of time. Those from 1600 to 1900 are yearly or periodic averages from Michael G. Mulhall, The Dictionary of Statistics, *4th ed. (London: George Routledge and Sons, 1899) and E. J. Farmer,* The Conspiracy Against Silver, or a Plea for Bi-Metallism *(New York: Greenwood Press, 1969; originally published 1886), p. 13. The other statistics are from Steve Puetz's Investment Letter, or from our own records. Statistics after 1900 are not yearly averages, but lows or highs that generally did not obtain for long periods. In 1980 the ratio stayed below 20 to 1 for the first two and a half months only, and touched under 16 to 1 for only a few days in January.*

Menes, Egypt, 3200 B.C.	2.5 to 1
Egypt, 2700 B.C.	9.0 to 1
Hammurabi, Mesopotamia, 2700 B.C.	6.0 to 1
Egypt, 1000 B.C..	10.0 to 1
Croesus, Lydia, ca. 550 B.C.	13.33 to 1
Persia under Darius, son of Hystaspes (father of Xerxes)	13.0 to 1
Plato, ca. 445 B.C.	12.0 to 1
Xenophon (in Persia)	11.66 to 1
Menander, ca. 341 B.C.	10.0 to 1

Greece, ca. 300 B.C.	10.0 to 1
Rome, 207 B.C.	14.5 to 1
Rome, 189 B.C.	10.0 to 1
Rome, 40 B.C., Julius Caesar	7.5 to 1
Rome, Claudius	12.5 to 1
Constantine the Great	10.5 to 1
Theodosian Code	14.4 to 1
Medieval England	11.1 to 1
Medieval Italy	12.6 to 1
Spain, 1497, Edict of Medina	10.07 to 1
Germany, 1500	10.05 to 1
1600–20	12.1 to 1
1700–20	15.1 to 1
1800–20	15.3 to 1
1821–40	15.6 to 1
1841–60	15.6 to 1
1861–70	15.6 to 1
1871–80	16.7 to 1
1881–82	17.6 to 1
1883–84	18.4 to 1
1885–86	19.9 to 1
1887–88	21.2 to 1
1890	18.3 to 1
1932	75.0 to 1
1940–41	100.0 to 1
1980	16.0 to 1
1991 (February)	100.0 to 1
1994 (July)	73.25 to 1

Is the ratio significant? Yes, to see very long-term, stable relations like the gold–silver ratio turn and confirm the trend you suspect, dropping steadily from that historic high of 100:1, offers powerful comfort to any careful investor.

Although the ratio seems mysterious, there is nothing magical about it. Still, it makes you wonder, What is going on here? When gold and silver were both everyday money, we could offer some explanation for the price movements. However, when their *official* monetary links have long been cut, why do they move together? What attraction between them drives the ratio? Not to put too mystical a cast on it, when you look at the ratio, you are observing some unseen force. *What is it?*

We confess, we don't know just how meaningful or trustworthy the gold-silver ratio is. Maybe it is some "natural" ratio, and tends toward the ratio of gold and silver in natural occurrence, 10 to 1 or 12 to 1. That, however, ignores the bulk of present-day demand analysis for silver and gold. There's a lot more *dirt* in the world than air, too, but there's no fixed ratio of price between them (unless you're a real estate agent).

Maybe the action of the ratio just stems from human psychology. Maybe traders watching the market cue off magic round numbers like 100 to 1 or 50 to 1 and make long-term decisions from that. Maybe the irrecoverable loss of silver through usage, a loss that gold doesn't share, and the ever-increasing uses for silver mean that the ratio of value should narrow in silver's favor over the years.

Estimates of the present world gold stock range from 3.2 billion ounces to 3.5 billion ounces. Of all the gold mined, very little has been lost. Certainly there is no ongoing, irrecoverable loss of gold that even remotely compares with irrecoverable silver loss. The CRA estimate of world silver production since 4000 B.C. of 37.45 billion ounces[1] offers a basis to estimate the *physical,* if not the market, gold–silver ratio. Assuming that very little gold has been lost, then all the gold humans have ever mined is about one tenth or one twelfth the weight of all the silver mined, a range of 10 to 1 to 12 to 1.

If gold and silver are both equally remonetized, then this ratio of all silver ever mined to all gold ever mined must be reduced farther still to account for the present physical balance of the precious metals. CRA estimates total world silver stocks *still in existence* to be 19 billion ounces.[2] If the total world gold supply is 3.2 billion ounces to 3.5 billion ounces, that makes the physical gold–silver ratio 5.95 to 1 to 5.44 to 1.

We also have to factor in the ongoing irrecoverable loss of silver, proceeding much, much faster than the loss of gold. Merely to reflect the physical gold–silver ratio, the ratio should easily drop *below 7 to 1*. From this viewpoint, Bunker Hunt's old saw—that he was holding silver until the ratio hit 5 to 1—doesn't seem so crazy after all.

Whatever mysterious force moves the gold–silver ratio, we have to face this: A ratio that has only twice in the past sixty years reached 100 to 1 is probably way out of line anywhere near that level. Besides, silver's performance relative to gold, rising 150 percent to 200 percent as fast as gold in bull markets, makes silver historically more attractive than gold, *understanding that past performance is no guarantee of future performance.*

RATIO TRADING

During the 1970s and early 1980s, when the ratio was very volatile, it fluctuated from 45 to 1 to 20 to 1, more narrowly from about 30 to 1 to about 40 to 1, a range of 33 percent. This volatility offered a superb *arbitrage* opportunity for sophisticated traders. You simply traded silver for gold when the ratio neared the lowest part of the range (around 30 to 1), waited until it hit 40 to 1, and then swapped the silver back into gold. Assuming you kept transaction costs low, you could easily double the amount of silver you held in a short time.

However, nothing lasts forever in this world. In the mid-'80s silver crossed the fateful ratio of 50 to 1 and hasn't returned since. Since the 1991 high at 100 to 1, the ratio has trended downward, more significantly since early 1993.

SOURCE: TONY HENFREY

What does this mean for precious metals investors today? If you believe that the ratio has turned in silver's favor for a long time, when you buy any more precious metals you should heavily favor silver, *remembering that there is no guarantee that the ratio will continue to improve in silver's favor*. However, the data we present in this book, especially the fundamental supply-demand data, along with silver's initial performance rising twice as fast as gold off the 1993 bottom, lead us to believe that the ratio has turned down for a long time.

Look at the Gold–Silver Ratio chart. Technically, that chart also indicates that *the ratio has made a major, long-term downward turn* that will continue for several years. Aggressive silver investors who eventually want to acquire a position in gold as well should concentrate buying on silver, planning to swap silver for gold at a ratio under 40 to 1, or 50 to 1 for nervous types. (Formerly, for income tax purposes, these trades were considered "like-kind" exchanges and were not taxable. Unhappily, that rule was changed for gold-silver swaps in 1982. The tax consequences may severely alter the profitability of the strategy. Under limitations, capital gains can be credited against capital losses, so check with your tax adviser to determine the exact income tax consequences in your own situation.)

On the way down, the round numbers will offer strong support to the ratio (i.e., resistance to further downward moves), especially around 70 to 1, 60 to 1, 50 to 1, and 40 to 1. Expect to see great volatility in the ratio, too. Remember that silver tends to rise one-and-a-half to two times as fast as gold but also tends to fall somewhat faster as well. Mathematically, this makes the ratio more volatile, so if you are trading the ratio, buckle up your seat belt, grab hold of the bars, and brace yourself for a wild ride.

Chapter 5

THE TECHNICAL EDGE

Once you've decided to invest in silver—bullion, coins, futures, options, or mining shares—you can enjoy an extra edge by learning basic technical analysis. Technical analysis can do two things: get you into the market at the right time, or keep you from cleaning your own plow. You either learn it, or you fly your money blind into the clouds, following the advice of the latest newsletter gurus. If that's your choice, we can only wish you happy landings.

Technical analysis is both an art and a science, and experts spend years learning it. However, you can carefully read the following short summary and learn at least a little something to aid you in deciding when to buy, sell, or trade. In the Resource Appendix you will find the names of several newsletters that offer technical analysis. Because the principles of technical analysis apply to stocks or commodities, serious students should start with the classic work on the subject, *Technical Analysis of Stock Market Trends* by Edwards and Magee (Boston: John Magee).

The most sophisticated technical analysis of them all is Elliott Wave Theory, and it points to a very strong future for silver. The most accomplished and expert Elliott Wave publication is *The Elliott Wave Theorist* (see Appendix 1) which is predicting a powerful bull market in silver.

TECHNICIANS VS. FUNDAMENTALISTS

There are two ways to approach investing: *fundamental analysis and technical analysis*. Fundamentalists throw rocks at technicians, and technicians cheerfully return the compliment, but we will not join their fray. As veteran analyst Ian McAvity says, trying to invest using only one form of analysis is like "trying to run a footrace with one foot tied behind your back."

Fundamental analysis did not get its name because its proponents shun dancing, drinking, and smoking. Rather, they believe that you cannot wholly rely on past price action to forecast future prices. Fundamentalists believe people continuously change their subjective views in response to fundamental factors in the marketplace (such as supply and demand). Because people make rational decisions based on those factors (an optimistic assumption), analyzing them should enable one to forecast market events accurately. The rationale of fundamental analysis is, in other words, that physical factors determine price.

The fundamentalist gathers all possible data to forecast supply and demand, and uses the results to forecast prices. Logical—but not always reliable. The shortcoming of fundamental analysis is that it can tell you *whether* a market is headed up or down, but not *when*. And timing, as every air traffic controller will tell you, is everything.

On the other hand, the rationale of technical analysis is that the price of a commodity contains all the information the market possesses. Price embraces not only all the fundamental physical factors (supply and demand), but also all the decisions of everyone buying and selling. Almost single-handedly, the price mechanism makes free markets work. Prices communicate all the knowledge and every preference of every buyer and seller in the marketplace. When prices rise, producers recognize that supply is getting short or consumer demand is increasing, and they can safely produce more. When prices drop, producers are put on notice that supply is increasing, or consumer demand is dropping, and they had better cut back production. For the technician, then, everything he or she needs to know is "already in the price" (another optimistic assumption).

Technical analysts or technicians are sometimes referred to as "chartists" because they analyze and interpret formations on price charts (or related data). When charted, these prices form patterns and establish trend lines that can be used to forecast future price action. Technical analysis is also based on human behavior and the assumption that large masses of humans will behave in the future as they have in the past. Therefore, yesterday's price action helps to forecast tomorrow's. Technical analysis relies on the common human tendency to continue a path of action once begun. The cardinal tenet is that "a trend in force remains in force until broken," or "the trend is your friend." Technical analysts assume that prices move in trends over time. Chart formations forecast and confirm trend changes.

Chartists graph price and other data and then analyze the formations. About a dozen of these are the classics. Generally, patterns generated from only a few days' data are much less trustworthy than massive formations created from months or years of data. Logical, but again, not always reliable. Chart interpretation is far from being a precise science, and different analysts looking at the same chart can differ in their conclusions.

At least, technicians will claim, their emphasis is on specific opinions within workable time frames. Fundamentalists, they retort, have no idea *when* a trend change will occur, only that it will. Fundamentalists deal with what ought to be, while technicians (they claim) deal exactly with what was, what is, and what that implies for the future.

In truth, both technicians and fundamentalists offer us indispensable investment tools. We want to know that the silver market's underlying fundamental facts are in our favor. We don't want to be buying silver, for example, when new mining techniques are about to halve the cost of producing it—no matter what the price action looks like. On the other hand, fundamentalists might be right about silver rising in the long term, but buy long before all the factors mature. The investor buys, gets tired of waiting, and throws in the towel just as silver is about to boom. Timing, for technicians, is everything. For this reason we offer you both technical and fundamental analysis, because a prudent investor looks at both.

IMPORTANT BENEFITS OF TECHNICAL ANALYSIS

Here are some of the benefits that chartists frequently cite for technical analysis:

It can cut the chance of analytical errors by half. Fundamental analysis relies heavily on data that necessarily contains subjective estimates. Just *how much* silver will come out of kitchen drawers when the price reaches $15? *How accurate* are the estimates of silver supply in India? Technicians, on the other hand, almost always start with solid data from highly reliable, objective sources, such as commodity exchange statistics. For silver, these include daily prices for physical silver, futures and options, mining shares, and mining share indices. Important comparison data for confirming an analysis include the gold–silver ratio (gold's price divided by silver's price), the platinum–gold spread (price of platinum minus the price of gold), silver bullion's relative performance against precious metals mining shares, the broad stock market, put/call ratios on options for silver futures and mining shares, trading volume, and exchange warehouse stock levels.

- Technicians are geared to forecast specific time and price targets. These forecasts have been greatly improved by advances in cycle analysis. Chartists' short-, medium-, and long-term targets offer a practical action framework and give us reasonable percentage probabilities within workable time frames. The fundamentalist can't really offer this. Timing is what technical analysis is all about.
- Basic technical signals are very helpful in timing buy and sell decisions and make possible risk-limiting techniques such as stop-loss orders. Technical analysis gives early warning of forthcoming trend changes by tracking data such as trading volume and lead/lag correlations between bullion and mining shares. Technicians have developed whole systems to pick major tops and bottoms.
- Charts and graphs give the investor an accurate picture of a vast array of information—far more than simply reading fundamentals. If a picture is worth a thousand words, a long-term chart has to be worth several million. This alone is one of the most forceful arguments for investors to learn some technical analysis and charting. It is the most time- and cost-effective way to stay current (or even ahead) of the ever-changing silver scene.

TRADING HINTS AND GUIDELINES

Silver is notoriously one of the most "emotional" (some would say "schizophrenic") commodities, so you have to take extra care predicting its behavior. Here are some technical insights to help small investors and speculators do a better job trading "the slippery metal."

• In bear markets, silver tends to move lower in "stairsteps": sideways price action followed by drops of 20 cents or so, and then more sideways movement. During silver bear markets, low trading volumes exaggerate this tendency. Longer-term investors need to keep their eye on multi-year, weekly, and monthly price-range charts to avoid buying too early.

• Because silver is the smaller speculator's metal of choice ("poor man's gold") and the global cash silver market is so small, percentage price swings are often exaggerated. This extra emotionalism will usually fuel several totally unexpected and quite violent bear market rallies or bull market collapses every year.

How Small Is the Silver Market?

With 250 million ounces on deposit in commodity exchange warehouses (a very high level) and silver at $5 an ounce, you could buy the whole pile for $1.25 billion—peanuts compared to the colossal market in U.S. stocks.

General Motors all by itself has a market capitalization of $38.5 *billion*. In other words, the stock of General Motors alone has a market value more than *twenty-seven times all the silver in warehouse exchanges!*

Or consider the Eurodollar market. A total of *$1 trillion* is flushed through that market *every day* it's open. Charles River Associates estimate that there are only 19.1 *billion* ounces of silver left. At $5 an ounce, you could buy *all the silver in the world* for a measly $100 billion, *only one tenth of the amount traded in the Eurodollar market in a single day.* From this perspective it's easy to understand that it won't require a mob of new investors, or a great amount of new money, to boost off silver's price like a Saturn 5 rocket.

• A strengthening U.S. dollar exchange rate will generally put downward pressure on all the precious metals, but particularly on silver.

• Once silver drops below $6, the gold–silver ratio tends to narrow at some point so that silver outperforms gold. Why? At those low levels, silver is much nearer than gold to its cost of production.

• The best buying opportunities in silver mining shares occur during classic accumulation bottoms. These sometimes take several years to work themselves out. What do they look like? Very low trading volume, and share and bullion prices that refuse to drop lower, even on fresh bearish news about silver. Accumulation bottoms are the periods when the public is paying very little attention to the precious metals while patient, savvy long-term investors are loading up.

• More and more, silver is viewed as an industrial metal (like copper or aluminum) and less as a monetary metal (like gold). Thus silver prices may respond more to industrial and economic outlook than to inflation forecasts. However—and this is one *big* however—because industrial demand is (compared to monetary demand) relatively unchanging in the short term, unpredictable changes in *monetary demand* probably drive the silver market in the short term. *This changing monetary demand is, we believe, the inscrutable key to silver's future.* One enormous component of that demand hides behind this practically unanswerable but crucial question: *To what extent will monetary-demand gold investors substitute silver?*

• The most volatile days in silver often occur on Fridays. Generally it is *not* a good idea to base decisions on such one-day price action.

• Buying silver off round dollar levels, such as $6 or $7, usually results in short-term profits.

• The most important technical silver trading rule of all is to develop the habit of *regularly* checking medium- to long-term charts (six months to five years) before making any major silver decisions. Reviewing the "big picture" helps keep dramatic precious metals news in perspective, avoids costly mistakes, and keeps you ahead of the herd before it stampedes.

CLASSIC CHART FORMATIONS

The chartist's basic tools are formations that have demonstrated good to excellent reliability for forecasting future prices. Most price data are shown in bar chart form: A vertical bar measures the price range for the chosen period (say, one day), and a small horizontal tick indicates the final price for the period. Data can also be displayed with line charts made up of closing prices only, although this is more commonly used for ratios, spreads, stock indices, and economic indicators. Most price charts show daily data, but multiyear charts may use weekly or monthly ranges to compact the data. We won't cover point-and-figure charting or semilogarithmic scales. These more specialized techniques are not essential to a basic understanding of practical technical analysis.

Critics liken charting to reading tea leaves or gazing into crystal balls. Actually, chart formations just mirror common human behavior patterns. For example, trends reflect the innate human tendency to continue a course of action once begun. Like a basic law of physics—an object in motion stays in uniform motion in a straight line unless acted on by an external force—price trends continue until something substantial alters the market participants' expectations.

A large part of chartists' success derives from other very human tendencies: thinking in terms of round numbers and broad percentage categories —for example, 60 percent, 50 percent, 33 percent. A quick review of almost *any* price chart shows just how common these standard moves and retracements are. Because these moves result from human action, chart formations show remarkable consistency.

Volume is commonly charted along with prices. Usually the higher the volume, the more valid a move, although to sustain itself, a drop often does not need as much volume as an upmove. Why? The public has a strong emotional bias to go long (buy), but normally will wait out periods of falling prices rather than go short (sell). Also, few people understand short selling, so that leaves downward price breaks in the domain of the professional short seller. We don't think this should be the case, but we recognize that it is.

MOVING AVERAGES

Moving averages delve into another layer of the market's condition and help confirm other technical indicators. Technical analysis is something like the physical examination the doctor gives you: He or she looks and pokes and thumps and punches. A moving average is like the electrocardiogram the doctor gives you before you walk out of the office.

Moving averages measure the internal dynamics of the market. They are very simple to construct. For a twenty-day moving average, you would simply add every closing price in the past twenty days' trading and divide that sum by 20. The next day you would subtract the oldest close from your series, add the latest day's close, and divide by 20. Because they *average* several days' prices, moving averages smooth out erratic price flurries and show market direction very plainly. The longer the term of the moving average, the more reliable it is.

Moving averages can be constructed for any time period: yearly, monthly, weekly, daily, or whatever you need. In arbitrage on the trading floors, one-, two-, three-, and five-*minute* moving averages are not unusual.

Moving averages are most often traded by comparing a short-term moving average with a longer term. For example, commodity charts that show daily price ranges and closes often show five-day and twenty-day moving averages as well. *Whenever the short-term moving average crosses the long-term average, that signals a change in market direction.* The direction will be the same as the direction of the short-term moving average. If the five-day average, for instance, heads upward and crosses the twenty-day average, that would signal an upturn in the market. If the five-day moving average crosses the twenty-day average headed downward, then the market should turn down.

The best ploy for heavy trading is to look at the popular chart services, determine which set of moving averages they use, and then construct a set slightly shorter to anticipate what the market will signal. For example, if a five-day to twenty-day comparison is very popular, you might construct four-day to nineteen-day or four-day to seventeen-day moving averages.

*Classic chart formations: (A) Channel (B) Head and Shoulders Bottom
(C) Trend Line (D) Island Reversal (E) Rising Wedge (F) Gaps.*

CHART FORMATIONS

Here are descriptions of major chart formations. Look at the sample chart
as you read them.

TREND LINES

Trend lines are the most basic formation. They tell us nothing about how
high or how low something may go, but they do warn of a possible
change in supply and demand, or a loss of momentum. The longer the
trend line, or the more times it has been tested and has held, the more
significant it becomes. A major trend can remain intact even if prices
retrace back through the trend line by as much as 60 percent. (In the first
push up, prices rise along a very steep line. As the market progresses,
these trends shed that steepness for a gentler slope.) The stronger the
trend move, the smaller such retracements will be. Trend lines are drawn

under an uptrend and above a downtrend by connecting the points where reversals (two or more bottoms that look like "Vs" or tops that look like upside-down "Vs") occur.

Usually you can draw a parallel trend line above an uptrend line or below a downtrend line. These parallel lines form a channel, and prices will trade within the channel's upper and lower boundaries. When minor trend trading fails to reach the top of the channel, it may signal weakness. Likewise, when trading fails to reach the bottom, it may indicate coming strength. When silver breaks out of a channel, either to the upside or the downside, it usually signals a strong move beginning (depending on volume and how long the trend has been in force).

RECTANGLES

Sometimes called boxes, these do not give consistent, dependable signals about the *direction* of the coming breakout. If they extend long enough and have sufficient depth, professionals will trade the smaller trends within the channel, selling off overhead resistance and buying at support. When a breakout occurs, it will usually carry at least as far as the height of the formation (not illustrated on the chart).

TRIANGLES

There are three basic types of triangles: symmetrical, ascending, and descending. About 75 percent of the time, a symmetrical triangle should not be drawn until there have been four minor trend reversals within the building formation. (You need two points to draw a line, so in a rising market, silver must rise and reverse twice, and drop and reverse twice, to form the triangle.) Breakouts from triangles offer the greatest predictability when prices break out about one half to three fourths of the way through the triangle's formation. When prices work their way too far into the triangle's tight end, the breakout's strength will be diminished. Symmetrical triangles are sometimes called *coils,* because of their behavior: The market is *coiling up* for a leap, but you can't tell which direction that leap will take. Contrary to expectation, the longer the coil, the weaker the leap.

Ascending triangles are quite dependable and generally form in a rising market. Ascending triangles are bounded by a flat top and a rising bottom. Equally dependable descending triangles form in downward trending markets; they sit on flat bottoms and show falling tops. Symmetrical triangles call for a move that is equal to the height of the second reversal. In descending triangles, however, look for the breakout to travel the height of the *first* reversal (not illustrated on the chart.)

FLAGS

This very reliable formation appears after a quick price run, generally on high volume. It signals a market consolidating after a fast move. The fast run-up forms what looks like a straight-up flagpole on the chart. As profit taking and consolidation set in, a sideways channel forms that slopes against the primary trend. Flags in rising markets slope downward, while flags in falling markets slope upward. Once prices break out of the flag, they tend to move very fast without a pullback. The target for the break-out from a flag is the length of the flagstaff, determined by the distance of the move from the previous congestion. The rule of thumb is: Flags always fly at half-staff (not illustrated on the chart).

Pennants are similar to flags but are usually smaller and can point horizontally or slope slightly downward. Breakouts from pennants are also fast movers (not illustrated on the chart).

WEDGES

These are also dependable and are formed by two lines that slant in the same direction, but at different angles. Rising wedges usually last two to four weeks. As time passes, volume declines and price ranges narrow. The rising wedge is bearish, and the downside breakout generally happens two thirds to three fourths of the way through the formation. The target price is at least the lowest point in the wedge. Falling wedges are just the opposite: bullish. As the falling wedge builds, both volume and selling interest will decline. The upside breakout generally occurs two thirds to three fourths of the way through the wedge. Falling wedge breakouts often form saucer bottoms.

DOUBLE TOPS AND BOTTOMS

Double tops or bottoms form when two rallies or breakdowns exhaust themselves at about the same level. Whether at tops or bottoms, the failure of the second move to exceed the first warns that the trend is weak and about to reverse. The target of the double top is the distance equal to the height of the rally from the bottom of the first sell-off. Occasionally, triple tops or bottoms will form. This only adds to the reliability of the indicator (not illustrated on the chart).

HEAD AND SHOULDERS—TOPS AND BOTTOMS

This formation begins after an extended move, and volume plays an important role. Genuine head and shoulders formations are very reliable reversal indicators, but callow chartists tend to see these patterns everywhere. Generally, a head and shoulders top begins with a rally on good volume. A second rally follows that exceeds the first, with volume slightly more or less than the first shoulder. This is the "head." A third rally, with noticeably less volume than the previous two and that *fails to exceed the top of the head,* forms the second shoulder.

From the top of this second shoulder, prices will decline until they break the neckline (formed by connecting the bottom of the two previous sell-offs). Once prices break the neckline, the minimum price objective is the height of the head. Frequently, after the price penetrates the neckline, it will pull back to the neckline one more time. Don't be fooled: This is only the death tremor of the corpse.

Head and shoulders bottoms are just the reverse of the tops (they stand on their heads) and are usually longer and flatter than tops. Volume will be lower due to the lack of interest in the still-declining market. However, on the breakout from the right (last) shoulder, volume should increase to confirm the breakout. Just remember this: Head and shoulder tops are bearish, and head and shoulder bottoms are bullish.

SAUCER TOPS AND BOTTOMS

Gently rounding saucer tops and bottoms reflect a more gradual shift in supply and demand than double tops and head and shoulder patterns. You will frequently find saucer bottoms in mining shares undergoing long accumulation periods at relatively stable prices. The target for a breakout from a rounding bottom is the depth of the saucer, but often the price will go much higher. Because saucer tops reflect indecision and nervousness about which direction the price will go, saucer tops are a more unstable formation (not illustrated on the chart).

GAPS

Gaps are unfilled spaces—holes—in price ranges formed by a clot of open orders. There are simply no trades in that price range. Gaps come in three types: *breakaway, continuation,* and *exhaustion.* Breakaway gaps occur after an accumulation or distribution just as prices break out of that congested formation at the start of a move. Its name describes it: breaking away from support (or resistance). You often hear traders say, "A gap is always filled." This is a truism almost as valuable as Every dog has his day or All good things must come to an end. The breakaway gap may or may not be filled.

Continuation gaps occur after prices break out of a congestion area. They are usually not filled and show a strong continuation of the new trend as they move straight up. When a number of these occur, they are frequently called runaway gaps. They usually show up about halfway through a move, so double their length to estimate a target for the move.

Exhaustion gaps occur at the end of a trend. They form after prices gap higher one last time, and then move sideways on heavy volume. Before collapsing, gaps are typical of powerful moves and extreme uncertainty. Precious metals price charts from 1978 to 1981 show plenty of gaps.

ISLAND REVERSALS

These usually occur at the end of a long, fast trend. The island reversal is created by two gaps isolating a trading area (the island) from the new trend. Island tops and bottoms can last from one to ten trading days and typically show up at major turning points. For example, the all-time high in gold was a two-day island reversal top.

A FEW MORE POINTS

Additional rules about support and resistance are used to analyze these formations. Old resistance becomes support once it has been penetrated, and vice versa. Remember also that the larger the formation, or the longer support or resistance holds, the more significant a breakout or penetration becomes.

In trading, it is crucial that you make decisions and stick with them. Don't let your emotional, psychological, or ideological attachment to silver (or anything else) override what the charts plainly tell you. There's a time to buy and a time to sell. Decide beforehand what your goals are, and stick with them. A couple of old Wall Street proverbs will stand you in good stead. First: *Nobody ever went broke taking profits.* Second: *Bears get rich and bulls get rich, but pigs get slaughtered.*

WINDING UP WITH SOME CAUTIONS

"A little learning is a dangerous thing." Technical analysis can be a wonderfully useful tool, but don't think you can become an expert technician overnight. For technical help, subscribe to the newsletters listed in Appendix 1, most of which give a regular monthly analysis of silver's technical situation. Check them to see if they confirm or deny your own analysis, and why. And although it seems to contradict what we just said, don't be afraid to act on what you see on the chart.

In general, you want to buy silver at *low risk points*. What are those? The most obvious is when silver has been dropping in price toward the bottom line of a trading channel. Often (but not always) silver will bounce off that bottom channel line, completing its correction. The opposite is also true: Buying silver near the top line (resistance) of a channel is bad business. More often than not, silver will bounce off that resistance line and trade downward for a while. Look at the trading channel marked (A) on our chart: If you had bought every time silver touched off the bottom (support) channel line, then two times out of three you would have won. Notice that the risk increases as the move gets older.

Another and very obvious *low-risk buy* is when silver breaks through resistance—for example, the top line of a trading channel or a triangle (note the end of "B" or "C" on the chart). Generally these breakouts mark the beginning of a long upward thrust. This move is confirmed if within three to five days silver backs down to (but not through) the resistance line it has just breached, then trades higher. This confirming touchback to resistance is a very, very strong buy signal.

There are also times when you don't ever want to buy. Whenever silver breaks through a support line (bottom line of a trading channel, triangle, or other formation), leave it alone until it settles. It will fall quite a ways before it stops.

In general, you want to do the opposite of what the public is doing. When silver has been dropping and everyone has lost interest in it, that probably means it has gotten cheap and it's time to buy. Never, never, never buy silver when the chart is headed straight up (hyperbolic rise) and everybody and his cousin is cheering for silver. That's just the time to be selling.

Be deliberate. Don't jump into silver (or any other investment) because of Joe's cousin's barber's hot tip. Before you make an investment decision, look at it from several viewpoints. Technically, always compare daily, weekly, and monthly charts. Because most readers will be investing in silver for the long term, you should try to buy when all three charts agree.

The best part of technical analysis is that it applies to every silver investment—bullion, stocks, futures, options—and every other investment. Whatever you learn trading silver you can apply to *all* your other investments.

Chapter 6

INVESTING IN SILVER: AN INTRODUCTION

You're convinced that silver is ready to blast off again. What do you do next? Two basic choices face the silver investor: paper or physicals. We'll cover these in detail in the coming chapters, but for now let's get a quick preview.

PAPER SILVER

By paper silver we mean any investment in silver where you do not take actual physical possession of the metal. There are leveraged and fully paid ways to do this. In general, the advantage of owning silver through paper is the leverage it offers.

Since 1980, the paper markets in silver have fundamentally altered. The opportunity to play stocks has almost vanished (with a few exceptions we'll mention), but new derivatives, such as put and call options on silver futures contracts, offer new ways to play the game.

SHARES

Silver shares or stocks are stocks in companies that mine silver. You can buy these on margin or outright. Note that they interpose an extra layer of risk on your silver investment: You can be right about the price of silver but wrong about the management of the company. Accidents can happen: mines can flood, cave in, or explode. EPA or other government agencies can attack a company. The management can make bad decisions, or the labor force can go on strike. Generally, however, when you buy shares in a silver producing firm, you are buying silver in the ground. Our difficulty here, as we will explain more fully, is that the long bear market in silver has decimated pure silver plays or primary silver producers. Two thirds of all the silver brought to market comes from mines where silver is only a byproduct. You could buy these stocks, but that dilutes your silver play by the value of gold, copper, lead, or zinc also produced.

MUTUAL FUNDS

Mutual funds are collections of stocks or other securities purchased by a group of investors and managed by professionals. *At present no pure silver mutual funds are available.* There is one with silver in its name—Lexington Strategic Silver Fund—but the proportion of the fund invested in silver is so small that it is practically diluted out of consideration.

COMMODITY FUTURES CONTRACTS

Commodity futures contracts are obligations to buy or sell a specified amount of silver at a specified price at some time in the future. These are traded on the Comex in New York (5,000-ounce lots per contract), the Chicago Board of Trade (5,000-ounce lots), and the Mid America Exchange (1,000-ounce lots). When you buy (or sell) a futures contract, you obligate yourself to buy or sell a specified amount of silver at a specified price at some definite future date.

Futures contracts are highly leveraged because you need not put up the entire value of the contract when you buy, but only a margin payment.

Think of this as collateral on a loan. When the value of the collateral dips below the percentage required to back the loan, you have to pony up more collateral.

If the market "goes against you" (drops when you buy or are long, or rises when you sell or are short), you must put up additional margin money, called *variation margin,* to make up for the decreased value of the contract. Risk is unlimited by anything but the rise or fall in price of the underlying commodity. The leverage of futures contracts can work for you or against you. If you are right about the direction of the market, profits mount very quickly. If you are wrong, losses mount just as quickly on the downside. These are *not* markets for amateurs.

Futures contracts offer several advantages over physical silver. First, they eliminate the trouble and expense of taking physical delivery of the silver. Second, they offer the slight advantage over physicals that you need not put up cash for the option margin, provided you put up a Treasury bill equal to or greater in value than the margin requirement. In that way you earn interest on your money while it is invested in silver. Third, commissions, spreads, storage, and freight costs may be lower than those for physicals.

COMMODITY FUTURES OPTIONS

Commodity futures options are the right but not the obligation to buy or sell commodity future silver contracts (not the physical metal!) at a specified price ("strike price") at some time up to or including a specified date ("expiration date"). The price you pay for the option is called a "premium."

Options are really very simple. Most people are familiar with real estate options. You think you want to buy a piece of land but haven't quite decided. For a very small payment (the "premium"), the owner of the land grants you the right until a specified time ("expiration date") to buy the land at a certain price ("strike price"). If you decide to buy the land, you exercise the right to buy within the specified time. If you decide against buying it, you do nothing and the option expires, worthless. You forfeit the premium. Simple.

Options that grant the right to buy carry the name "call" options. You can "go long" silver by buying a call option. Options that grant the right to sell are called "put" options (perhaps because you "put it to" the buyer). You "go short" silver by buying a put option.

Here's where it gets confusing. The person who sells a call option undertakes the obligation to sell the underlying futures contracts. Once he or she sells the call, that person is "short" silver. Selling a call also goes by the name "writing a call." The person who sells ("writes") a put option undertakes the obligation to buy the underlying silver futures contracts. Selling a put makes the seller "long" silver.

Writing puts or calls is a tricky business. When you do not own the underlying silver futures contracts (long contracts or short contracts), you are writing "naked" options. You receive the premium when you write a put or call, but if the market goes against you, you must be prepared to buy the underlying futures contracts for which the option obligates you. When you own the underlying silver futures contracts upon which you have written options, you are writing "covered" options.

The chief advantage of buying options is that they *limit your risk*. Whether you buy calls or puts, the worst thing that can happen is this: The option expires worthless; you lose the entire premium. Options carry a *time value*. When you buy an option you are really buying time. Other things being equal, the closer the option comes to its expiration date, the more quickly its value falls. Options are *highly leveraged* and can bring enormous profits—or lose the whole premium. Because the risk of options can be known in advance, they can be superb risk management vehicles.

Options come in three colors: *in the money, out of the money, and at the money*. An in-the-money option is already profitable. For example, if you bought a July silver futures call option in January with a strike price of $7, as soon as the price of silver goes above $7, your option value increases cent for cent with the price of silver. It is then "in the money." An out-of-the-money option is not yet profitable (and may never be). If you bought a July silver futures call option in January with a strike price of $7, that call option does not increase cent for cent with the rise in silver until silver rises above $7. An at-the-money option is one in which the strike price is exactly the same as the market price. In our example above, when the price of July silver futures reaches $7, the option is at the money.

For most people these three "colors" are a little harder to grasp on the downside. When you buy a put option, that option is out of the money whenever the price of the underlying silver futures contract rises above the strike price. A put option is in the money whenever the price of the underlying silver futures is below the strike price. A put option is at the money whenever the strike price is the same as the market price. For example, if you bought a July silver futures put option with a strike price of $7, at any price above your $7 strike, the option is out of the money. Nobody wants the right to sell silver at $7 when the price is, say, $8. However, when the price of the underlying silver futures is below $7, the put option is in the money and gains in value cent for cent with the drop in silver's price. When silver drops to $6, your silver futures put with a $7 strike is worth $1 an ounce.

SILVER CERTIFICATES

Silver certificate programs or storage programs are generally run through banks, brokerage firms, or off-exchange bullion dealers. You buy the silver, and the broker stores it and issues you a certificate. The certificate obligates the issuer to deliver the silver to you on demand. You may take physical possession of the silver or leave it on deposit. Normally these deposits are subject to a storage charge. Certificate programs save you the trouble and cost of actually taking physical delivery. However, because you do not take delivery of the silver, you forgo the benefits of physical possession and must be very careful of the liquidity, stability, and integrity of the dealer. Horror stories abound about unscrupulous storage programs where promoters take the customer's money and never buy the silver.

OFF-EXCHANGE LEVERAGED CONTRACTS

A few companies that are *not* brokers on the commodities futures exchanges write "leveraged contracts." These are similar to futures contracts. Typically you put down 25 percent of the value of the contract (generally 1,000 ounces of silver) and must pay interest on the balance of the contract's value. Because this down payment is called "margin," these are often called "margin" contracts. Since these dealers are not commodity futures brokers, they are not subject to the same financial requirements. We recommend *extreme caution* in dealing with this sort of contract.

PHYSICAL SILVER

Physical silver investments include any method of buying silver where you take actual physical possession of the metal. This means you pay the full amount of the price of the silver investment when you buy it, and then have it delivered to you. The chief advantage of physical silver is having physical ownership and control of your investment.

SILVER BARS

Silver bars are minted by reputable and not-so-reputable refiners. They come in 1000-, 100-, 50-, 10-, and 1-ounce sizes, and should be at least .999 fine (99.9 percent pure silver). The most common and popular brand names in the United States are Engelhard and Johnson-Matthey.

Generally, 1,000-ounce bars are not appropriate for most investors. They are about the size of a large videocassette recorder and weigh about seventy pounds. In case of emergency, you will not strap these babies to your back and run down the street with them. Thousand-ounce bars are the only bars acceptable for delivery on the futures exchanges. If you want to buy silver this way, simply buy it on the futures exchanges and have it delivered to you.

One-hundred-ounce bars are usually an inexpensive way to invest in silver. Expect to pay a small premium, sometimes called a "bar charge," over the silver price, perhaps as much as 40 cents an ounce. Bars that do not carry the Engelhard or Johnson-Matthey marks are cheaper, but they bring less when you sell them.

Ten-ounce bars and one-ounce wafers, bars, and coins were once very common in the dealer market, but in the past few years have not been seen as often. The major refiners have stopped making them. In general these are now available only as "rounds," or privately made 1-troy-ounce coins. Generally, the smaller the bar size, the higher the cost per ounce. Expect to pay as much as 50 cents an ounce premium for rounds.

U.S. SILVER COINS

The United States minted dollars, half dollars, quarters, and dimes in 90 percent silver from 1834 through 1965. Since 1965, the U.S. government has minted a few silver coins, but mostly as commemoratives with high premiums over their silver content. From 1965 through 1970, the United States minted 40 percent silver half dollars. Regardless of denomination, these coins are all traded in *bags* of $1,000 face value.

Circulated U.S. silver dollars contain 0.765 troy ounce of fine silver (765 ounces to the $1,000 bag). They were minted at 0.7734 troy ounce per dollar, so our 0.765 figure allows for some wear. Expect to pay a 100 percent to 200 percent premium for dollars.

Circulated U.S. 90 percent silver dimes, quarters, and half dollars minted before 1965 contain 0.715 troy ounce of silver per dollar face value and are 90 percent silver by weight. These coins were minted at 0.7234 troy ounce of fine silver, so the 0.715 figure allows for some wear. Ninety-percent silver coin bags are also called "nineties" or "junk coins." Expect to pay a premium of 5 percent or less for nineties.

U.S. 40 percent silver dollars contain 0.295 troy ounce of fine silver each. They are also traded in bags of $1,000 face value and carry a premium of 6 percent or less. Less commonly traded are *silver war nickels*, the five-cent pieces minted between 1942 and 1945. They are 35 percent silver by weight and contain about 1.1 troy ounces of silver per dollar face value.

Official Silver Bullion Coins

During the early 1980s, the Mexican mint introduced a legal tender 1-troy-ounce .999 fine silver coin, the *Libertad*. Other nations quickly followed suit. In 1986, the United States introduced the 1-troy-ounce, .999 fine American Silver Liberty Coin, now commonly called the American Silver Eagle. The comparable Canadian coin is the Silver Maple Leaf, and Australia mints a 1-troy-ounce Silver Kookaburra.

The introduction of the American Silver Eagle attracted so much public investment demand that the premiums on U.S. 90 percent silver coin, which previously had been the most popular bullion silver investment, dropped drastically. The American Silver Eagles and similar ones from other countries carry a hefty premium, nearly $1.50 an ounce at retail. Nevertheless, they continue to be quite popular.

PHYSICAL SILVER ON THE FUTURES MARKET

You can also buy physical silver off the futures exchanges. Simply tender the full amount of the price of the contract and tell your broker you want to take delivery. Delivery can be accomplished through certificates ("warehouse receipts") or physically. If you choose to buy silver this way, it is to your advantage to leave it on deposit in an exchange-approved warehouse. When you take physical delivery, you must pay all delivery charges plus sales tax in some states. When you retender the silver for sale, if you have taken it out of the warehouse, you will have to have it assayed and pay all those costs. Leaving the silver on deposit will incur only a nominal storage fee yearly.

THE DARK SIDE OF TRADING SILVER: GOING SHORT

For reasons mysterious to the human mind, most people can't understand how you can make money "going short," or selling silver you don't yet own. Actually, it's very simple. Think of a price graph as a vertical line. Your profit *is the piece of that line between the buy point and the sell point.* It makes no difference where you start on the line.

Imagine you have a booth at a flea market. You're selling flower pots you buy in Mexico. You buy the pots for $10 each in Guadalajara and sell them for $20 in Sioux City. This Saturday, the flea market is full, and you sell every single pot except for your sample. A lady walks by, sees the sample, and wants to buy a hundred pots. "Ma'am, I'm sorry," you say, "but that's the only pot I've got left. But I'm going down to Mexico next week, and I can pick up your hundred pots then and deliver them next Saturday." She agrees to wait a week, and gives you $2,000 for a hundred pots. You have just *gone short* flower pots.

Now, watch closely: It didn't make a bit of difference whether you *bought* the pots first, or *sold* them first. You made the same $10 a pot either way. You just took a piece out of the line between "buy" and "sell." Simple.

In just the same way, if you expect the price of silver to drop, you can "go short" by selling futures contracts or buying put options. This can be very profitable for two reasons. First, markets drop faster than they rise.

109

Second, most people don't understand (and refuse to try to understand) shorting, so fewer people do it.

Sophisticated silver traders can significantly add to profits by going short against existing long positions ("shorting against the box"). For traders who are willing to master technical analysis and ready to take the increased risk of temporarily going short in a bull market, this can be a very profitable strategy. If you're not ready to do that homework, *don't short.*

And remember this market proverb: *He who sells what isn't his'n, buys it back or goes to prison.*

Chapter 7

INVESTING IN PHYSICAL SILVER

WHICH FORM OF SILVER SHOULD I BUY?

The answer to this question depends on your personal circumstances and goals. If you want your silver investment to perform the dual functions of an investment in silver and a stash against monetary catastrophe, then stick with silver coins. If you are not worried about catastrophe, then you have other options. The only rational, *quantitative* way to choose is to determine which form offers you the most silver for your money—that is to say, the lowest cost per ounce.

The cost of any form of silver *above* the value of its silver content ("melt" or "bullion" value) is the *premium*. Premiums may include *seigniorage* (the manufacturing charge for coins levied by the minting country), fabrication charges (for bars or medallions), commissions, and whatever fragile or intangible extra value the market happens to place on a given form of silver.

To figure the cost of silver in any investment, remember this rule: *Divide cost by content.* The silver content of the silver dollar, for example, is 0.765 troy ounce. At $7.50 per coin, silver dollars cost (7.50/0.765 =) $9.80 per ounce of fine silver. Amazingly enough, some forms of silver actually trade at a *discount*. A discount is the amount by which the cost of any form of silver is *beneath* its silver value.

To calculate the melt or bullion value of any physical silver investment, simply multiply the fine silver in ounces by the current price of silver. To figure premium or discount as a percentage, just divide the cost you pay by the melt value.

To calculate price per ounce of any silver investment, divide cost by content—cost per unit by content in fine ounces. However, to figure the total transaction cost of any silver investment, you should also consider the "spread." All commodities (and stocks, too) are traded on a "spread" between buy and sell. The "spread" is the difference between the price at which dealers will *buy* ("bid") and *sell* ("ask" or "offer") a particular form of investment silver. For instance, bags of 90 percent silver coin might be quoted "3325 at 3475," a $150 spread. When you sell your silver, this spread will form part of the total transaction cost. *You do not break even until the price of silver has risen enough to cover the spread on your investment.*

If privacy is a concern, you should consider whether the sale of your silver will be reported. No purchases are reported unless you pay with more than $10,000 in cash. Don't even think about asking a dealer to sell you more than $10,000 worth of silver for cash, because both he or she and you can land in jail for money laundering if you do. You can also go to jail for "structuring" a transaction if you make related purchases below the required reporting amounts to avoid the reporting requirement. Don't, for example, walk in and buy $9,000 worth of silver for cash on Monday and repeat the transaction on Tuesday. *It is not necessary for the government to prove that your money was the proceeds of some crime. It is not necessary for the government to prove that you had any "criminal intent."* The courts construe money laundering statutes as "strict liability" statutes, and you can go to jail whether you meant to break the law or not—or even if you didn't know that the law existed. We think this is unreasonable—indeed, criminally tyrannical—but it is the present state of the law we have to face.

IRS REPORTING REQUIREMENTS

In general, U.S. 90 percent silver coins (or any other form of silver bought in the dealer market) offer greater privacy than silver held in a public exchange warehouse. However, one minor drawback to trading nineties is that when you sell them back to a dealer *in lots of five bags or more*

($5,000 face value), the dealer must report that transaction to the Internal Revenue Service. At present silver dollars, 40 percent silver halves, and American Silver Eagles are not reportable. One dealer trade association, the Industry Council for Tangible Assets (ICTA), maintains that sales of 1,000 troy ounces in 100-ounce bars are reportable. Others, however, maintain that only sales of 1,000-ounce bars are reportable because ten 100-ounce bars are not tenderable against a futures exchange contract, and the regulations are based on what is or was tenderable against futures contracts. The ultimate interpretation of these IRS regulations has plagued the dealer market with fear and uncertainty for years. The recent resolution and clarification of those regulations can only help the dealer industry.

HOW TO INVEST IN PHYSICAL SILVER

Physical silver investments come in several forms, each with its own benefits and drawbacks. Basically you can choose from silver bars on the futures exchanges, silver bars from dealers, or silver coins from dealers.

BUYING OFF THE FUTURES EXCHANGES

The Mid America exchange in Chicago offers silver futures contracts in 1,000-troy-ounce lots. The Chicago Board of Trade (CBOT) and the Comex futures exchanges trade a 5,000-troy-ounce lot. If you plan to take delivery, put up margin for the contract by paying half the contract's value or leaving a T-bill with the broker (you get both credit for margin *and* interest on the T-bill). When the contract expires, you "take delivery" by paying the balance of the contract. If you buy silver through a futures exchange, *leave the metal on deposit in an exchange-approved depository, and the broker will send you a warehouse receipt.* These warehouse receipts are recognized all over the world. No investor has ever lost a penny on the American futures exchanges since they opened in 1856—from failure to make good on the contracts, that is. Obviously, plenty have lost their shirts when they bet the wrong way on the market or when the exchanges changed the rules.

Once you have the warehouse receipt, it's the same as having the silver —almost. You can take the receipt to any bank and use it as collateral for a loan. When the price reaches your long-term target, you can sell the metal by tendering the warehouse receipt to your broker. You have to pay storage in the meantime (maybe as little as $30 a year), but that's nothing compared to what you'd pay to store it yourself locally or the cost of taking personal physical delivery, paying freight, and then re-tendering the physical silver. Depending on commissions, the round trip cost is about $150.

If you buy silver off a futures exchange, *under no circumstances* should you take delivery on it—that is, have the physical metal delivered to you. In many states, if you take delivery of the silver, your brokerage house will charge you sales tax. Once it leaves the warehouse, the silver is no longer certified *good delivery*. That means you will have to pay to ship it back to an exchange-approved warehouse, usually by air freight. Theoretically 1,000-troy-ounce bars weigh 68.57 avoirdupois pounds, but exchange bars can weigh up to 1,060 ounces or 72.69 avoirdupois pounds. With packaging they almost always weigh more than 70 pounds, too heavy for UPS or the post office. Once the bar returns to an exchange warehouse, you will have to wait (and pay) for the silver to be assayed and recertified so you can sell it back on the exchange. If you try to sell 1,000-ounce bars on the off-exchange dealer market, you may have to take a discount.

The chief advantages of buying silver bullion on the futures exchanges are the *low transaction and storage costs*. The major drawback is your inability to keep ownership private and the lack of physical control. If the U.S. government ever decides to nationalize silver again, you'll be a sitting duck. However, we believe that another nationalization is a very remote possibility—possible, but not likely.

SILVER DOLLARS

In the off-exchange precious metals dealer market, *circulated* silver dollars are traded in "bags" of $1,000 face value, but you can buy less than a full bag. Expect to pay a bit extra for buying smaller amounts.

Although they were minted at 0.7734 troy ounce each, the market counts them as 0.765 ounce (765 ounces to the bag) to allow for wear. Dealers quote these coins in various ways. If they are selling for $7.50

each, dealers may quote them as "seven-fifty," "seventy-five," or "seventy-five hundred." They all mean the same thing.

If you are counting on finding the Priceless Life-Changing Coin in a bag of circulated dollars, forget it. By the time they get to you they have been combed through thoroughly by dealers. The dollars generally available were minted from 1878 through 1935. From 1878 through 1904, and again in 1921, the design of engraver Charles Morgan was used, hence the name "Morgan" dollars. These issues are the most popular with collectors, so your circulated bag of dollars will contain very few of them, and those will be heavily circulated. In 1921, the United States minted millions of Morgan dollars under the Pittman Act, so these will also be plentiful, making up about 20 percent of the typical bag. From 1921 through 1935, the "Peace" dollar was minted, and these are the most common in circulated bags. Eighty percent or so of the bag will be Peace-type dollars, minted from 1921 to 1934. Twenty percent will be 1921 Morgan-type dollars or heavily worn pre-1905 Morgans.

Other than a Bernini silver salt cellar or similar artifact, silver dollars are the most expensive way to buy silver. They carry a high *premium*. The premium on silver dollars varies, but generally is at least 100 percent over their silver content, and may rise as high as 200 percent—a *very* expensive way to buy silver.

ALWAYS take personal delivery on coins you buy from a dealer. Never leave them on deposit with a dealer. When you take delivery, some states levy a sales tax. If you buy them in another state, or if they are shipped out of state, you can avoid the sales tax. However, some states levy a compensating use tax and may consider you liable to pay a *use tax* for coins bought out of state. Check with local tax authorities to learn the local rules.

When you buy coins from an off-exchange dealer, you may have to wait several weeks for delivery. Some dealers will charge postage to deliver the coins to you; some will not. A fair shipping charge is $50 to $65 per bag, and the bags may be sent by registered, insured mail or by UPS. A bag of silver dollars weighs a little over 58 pounds, so don't send your 98-pound grandmother to pick it up at the post office.

U.S. 90 PERCENT SILVER COIN

U.S. 90 percent silver dimes, quarters, and halves ("nineties") were minted to the same weight and fineness standards from 1853 through 1964. They are traded in bags of $1,000 face value: 10,000 dimes, 4,000 quarters, or 2,000 half dollars. Although they were minted at 0.7234 troy ounce of fine silver to the dollar, the market counts them as 0.715 troy ounce per dollar face value (715 troy ounces to the bag). Some dealers even count them as 710 ounces to the $1,000 bag. Fourteen dimes ($1.40) contain roughly an ounce of pure silver.

Dealers usually quote bags in terms of paper dollars times face value. For example, if bags are selling for $3,725 per $1,000 bag, dealers will quote them as "three point seven two five times face." They might also quote them as "thirty-seven twenty-five" or "three point seven two five." As with the dollars, you can buy less than a full bag of 90 percent coin, but you may have to pay a little extra and pay freight. Most dealers charge a premium of $50 to $100 if you specify *half dollars*. If you take pot luck, you'll probably get quarters.

Ninety percent coins are also called "junk" coins or "junk bags." This doesn't mean that they are literally junk, but simply that they are circulated coins. They will show some wear, a few perhaps heavy wear, but there should be no bent coins or coins with holes. Check through the coins yourself to see that the bag contains no rejects and no coins minted after 1964.

Just like silver dollars, you may have to wait several weeks for delivery of your 90 percent coins. Some dealers will charge postage to deliver the coins to you; some will not. A fair shipping charge is $50 to $65 per bag, and the bags may be sent by registered, insured mail or by UPS. A bag of silver coins weighs a little over 55 pounds.

Nineties used to be the public's most popular form of silver investment. Survivalists combined a survival motive with investment by buying silver coins as a means of barter in case the paper monetary system broke down. At midsummer 1982, when silver hit a cyclical low, bags carried a *premium* of 40 percent to 50 percent. Now they are just about your cheapest way to buy silver.

What happened? In 1986 the United States mint began issuing the American Silver Eagle "dollar." We put quotation marks around the word "dollar" because the American Silver Eagle coin does not contain a constitutional or statutory dollar's worth of silver ($1.2929 per ounce, 0.7734 troy ounce per dollar). Rather, it contains .999 troy ounce of fine (.9999) silver.

In spite of the very high premium on the American Silver Eagle coins, the public has bought loads of them. This demand shift undercut the premium on nineties, and for the past several years they have traded at or near their silver content. That would make them the best buy on the silver market, except the *spread* (the difference between dealer's buying price and selling price) is a bit wider on bags than it is on silver bars. However, the nineties are more divisible than 100-ounce silver bars. You can't take your band saw to a 100-ounce bar and cut off 2.5 ounces to liquidate it without ruining the bar and garbaging your investment.

To determine the price per ounce of 90 percent silver coins, divide *cost by content.* If a bag of nineties sells for $3,700, that's (3700/715 or 3.700/.715 =) $5.17 per ounce of pure silver.

Despite changing fashion, we consider U.S. 90 percent silver coins to be one of the very best ways to invest in physical silver. The October 1992 Charles River Associates *Stocks of Silver Around the World* study estimated that 335 million troy ounces of silver coinage remain in the United States. If none of this was silver dollars (and some in fact is), that would total only 468,531 bags. CRA estimates that 151 million troy ounces are stockpiled by investors or actively traded (211,188 bags). Conservative investors who hold these coins as a disaster hedge are *not* going to sell them readily. Moreover, dealers are *still melting 90 percent silver coins!* If, as we expect, investment demand for silver increases, demand for nineties will increase as well. Because the number of bags is continuously shrinking, strong premiums could develop on these coins.

U.S. 40 PERCENT SILVER HALF DOLLARS

From 1965 through 1970, the United States minted silver-cladded half dollars (only). In this laminated coin, outer layers of 80 percent silver are cladded to core layers of copper-nickel and copper core. The weight of the finished coin is 40 percent silver, and two of these halves contain 0.29584 troy ounce of silver. The trade counts them as 295 ounces in the common trading unit of $1,000 face value bags.

To determine the price per ounce of 40 percent silver coin, divide *cost by content*. If a bag of forties sells for $1,600, that's (1600/295 or 1.600/.295 =) $5.42 per ounce of pure silver.

The advantage of 40 percent silver coins is their low cost in relation to their silver content. If you bought a bag and the price of silver got so cheap they were paying people to haul it off in trucks, the bag of forties would still be worth $1,000 in face value. The maximum risk on forties is the amount you pay above their $1,000 face value.

The drawback of forties, however, is their bulk in relation to their silver content. Three 100-ounce silver bars take up about the same space as nine packages of cigarettes laid side by side, three high and three wide. The same amount of silver in the form of 40 percent halves is roughly the same size as a gallon jug of milk. Any sizable silver investment in the form of forties could be, in terms of storage, an embarrassment of riches.

One further note about the 40-percent standard: The United States issued a few Eisenhower silver dollars in 40 percent. The net silver content is 0.31625 troy ounce per $1 coin. These coins were all issued between 1971 and 1974 inclusive, and all were issued from the San Francisco mint. You can distinguish between the cupro-nickel variety and the silver variety by the color: The silver version is white, the base metal is dull gray. If that's not clear enough, only the San Francisco mint issued the silver variety, so look above the date for the little "S" under Eisenhower's neck. Caution: In 1974 the San Francisco mint coined both cupro-nickel and silver varieties.

The U.S. mint also issued silver-clad Eisenhower *Bicentennial* dollars, dated 1776–1976 only and from the San Francisco mint only. The Bicentennial was also the excuse for the San Francisco mint (only) to issue silver-clad *quarters*. These are dated 1776–1976, show a weight lifter playing a drum on the reverse, and contain 0.07396 troy ounce of pure silver each; in other words, four silver-clad quarters have 0.295 troy ounce of silver, the same as two 40 percent half dollars.

Both the silver-clad Eisenhower dollars and the Bicentennial quarters were issued in proof and uncirculated sets, so they have never been traded in any sort of volume, even in the dealer market. Chances are, you'll never see any.

AMERICAN SILVER EAGLES AND OTHER BULLION COINS

Since 1986, the United States has minted a 1-troy ounce .9999 fine silver coin, the American Silver Eagle coin. This coin has proven very popular with the public, so much so (as we noted above) that it has drawn a large part of silver investment away from other traditionally favored forms. We must admit, the silver American Eagle with the A. A. Weinman "walking Liberty" device that appeared on the old 90 percent half dollars is the most beautiful coin the U.S. Mint has issued in a long, long time. It far surpasses the studied ugliness of the designs the mint has favored in the past three decades.

What's amazing about this shift in demand to the American Silver Eagle? It is not an economical way to buy silver. The U.S. Mint sells these coins to major dealers at about $1.06 an ounce over the silver price. Dealer-to-dealer prices usually run $1.25 over spot, so by the time the retail customer gets the coin he or she is paying $1.50 or more per ounce over silver. At $5 silver, that's a *30 percent premium!* Nevertheless, the public loves them.

OFFICIAL ISSUE BULLION COINS

Since the early 1980s a growing number of nations around the world have issued gold and silver bullion coins. A bullion coin is one sold for its bullion content alone, without any numismatic or collector value. The Mexicans led the way with the *Libertad,* Canada issued the Silver Maple Leaf, and Australia issued the Silver Kookaburra. These are all masterfully executed coins, lovely to own and to gaze upon, but some may be even more expensive than the American Silver Eagle.

SILVER BULLION BARS AND COINS

The market for silver bullion bars has changed dramatically in the past ten years. In the late 1970s all sorts of brands circulated, generally at about the same price. As the price of silver skyrocketed into 1980, all bars went to a discount to their silver value (see below). However, as the

1980s bear market ground down investment demand for silver, marketing took over.

Many of the pre-1980 bars were crudely melted lumps of silver stamped simply ".999 fine silver." In the early 1980s, Engelhard and Johnson-Matthey bars carried a premium to all the others. Then both Engelhard and Johnson-Matthey introduced a machined bar, and finally a very clean, fancy bar packaged in a hard, clear plastic wrapper. These are now the premium bars in the 100-ounce bar market, and they trade 10 cents to 25 cents an ounce above other bars.

The advantages of 100-troy ounce silver bullion bars are chiefly their compact size and their narrow spread between buy and sell. They do not offer the divisibility of 90 percent or 40 percent silver coins, and nonname brand bars may be discounted when you sell them.

The major refiners as well as regional firms used to make 10-ounce bars, and to a lesser extent 25- and 50-ouncers. These are all hardly seen now. One-ounce bars before 1980 were available primarily as "art bars," fancy stamped bars issued by companies such as the Franklin Mint or the Danbury Mint. In the 1980s, these gave way to very professionally minted 1-ounce rounds from Johnson-Matthey, Engelhard, and several regional refiners and dealers. As a general rule, the smaller the bar, the higher the premium you will pay. Today the 10-ounce bars are seldom seen, and the major refiners no longer mint 1-ounce rounds. Smaller refiners do mint 1-ounce rounds, and these are usually available at about 40 cents per ounce over spot silver.

Again, *ALWAYS take personal delivery on bullion you buy from a dealer.*

You may have to wait several weeks for delivery of your silver bullion. Some dealers will charge postage to deliver the bars to you; some will not. A fair shipping charge is $50 to $65 per 1,000 ounces, and the bullion may be sent by registered, insured mail or by UPS. A 100-ounce silver bar weighs 6.857 avoirdupois pounds, so 1,000 ounces weigh 68.57 pounds. Watch your back when you pick it up at the post office!

A few years ago there was a flap about *counterfeit* or *altered* silver bars. At least one hard money newsletter ran terrifying stories, complete with pictures of bars that had been drilled out and filled with lead. However, these counterfeits should be easy to detect. Silver is the most resonant metal. If you will hold a 100-ounce bar loosely in each hand and lightly tap them together at the corners, you will notice a sweet, long-lasting metallic ring. Bars filled with lead will only say "Thud." If your bars say "Thud," run back to your dealer and demand a replacement.

Pure silver is resistant to oxidation but reacts quickly to sulfur compounds in the air or in paper wrapped around the bars. It is not unusual for silver bars to turn completely black, deep blue, purple, or even yellow. Numerous solutions sold in grocery stores and drugstores as silver "dips" will remove this discoloration quickly and inexpensively.

ARBITRAGE OPPORTUNITIES

In the past, the premiums on various forms of silver, especially silver coin, have fluctuated considerably. If you have access to a dealer who will work on a narrow spread, you can profit from this change in premiums by *arbitrage*. When the premium on silver dollars, for example, reaches historic highs, you swap silver dollars for the cheapest form of silver—say, 100-ounce silver bars or 40 percent silver coins—and dramatically increase the amount of silver you own. If silver dollars are carrying a 100 percent premium, you can swap the dollars for bars and nearly *double* your total ounces of silver. For those who now hold bags of circulated dollars, we recommend this trade. However, you have to reckon with fairly wide spreads in the physical silver market and the fact that your *estimate* of which way premiums will move is just that: an estimate.

In the market of the early 1980s, this strategy worked very well. However, since 1986 and the advent of the American Silver Eagle, which siphoned demand away from other forms of silver, the premiums on all forms of coin have tended downward. This means that the strategy no longer works very well. Because of the limited number of 90 percent and 40 percent bags—a number that shrinks all the time due to continuing melting—there is the possibility that the premium on these forms will rise as the silver market heats up. Therefore, we would rather hold these forms than silver dollars or silver bars.

Why? First, the premium on dollars now is about 100 percent. Even if it goes higher, it won't happen quickly. Will it ever see 200 percent again? We doubt it. If you swap now, you can roughly double the number of ounces you hold. Second, the 90 percent—and to a much lesser degree the 40 percent—at least has the *chance* to develop a premium later in a hot silver market. Whenever that happens, you should switch out of coins and into bars or any other cheaper form. Silver bars never develop any great premium. When the premium on 90 percent bags gets to 25 percent or 30 percent, you should consider trading 90 percent for bullion or 40 percent. When the premium on 40 percent gets to 7.5 percent, you should trade 40 percent for bullion.

Remember, however, that in 1979–80 the premium on all forms of physical silver (other than bars on deposit in commodity exchange warehouses) disappeared. In fact, these forms of silver went to a deep discount to their silver content. Investors should not expect this silver bull market to behave exactly like the last market. The only solution is to watch the premiums closely, chart them, and make a decision based on their direction at the time.

A similar arbitrage opportunity exists between gold and silver. When the ratio of silver to gold reaches *extreme levels,* as it has recently, you can swap your gold for silver. At a ratio of 80 to 1, if you sold an ounce of gold and bought silver, you would end up with 80 ounces of silver (ignoring premiums). When (and if) the ratio of silver drops to 40 to 1, you swap back out of silver and into gold, and double your gold for your trouble. The drawback here is that the gold–silver ratio in the past few years has gone to its highest level in history, more than 100 to 1. For investors who are serious enough to track the ratio and are satisfied that silver will rise faster than gold, this could be a very profitable long-term trade.

THE 1980 SILVER TRAP: PITFALLS OF PHYSICAL SILVER INVESTING

Why would you want to forgo the pleasure and security of actually holding the metal? *The experience of the 1980s gold and silver top,* which especially affected the investor's ability to sell silver. Only those who lived through this time and saw it happen understand how you might be holding the right metal at the right time and yet remain *unable to realize the full value of your investment.* In the main, gold did not suffer from the same problem.

Beginning in September 1979, silver ran up so fast that the volume of scrap flooding onto the market literally overwhelmed refineries and dealers. Quoted turnaround times stretched out to three months, six months, a year, or more. But overloading the refining system wasn't the only problem. Typically, refineries and dealers "hedge" or "lay off" their physical silver purchases by selling silver futures contracts at the same time they buy physical silver, and vice versa. Their job is *not* to speculate in silver, but to make a middleman's profit. They don't care which way the market moves as long as it doesn't stand still. Selling doesn't hurt them, buying doesn't hurt them, but a market going nowhere *kills* them. They buy 5,000 ounces of physical silver and sell a 5,000 silver futures contract. They lock in a profit and keep their "position fully hedged," in the jargon of the trade.

In 1979–80, however, exchange brokers kept shorting (selling) silver all the way up, and their pain increased to the breaking point. Even though their actual position, balancing futures against physicals, might have been flat (neither long nor short), they still had to meet phenomenal margin calls against their short futures contracts. By January 1980 they were actually threatened with *losing* (a once-in-a-millennium experience), so they did what powerful financial interests always do when a loss threatens: *They changed the rules.*

On January 21, 1980, the Comex effectively closed trading in silver. You could only buy or sell to liquidate existing positions. Off-exchange physicals dealers and investors were trapped. The price of silver began to break. Trading volume statistics from the Comex and Chicago Board of Trade eloquently tell the tale. In 1979, total trading volume was 34 billion ounces. In 1980, volume dropped to 6.99 billion ounces. From 1.1 billion ounces in 1979, open interest dropped to 309.3 million ounces in 1980.

Silver on the commodity exchanges may have been trading at $50 an ounce, but unless investors already had the silver on deposit in an exchange warehouse, *they couldn't get more than 65 percent of its value.* Coins, silver dollars, wafers, ingots, sterling silver, and bars all went to huge discounts because of the refinery overload. Dealers and refiners discounted everything. Some refused to buy at any price.

TODAY'S MARKET

What's happened since 1980? The populous, well-developed, liquid off-exchange dealer market of the 1970s and 1980s has all but disappeared, its ranks decimated once, twice, and yet again by the deadly slow bear market of the past thirteen years. Numerous refineries have closed their doors since those hectic days. Thus your problem becomes: *Where can you sell the silver for full market price in the event of a panic-top blowoff?* The only certain solution is to buy and sell on the commodity exchanges—unless you buy silver through a Swiss or other foreign bank. In 1980, until silver trading was closed off, only warehouse receipt holders were able to get the full price quoted on exchanges.

Does this mean you shouldn't buy and hold physical silver in your own possession? Not at all; but it does mean you ought to understand this past difficulty and be prepared for it. This time, when you see the silver spike building, make your preparations early.

OFF-EXCHANGE PHYSICALS: SOME PROS AND CONS

Which form of physical silver should you hold outside the exchanges? U.S. 90 percent silver coin beats everything else. But you can't tender that on the commodity exchanges, some might complain. Right; but you can't tender 100-ounce Engelhard bars either, even though Engelhard is a commodity exchange-approved refiner. They're 100-ounce bars, not thousands, and they're outside an approved warehouse, so they might as well be Granny's sterling silver spoons as 100-ounce bars—you still can't tender them. Besides, a $1,000 face value bag of U.S. 90 percent silver coins in dimes contains 10,000 pieces of silver, 14 pieces to the ounce. If you need them to barter, a bag of dimes offers potentially 10,000 transactions. The 90-percent coins serve a dual purpose, namely, an investment in physical silver and a universally recognized barter medium in the event of the most terrible social upheavals.

PRIVACY, PRIVACY, *TOUJOURS* PRIVACY

Finally, there's another advantage to holding silver or gold outside commodity exchanges. It's a private form of wealth no one, especially not the government, knows about. (We're not talking about evading taxes here. If you owe taxes, you have an obligation to pay them.) Face it: At the rate our government is moving toward a police state (114 mph on a slow day), you may be glad to have something hidey-holed that *they* don't know about. What's the value *to you* of that kind of privacy? I have personally heard many eyewitness tales about the conflagrations, escapes, bombings, and turmoil of World War II, when a stash of gold, silver, or diamonds proved to be the difference between life and death for whole families.

One friend of ours, a Hungarian who made his way to the United States, recounts a boyhood memory from Budapest at the end of World War II. His house was in rubble, but he and his father sneaked into the basement at night. His father had buried a small strongbox there with precious metals and a few diamonds. They dug frantically in the dark, not knowing whether the box was still there. Our friend says that when he heard his father's shovel strike the box, the sound told him they would survive.

WHEN TO BUY?

When you have concluded that the long-term trend for the metals is up, *buy your position* in stocks, futures, or physicals, and stick with it. Don't act like a maniac wholly ignoring current price action, but don't pay overmuch attention to short-term prices, either. Look to buy on a reaction after a move up. Don't torture or delude yourself with greed. You won't buy at the very low (you *already* missed that), you won't sell at the very high; you only want to take a piece out of the middle. Keep your perspective.

WHEN TO SELL?

Sell when everyone else is buying . . . when the headlines in *The Wall Street Journal* and *Newsweek* and *Time* begin to write about the fortunes being made in silver . . . when your paper boy tells you about the killing his grandmother intends to make in silver. These are all signs of a blowoff top. Look for a chart formation that shows the price moving straight up. It is very difficult to set a target in advance, because markets so often overshoot the mark. From the perspective of $5 silver in 1978, $50 silver looked impossible, *but it happened.* Remember that buying at the right time offers you no advantage at all if you don't also sell at the right time.

FINAL TIPS

You may wonder how much of your investment portfolio you should put in physical silver. In general, the less you have to invest in silver, the more you should concentrate on physicals. Because silver is volatile, you should never invest more than you can afford to walk away from. Ask yourself: If silver went bust, could I still sleep nights? The amount you invest in silver depends on your personal circumstances. The younger you are, the more money you have, the more you can risk.

In general, the less you have to invest, the more you should concentrate on the most standard and least troublesome forms: U.S. 90 percent silver coins, or 1-ounce bullion coins at their slightly higher cost per ounce. Always try to buy the form that gives you the most silver for your money. See Chapter 8 to learn how to calculate exactly what you are paying per pure ounce of silver. If you plan to buy a lot of silver, you should think of buying it off the futures exchange as bullion and leaving it in storage.

Speaking of storage, silver in quantity can be quite heavy and quite bulky, so make storage preparations in advance.

The long bear market in silver has thoroughly cleaned out the dealer market. Most of the ones left are financially sound and good as their word. You should remember that when you place an order with a dealer, that is a *binding contract,* just like buying stocks from a stockbroker.

If you can find a local dealer you can trust (check him or her out with the Better Business Bureau and local coin collectors), so much the better. If not, pick up a copy of *Coin World* or *Numismatic News* at your newsstand and check out the advertisers. If they are out of state, call their local Better Business Bureau before you send them money—it's well worth the call. It usually pays to shop prices.

Most of all, avoid like the plague dealers or salesmen who pester you to buy or pressure you to buy something you don't want. If you call and ask for U.S. 90 percent coin and they press you to buy something else, hang up. When the silver market heats up, these boiler room artists will reappear, and they're nothing but trouble.

We list our own gold and silver brokerage, Jefferson Coin and Bullion, Inc., in Appendix 1. Feel free to shop our prices. You have a right to compare, and make sure you compare *final* prices, including shipping, commissions, and all the extras a dealer might tack on.

Chapter 8

COLLECTIBLES, NUMISMATICS, AND THE MATHEMATICS OF SILVER

Many things made of silver are touted as investments in silver. Unfortunately, they aren't. Silver collectibles or silver numismatic (collector's) coins may gain in value at the same time as silver, but the demand that generates that price rise is not identical to the demand for silver. Silver art forms, silverware, silver jewelry and rare silver coins may be good investments in themselves, but their value is so distantly related to their silver content that the price of silver exerts no practical effect on their performance.

NUMISMATIC COINS

During inflations, *things* tend to appreciate. A "hard asset" is any asset that has some sort of value in itself, as opposed to "paper assets," whose value is derived from some underlying obligation.

During the inflation of the 1970s, *things*—land, real estate, diamonds, old cars, baseball cards, rare coins, gold, and silver—all appreciated, many of them much faster than inflation. Note that the demand for these items is much the same, perhaps even spurred by similar factors, *but not identical to, the demand for silver.*

For example, a U.S. Type I $1 gold piece contains about 0.05 ounce (0.048375 troy ounce exactly) of fine gold. In the lowest uncirculated grade, Mint State-60 or MS-60, the gold in that coin costs about $2,200, or *$45,478 an ounce!* With a gold price at such cosmic distance from the market price of gold, no one can honestly call this coin *an investment in gold*. The same principle holds for numismatic silver coins. It is true that hot gold and silver markets frequently heat up the numismatic market, but the basic demand underlying the values of these investments is not the same. In the past decade we have more than once seen raging bull markets in numismatic coins while gold and silver went nowhere.

The value of gold and silver arises from their underlying *industrial* and *monetary* demand. The fundamental value of *numismatic* or collector's coins arises not from their gold or silver content but from their *numismatic rarity*.

A LEVERAGED SILVER PLAY THROUGH NUMISMATICS

However, the excitement that this bull market in silver will ultimately generate offers a *leveraged silver play through silver numismatics*. In frenzied bull markets, when panic buying sets in, rare silver coins tend to rise by a higher percentage than silver bullion. Why? Because the market is so tight—the supply of rare silver coin is very, very limited. When thousands and then millions of buyers try to get through that tiny Rare Silver Coin Door all at once, something has to give. Rare silver coin prices must skyrocket to clear the market. If you have this sort of play in mind, buy very-high-grade U.S. Morgan or Liberty Seated silver dollars grading at least Mint State-65, certified by the Professional Coin Grading Service

(PCGS) or the Numismatic Guaranty Corporation (NGC). Dealers will call these "slabbed MS-65" or "better Morgans."

ASSESSING NUMISMATIC COINS

Rarity is a combination of *scarcity, strike,* and *state of preservation.* How many coins were minted, and how many survive? Was the coin well or weakly struck? Does its beauty irresistibly draw your eye? How well is the coin preserved? Is it heavily worn, or does it retain the same pristine effulgence it took from the mint? Has time beautified or ravaged it?

GRADING

Grading has always been the chief problem in the numismatic market. Grading coins is half art and half science. A coin may *technically* have all the characteristics of a certain grade, yet so utterly lack *eye appeal* that it will never command the price its technical grade deserves. Expertise in grading coins simply requires years and years of experience and practice.

For years, unscrupulous coin dealers have taken advantage of the public's ignorance. These chicken-stealers have two different grading standards, depending on whether they are buying or selling. They sell coins at one grade, but when it comes time to buy them back, they discover that "grading has become tougher" and now the coin only merits the next lower grade. Thus when you offer to sell back to them the "wonder coin" they sold you two years ago at Mint State-65, they discover that now it grades only MS-62 or MS-60.

We have even met one customer to whom a dealer had sold "whizzed" (mechanically polished) coins graded no better than Extremely Fine-40 (a midrange circulated grade) as *choice brilliant uncirculated!* He had relied on the old saw, "If you don't know coins, know your dealer." The problem was, he never even checked out his dealer.

CERTIFIED COIN GRADING

Coin grading has faced two problems: the intangible, hard-to-quantify *aesthetic* quality; and *bracket creep,* the tightening of grading standards over the years. To address these problems, a number of dealers banded together in the 1980s and formed the Professional Coin Grading Service (PCGS). At about the same time, several independent grading services were founded, such as the Numismatic Guaranty Corporation (NGC). Their goal was to make coins a fungible commodity, like wheat or bean curd. Under this plan, every MS-60 coin would be the equal of every other MS-60 coin, so that you could buy them sight unseen and know you were getting the real merchandise. Several grading experts independently examine and evaluate every coin to assign it a grade. The coin is then ultrasonically sealed in a plastic slab (hence the term "slabbed coin") along with a certificate of authenticity and grade.

The ultimate hardship with that approach is that hard-to-define irreducible aesthetic content. In the end, a coin is a work of art. For example, a weakly struck, lackluster New Orleans Morgan dollar will never be the equal of a strongly struck Philadelphia dollar with brilliant luster and understated pink toning. *Each coin is an individual.* However, for the investor who knows absolutely nothing about coin grading but wants to invest in rare coins, the certified coin grading system at least offers some basic evaluation level. It has also hugely enhanced market liquidity and reduced dealer spreads and customer vulnerability.

A few years ago PCGS dealers experienced large losses when counterfeit slabs suddenly invaded the market, but they managed to remove the counterfeits and survive. For all its problems, certified coin grading is here to stay. *Investors untrained in numismatics who buy anything but certified numismatic coins are simply throwing their money away.*

BOILER ROOMS

During the boom times of the 1970s and 1980s, numerous hungry coin dealers set up WATS line *boiler rooms.* Regiments of salesmen beat the telephones day in and day out, calling prospective coin buyers and wheedling until they bought *something* just to get off the telephone. These dealers sold primarily *what they could buy easily,* the so-called half-numismatic coins, and at inflated prices. As you can imagine, half-numismatic is about as good as "half-witted." If boiler rooms could find a large, steady supply of these coins, then by definition they lacked the primary characteristic of a genuine numismatic coin: *scarcity.*

Because boiler rooms were so successful in creating a market for lower-grade uncirculated silver dollars ("unc. dollars" in rolls of twenty coins), investors who had bought in the early 1970s saw fantastic gains. Unhappily, only a few sold in time to realize these gains. Even if they had sold, wide dealer spreads could have consumed a large chunk of their profits. Worse yet, under frenzied market conditions many boiler rooms suffered a severe lapse of eyesight when grading incoming coins. Some sent out *sliders,* attractive coins that are *almost but not quite* uncirculated. The worst sent out junk that wouldn't have graded uncirculated in the depths of Carlsbad Caverns during a power outage.

But the boiler room salesmen could point to two things to incite the buyer's greed: the gold and silver price spikes, and the Salomon Brothers investment performance studies. In fact, the 1980 price spikes should have warned investors to be wary of gold and silver for a number of years. The Salomon Brothers studies showed that numismatic coins had been the top investment performers for years on end—never mind that the studies didn't take into account market reefs such as changes in grading standards, choice of issues, dealer spreads, and other quirks of numismatic markets. As long as the public kept on buying, the market for these coins remained high. As public interest in the precious metals shrank, however, quasi-numismatic coins lost their appeal, and many boiler rooms went belly up. At last the market for common uncirculated silver dollar rolls busted, too, and dollars dropped from $1,250 or $1,500 a roll to $240 or lower.

Uncirculated rolls of silver dollars are beautiful coins. They're fun to own and gaze at, fascinating for their history and diversity. But at $300 a roll (twenty coins), you're paying $19.39 an ounce for silver. Reasonably speaking, that must be defined as an investment in rare coins and *not* an investment in silver bullion.

The point to remember is that the rare coin market often operates *completely independently* from the silver and gold markets. While rare coins tend to rise when silver and gold are rising, they can also behave in a completely opposite fashion when the metals are falling or moving sideways. Last but not least, rare silver coins offer a *leveraged silver play* when silver bull markets really heat up.

MODERN RARITIES

So-called modern rarities offer plenty of hype potential for boiler rooms. They purchase dump-truck loads of these coins and then "discover" how rare they are: "We bought all we could find and now they've disappeared from the market!"

What you will not discover until it's too late, however, is that there is absolutely no secondary market for most of these coins at anything near what you paid for them. Even the limited editions of major nations, which are usually issued for double their melt value in gold and three to five times their melt value in silver, will immediately fall to melt value or slightly more than melt in the resale or secondary market.

For smaller countries, you'll have to discount the silver content to persuade even a scrap dealer to buy them. If the *Mbezeland 20-qotutu* silver coin with the picture of the rare Dongeli swamp gnu (contains 3.05839 guzzlalis of silver, the traditional *Mbezeland* silver weight—sorry, we can't find a conversion table that translates guzzlalis into troy ounces, but it's a *big* coin and really shiny!) is such a great buy, why didn't the collectors in Mbezeland buy them all up? Because only eight people live there, and the country's thinking about going out of business next year. Avoid this stuff like it was your worst enemy with the flu the day before you leave for vacation.

NUMISMATIC "INVESTMENT"

Some financial advisers and writers may call the purchase of rare coins "investing," but for most folks it's just snipe-shooting in the dark. A *genuine* numismatic investment with a real shot at appreciation over time must begin as a *genuine* rarity. How many were originally minted? How many survived? In what grades? The demand for that particular coin by date or denomination or grade must increase over time. Often that depends on nothing more than numismatic fashion in the collectors' market. This year they like halves; next year it's three-cent pieces.

The euphoria of a silver and gold bull market tends to overflow into the rare coin market. When this has happened in the past, many high-grade, truly rare U.S. coins have actually outperformed silver and gold bullion by a very large margin.

Numismatics can be a worthwhile pastime or avocation and bring countless hours of joyful fascination. You can never go wrong if you take pleasure in it for that alone. If you want to treat numismatics as an investment, your judgment in picking a particular issue may or may not pay off, but that will be determined practically independent of the factors governing the price of silver. Numismatic coins may be a great investment, *but they are an investment in coins, not in silver.*

We've painted things with a pretty broad brush here. There are people of integrity in the coin business. Still, in this investment field you must be willing to educate yourself, or you will have no idea how to evaluate coins or dealers. Knowledgeable, prudent, marketwise dealers can steer you to genuinely rare, undervalued issues with real potential for excellent appreciation. We founded Jefferson Coin and Bullion, Inc., precisely for that purpose. For more information, call or write to Jefferson Coin and Bullion, 2400 Jefferson Highway, Jefferson, LA 70121; tel. 800-593-2585.

ANCIENT COINS

Ancient coins are a fascinating niche in numismatics. Expertise and skill are even more critical here, but the entire market is fundamentally undervalued relative to U.S. coins.

Counterfeiting and correct appraisal have always been problematical for the collector of ancient coins, but now there is the Ancient Coin Certification Service (ACCS). As with the issues of later days, certification will be worth much more than it costs you.

COLLECTIBLES

Silver is an extraordinarily beautiful metal. Metal craftsmen love its forgiving, cooperative nature, and throughout the ages people have wrought silver into exquisite works of art. However, you should acquire collectibles—art bars, medallions, silver statuary, *objets de vertu* and *objets d'art* —only if you have an underlying interest in the aesthetics and lore of the field. If an article in your field of interest also happens to be made out of silver, great, but don't buy it for any alleged investment value. There are only two real reasons to buy silver collectibles. First, buy them for enjoyment without any investment intent. Frequently that will be your biggest return. Second, buy an object made of silver because the silver *enhances* an object in a field you already know. Basically silver "collectibles" are not an investment in the silver market but in the art market.

From the middle 1960s into the 1970s, the general interest in silver brought forth a booming market in silver collectibles. Private "mints" sprang up and put silver to every imaginable use. They cranked out plates, napkin rings, bars, spoons, sculptures, plaques, and medals in series, and touted them as great investments in collectible limited editions.

Many times, these silver objects were sold in baffling weight designations that were as unfamiliar and tricky to figure out as speed expressed in *furlongs per fortnight*. There were the 1000-grain sterling bars in the handcrafted walnut presentation case, one for every state in the Union. *Quick now:* What is the pure silver content of a 1000-grain bar of sterling silver? ("What's a grain?") Why, 1000 divided by 480 grains to the troy ounce ("or is silver measured in *avoirdupois* ounces?") times 92.5 percent purity—that makes 1.92708333 ounces of pure silver. Quite a buy at only $22.50 each when spot silver was $1.70 an ounce, even if it did work out to $11.68 an ounce. Most folks who bought items like these as an "investment" were only able to bail out when silver hit $30.00, $40.00, or $50.00 an ounce, and then only for about what they paid for them.

Lest you regard us crass Philistines, we certainly wouldn't say no one should ever buy silver artwork. Everyone knows the joy that works of art enhanced by the wondrous luster of pure silver can bring, whether you own them yourself or give them as gifts.

However, this illustration points out that these modern "rarities in limited editions" just couldn't stand on their own feet as investments in silver. Let's look at some silver standards so that in the future we can look a little more closely at offers like this.

SILVER STANDARDS: HOW FINE IS FINE?

The first critical question about any silver object is, *How pure is it?* Purity varies widely according to use, custom, and even legal mandate. Purity or *fineness* (in the jargon of the trade) is often expressed as a system of 1000 parts, or three or four numbers preceded by a decimal. Thus sterling silver (92.5 percent pure silver) may be expressed as .925, 925/1000, 92.5, 92.5 percent, or simply "sterling." Silver that is "800 fine" is 80 percent pure. In most countries, these stamps or hallmarks are defined by law.

Theoretically the purest silver—*fine* silver—would be 100 percent. However, as a practical matter, even electrolytically refined silver is only 99.99 percent fine (.9999, or "four nines fine"). The delivery requirement for a Comex futures contract is 5,000 troy ounces of silver, plus or minus 6 percent, .9990/.9999 fine. Because pure silver is very soft and wears rapidly under use, various alloys are used for silverware, holloware, and coinage.

BRITANNIA AND STERLING

Henry VIII so scandalously debased the English silver coinage that by 1551, a pound weight of coin contained only three ounces of silver. When young Elizabeth I ascended the throne, she appointed a commission to examine the state of the coinage and make recommendations. One of the members of that commission was Dr. Gresham, who enunciated the law *"bad money drives good money out of circulation,"* a principle that later became known as Gresham's Law. Actually, the English Parliament had already recognized that principle of economics in the 1200s, and before that, it was well known among the ancient Greeks.

Elizabeth's Great Recoinage definitively reestablished the ancient sterling standard of 11 ounces, 2 pennyweights (abbreviated "dwt.") of pure silver per 12 ounces of gross weight. Since there are 20 pennyweights to the ounce, 11 ounces, 2 pennyweights equal 11.1 ounces, and 11.1/12 = 925/1000 or 92.5 percent pure silver.

In the latter part of the seventeenth century, silver was being heavily exported to India, resulting in a scarcity of silver in the British Isles. Since wealthy persons kept their silver as plate (from the Spanish *plata,* meaning silver, not to be confused with silver*plated* ware), coins were melted for manufacturing silverware. In 1696, Parliament passed a law raising the silverware standard *above the coin standard* to 11 ounces 10 dwt. (11.5/12 = 95.833 percent). However, the older sterling standard was revived in 1719. Like all government interventions in the market, the new Britannia standard did not accomplish its intended purpose. Silversmiths added just enough pure silver to melted sterling coin to reach the higher standard. Furthermore, sterlingware was far more durable than the softer Britanniaware. From 1719 on, British law left to the silversmiths' own discretion whether they would use the Britannia or the sterling standard. Silverware made in the Britannia standard, hallmarked with a figure of Britannia, is almost never seen in the United States.

STERLING SILVER

The sterling standard (925 parts out of 1000) is so ancient in Britain that its origins are shrouded in the mists of time. Wyler[1] tells a wonderfully precise story detailing how King John in 1300 called a band of immigrant Germans (from the East, so "Easterlings") to refine silver for coinage. Then a statute of 1343 dropped the first two letters and the term "sterling" began. Fascinating, but most likely apocryphal, since John died in 1216.

Silver mines had been worked in England since at least Roman times. The Saxons revived and worked these same mines, but so low was the state of their native culture in monetary affairs that they copied Moslem coins. Later they issued "pennies" in imitation of the Roman *denarius* (hence the English abbreviation for penny, d.), which were 92.5 percent pure silver and weighed about 20 grains.

Another version of the "sterling" story holds that the Saxons gave their name to the British coinage because they were "Easterlings," Eastmen, Ostermanni (Eastmen), or Ostrogoths (eastern Goths).[2] *The Oxford English Dictionary* offers several alternatives. Either the coins of 92.5 percent fine silver took their name from *stars* imprinted on them (*steorling*, coin with a star), or from the four birds, *starlings*, on the coins of Edward the Confessor.

Whatever the actual origin, the Saxons had already given their coins wide circulation in northern Europe by the time of Charlemagne. In his monetary reform, he adopted the sterling silver penny as standard and established the system of *pounds, shillings, and pence* (one pound = 20 shillings = 240 pence), harking back to the Roman system. England remained on a sterling coinage standard until 1920, when the fineness of English coin was reduced to 50 percent. In 1947, silver was removed from English coinage altogether.

AMERICAN STERLING

Before 1894, there were generally no laws in the United States regulating the stamping of content designations on silver items. Therefore items produced before this time may mislead the consumer either way. In 1906, the U.S. Congress passed a national gold and silver stamping act. In the United States today, the law requires that silver objects that contain at least 92.5 percent silver be stamped "sterling." The designation may appear as "925/1000s," "925/1000," ".925," or even "925." Coin silver (90 percent fine) may be stamped "coin," "coin silver," "900," or "900/1000."

ENGLISH STERLING

English silver hallmarks are a study unto themselves. Each sterling piece carries several hallmarks, including makers' marks and duty marks. Since 1300, all sterling silver pieces have been required to carry the hallmark called a "leopard's head." This was actually a mistranslation of the French in the statute, as the head was that of a lion. The leopard will always appear on English sterling, and since 1554, an additional mark, a lion passant, has been required for all London silver. As many as six hallmarks may appear on English silver.[3]

GERMAN SILVER STANDARDS

According to Germany's *Law Concerning the Fine Content of Gold and Silver Wares* of July 16, 1884, no silver item of less than 80 percent purity (800/1000) may be stamped. The indication of the fine silver content consists of several legally controlled signs. Under the *Law Concerning the Form of Stamp Marks upon Gold and Silver Items to Indicate the Fine Content* of January 7, 1886, the stamps upon silver must include: the imperial crown (see picture); the crescent moon sign; the indication of the fine silver content in thousandths—for example, 800/1000; and the authorized trademark of the manufacturer. The imperial crown must appear immediately to the right of the crescent moon.

Sterling Silver as an Investment

In general, decorative forms of silver—jewelry, flatware, holloware, etc.
—should be bought for the luxurious, elegant pleasure of silver they give
you in themselves. Buy them and use them with pleasure, and bequeath
them to your family as part of their treasured inheritance. Sterling silver
has long been a traditional wedding gift. However, sterling silver bought
at retail is an investment in your future enjoyment, not an investment in
silver. A typical place setting of silver flatware—knife, salad fork, tea-
spoon and dinner fork—in the lighter "place" size (as opposed to the
heavier "dinner" size) costs about $175 and contains at most four ounces
of silver. Since that works out to $43.75 an ounce, it's not an economical
way to invest in silver.

Misleading Silver Hallmarks

*The following hallmarks are misleading and do not indicate any silver content
whatsoever. In the United States, silver-containing items are legally required
to bear the mark "sterling" or some variation of 925/1000. Items of coin silver
(90-percent pure) must be marked "coin silver," "coin," or 900/1000.*

Alaska Silver	Nickel Silver
Brazil Silver	Peru Silver
German Silver	Silverine
Guaranteed 12 DWT.	Silveroid
Silverode	Silverore

*Note well, however, that many fine sterling silver pieces are handcrafted in
Germany, Mexico, or Peru. These, however, will bear some variation of the
"925" mark in addition to the name of the country. Additionally, the marks
"International Silver" or "Rodgers Bros. Silver" must be accompanied by the
"sterling" mark or the pieces are not sterling.*

Coin Standards

Although there have been many different purity standards for silver coinage, the term "coin silver" generally (in the United States, legally) means 90 percent pure silver (900/1000 or .900). This standard has been used around the world, but was only adopted in the United States in 1834. For obscure reasons, the original American standard was 1485/1664 pure silver, or 89.24 percent.[4] In the nineteenth century, coins were often melted and made into silverware, so the mark "coin" or "coin silver" often appears on the back of old silver and indicates 90 percent fine silver. Antique coin silver may even be stamped "D" or "DOLLAR."

Other Coinage Standards

Canadian silver coins (dimes, quarters, and halves) were, like the British, also sterling until 1920, when they were reduced to 80 percent fineness (.800 or 800/1000). This was reduced to 50 percent (.500 or 500/1000) in 1967, and silver was removed from Canadian coin altogether in 1968. Thus Canadian silver dimes and quarters dated 1967 may be either 80 percent or 50 percent, and Canadian dimes and quarters dated 1968 may be silver or nickel.

Australia maintained the sterling standard until 1946, when it reduced the silver content of its coins to 50 percent. With a few exceptions, silver disappeared entirely from Australian coinage completely after 1963. Until 1933, New Zealanders used British and Australian coinage. In 1933, the first New Zealand shillings were struck in 50 percent silver, but this standard was abandoned in 1947.

France and the Latin Monetary Union

Until 1791, the standard under the *ancien régime* in France was the Scotch standard, 91.7 percent or .917. In 1791, this was briefly lowered to 66.6 percent (.666), before a tidal wave of paper money engulfed France. When Napoleon restored the integrity of the coinage in 1800, he employed the 90 percent standard for his new coinage. This continued until France initiated the Latin Monetary Union (France, Italy, Switzerland, and Belgium), which reduced the standard to 83.5 percent (.835) to attempt to stave off the drainage of silver from these countries. In 1914, France abandoned silver coinage completely. When coinage was resumed in 1920, the franc pieces were made of an aluminum-bronze alloy.

THE MARIA TERESA THALER

The Austrian Maria Teresa thaler is 83.33 percent fine silver and contains 0.7520 troy ounce fine silver. This splendid coin has been minted for use as a trade coin in the Middle East and Asia since it was first issued in 1780. It has been struck in the millions, always dated 1780, at the mints of Vienna, Rome, Paris, London, Brussels, Bombay, and Birmingham. In fact, you can still have them minted today at the Austrian mint, or buy them from dealers.

THE NETHERLANDS AND GERMANY

Netherlands standards vary considerably from coin to coin and period. The Gulden (100 cents) from 1818 through 1837 was minted in 89.3 percent fine silver; from 1840 through 1917, in 94.5-percent silver; from 1922 through 1967, in 72-percent pure silver; and from 1967 onward, silver disappeared. German issues of the period 1873 to 1915 from 20 pfennig through the 2-mark pieces were 90 percent silver.

MEXICO AND LATIN AMERICA

From 1863, the silver standard for Mexican Republican coinage was 90.3 percent. In 1905, the standard for most coins of the United States of Mexico became 80 percent silver, which was further reduced to 72 percent in 1925, and with a few exceptions abandoned altogether by 1945. The peso coins of 1947–49 were issued in 50 percent silver, reduced to 30 percent in 1950 and to 10 percent, 1957–67.[5] Silver coins of Latin America often reveal their silver content on their face with a designation such as "25 *gram(os) ley* .900" or "*ley* 0.900 gr. 12.5." The first indicates "25 grams of silver 900/1000ths fine by law"; the second, "12.5 grams of silver 900/1000ths fine by law."

SILVER FINENESS STANDARDS

Name	Purity	Fineness
Fine silver	99.99%	999.9/1000
Britannia standard	95.83%	958.3/1000
Sterling standard	92.50%	925/1000
Scotch standard	91.67%	917/1000
Coin standard, United States, 1834–1964	90.00%	900/1000
1792 U.S. standard	89.24%	892.4/1000
Latin Monetary Union standard	83.50%	835/1000
Austrian Maria Teresa thaler	83.33%	833/1000
U.S. half dollar, 1965–70	40.00%	400/1000
U.S. silver war nickels, 1942–45	35.00%	350/1000

SILVER CONTENT OF $1 FACE VALUE IN COIN

(In troy ounces. To allow for wear, mint values are given in one column, trade values in the second two columns. For some coins, the mint and trade content are the same because as a practical matter they never circulated.)

	Mint Content Each	Trade Content Each One	Trade Content in Coin Dollar
U.S. 90%			
U.S. silver dollar	0.7734	0.765	0.765
U.S. silver half dollar	0.36169	0.3575	0.715
U.S. silver quarter	0.18084	0.17875	0.715
U.S. silver dime	0.07234	0.0715	0.715
U.S. 40%			
U.S. 40% Eisenhower dollar	0.31625	0.31625	0.31625
U.S. 40% silver half, 1965–70	0.1492	0.1475	0.295
U.S. 40% silver quarter	0.07396	0.07396	0.295
U.S. 35% war nickel	0.05626	0.055	1.100

Canadian 80%			
Dollar	0.600	0.600	0.600
Half dollar	0.3000	0.2925	0.585
Quarter	0.1500	0.14625	0.585
Dime	0.0600	0.0585	0.585
Canadian 50%			
Quarter	0.0937	0.3748	0.3748
Dime	0.0375	0.3748	0.3748
Maria Teresa thaler	0.7520	0.7520	0.7520

SELLING SCRAP SILVER

Before you sell sterling silver, you should have it examined or appraised by more than one knowledgeable dealer to determine if it has any antique value. Be careful: Even silverplated ware may have substantial value as an antique. Be sure to take your item to more than one dealer. We hate to admit it, but some folks would steal the quarters off a dead man's eyes.

If you have scrap silver you no longer need or want, look in the yellow pages under "Precious Metals Dealers" or "Gold and Silver Dealers" to find a dealer. Give them a call and ask what they are paying per ounce for scrap silver. Once they tell you, you still won't know much. Here's how to figure out what they're actually paying per fine ounce.

If they say they're paying $3.25 an ounce for scrap sterling, divide their price by .925 (remember, *cost divided by content*); $3.25/.925 = $3.51 per fine troy ounce. To figure what percentage of the melt value they are paying, divide the price per fine troy ounce by the spot silver price. If spot silver in this example was at $5, then 3.51/5.00 = .702. They're paying 70.2 percent of the silver value.

Generally, you can expect to take a deep discount when you sell scrap silver to dealers, as much as 35 percent to 40 percent off the spot silver price, so it pays to shop around. Don't get too irate, however. The dealers have to make a profit. While they're trying to buy enough silver to make a trip to the refinery, they have to carry the risk of the market moving against them. Check the flea markets and antiques shops: There may be dealers in sterling there who will give you more for your scrap as *silverware* than you can get for it as scrap silver. (It works the other way, too.

You may find a dealer in sterling who will sell you reconditioned sterling silver at much less than the retail price for new tableware.)

If you have sterling silver knives, candlesticks, candelabra, or candy dishes, remember that the handles and bases of most of these are *not* solid sterling silver. Most are filled with epoxy or cement and wrapped with sterling silver foil. The typical table knife has only about 0.5 troy ounce of sterling silver; the blade is stainless steel.

If you decide to try to sell your sterling silverware yourself through a classified newspaper ad, *play it smart*. Don't use your home telephone number or address. Use your office telephone number only. Don't run the risk of having your home burglarized.

Weighing Silver

The troy system is used to weigh silver and gold. The avoirdupois system is the customary system used in the United States. Be careful: Grains are abbreviated "gr.," grams are abbreviated "g."

Troy	Avoirdupois

grain = the smallest unit, identical in both systems

Troy	Avoirdupois
24 grains = 1 pennyweight (dwt.)	1 dram = 27.344 grains
1 ounce = 480 grains	1 ounce = 437.5 grains
= 20 pennyweights	= 16 drams
1 pound = 12 ounces	1 pound = 16 ounces
= 240 pennyweights	= 256 drams
= 5,760 grains	= 7,000 grains

CONVERTING AVOIRDUPOIS TO TROY WEIGHT

1. **To convert avoirdupois ounces to troy ounces:**

   437.5 grains = 1 avoirdupois ounce = 0.911 troy ounce

   To convert avoirdupois ounces to troy ounces, multiply avoirdupois ounces by 0.911. Rule of thumb: For a quick approximation, multiply avoirdupois ounces by 0.9 to get troy ounces.

2. To convert troy ounces to avoirdupois ounces:

480 grains = 1 troy ounce = 1.097 avoirdupois ounces

To convert troy ounces to avoirdupois ounces, multiply by 1.097. Rule of thumb: For a quick estimate, multiply troy ounces by 1.1 to get avoirdupois ounces.

3. To convert avoirdupois pounds to troy ounces:

16 avoirdupois ounces = 1 avoirdupois pound = 14.583 troy ounces

To convert avoirdupois pounds to troy ounces, multiply avoirdupois pounds by 14.583. Rule of thumb: For a quick approximation, multiply avoirdupois pounds by 14.5 to get troy ounces.

4. To convert troy ounces to avoirdupois pounds:

480 grains = 1 troy ounce
7,000 grains = 1 avoirdupois pound = 14.583 troy ounces
1 troy ounce = 480/7000 = 0.06857 avoirdupois pound

To convert troy ounces to avoirdupois pounds, multiply troy ounces by 0.06857, or divide troy ounces by 14.583. Sorry, there's no quick way to work this one out.

Converting Troy Weight to Metric Weight

1. To convert grams to troy ounces:

1 grain = 64.8 milligrams = .06479891 grams
480 grains = 1 troy ounce = 31.1034 grams

To convert grams to troy ounces, divide grams by 31.1034. To convert troy ounces to grams, multiply troy ounces by 31.1034.

2. To convert troy ounces to kilograms:

32.1508 troy ounces = 1,000 grams = 1 kilogram

To convert troy ounces to kilograms, divide troy ounces by 32.1508. To convert kilograms to troy ounces, multiply kilograms by 32.1508.

3. To convert metric tons to troy ounces:

1,000 kilograms = 1 metric ton = 32,150.8 troy ounces

Precious metals are weighed in metric tons. To convert metric tons to troy ounces, multiply metric tons by 32,150.8. To convert troy ounces to metric tons, divide troy ounces by 32,150.8. Confusing point: Metric tons are sometimes indicated by the spelling "tonnes," but this is unnecessary. In references to precious metals, metric tons are always indicated.

Quick Conversion Table

To convert:

Avoirdupois ounces to troy ounces, multiply avoirdupois ounces by 0.911

Avoirdupois pounds to troy ounces, multiply avoirdupois pounds by 14.583

Troy ounces to avoirdupois ounces, multiply troy ounces by 1.097

Troy ounces to avoirdupois pounds, multiply troy ounces by .06857

Grams to grains, multiply grams by 15.4324

Grams to troy ounces, divide grams by 31.1034

Kilograms to troy ounces, multiply kilograms by 32.1508

Metric tons to troy ounces, multiply metric tons by 32,150.8

Grains to grams, divide grains by 15.4324

Troy ounces to grams, multiply troy ounces by 31.1034

Troy ounces to kilograms, divide troy ounces by 32.1508

Troy ounces to metric tons, divide troy ounces by 32,150.8

CALCULATING VALUE

How to Calculate the Melt or Market Value of Silver Scrap

To determine the silver content of silver items, you must use this formula:

Weight in troy ounces × fineness = fine silver content in troy ounces

Fineness must be expressed as a percentage with the decimal point in front. For example, sterling silver is 925/1000s fine silver, or 0.925 fine.

Here's how to convert:

1. *Weigh* your silver item. You can even ask your butcher to put it on his very accurate scales if you have no small scales.
2. *Convert* the weight to troy ounces. To express avoirdupois ounces in troy ounces, multiply avoirdupois ounces by 0.911, or avoirdupois pounds by 14.583:

   Avoirdupois ounces × 0.911 = troy ounces
   Avoirdupois pounds × 14.583 = troy ounces

3. *Calculate* the net silver content. Determine the fineness of your silver item. It will probably be sterling (92.5 percent pure silver), but it may be coin silver (90 percent pure), or 800 fine (80 percent), or even 750 (75 percent fine). Then multiply the gross weight in troy ounces by the percentage purity:

   Weight in troy ounces × fineness = silver content in troy ounces

To calculate the melt or market value of your silver item, you must use this formula:

Silver content in troy ounces × spot metal price = melt or market value

Example:

1. You have a sterling silver goblet. You take it to the grocery store, smile at the butcher, and ask him or her to do you a favor: "Please weigh this for me." The butcher rolls his or her eyes, smiles, puts it on the scale, and says, "0.42 pound." Thank the butcher, write down the weight, go home, and dig out your calculator.
2. You know the butcher's scale uses avoirdupois pounds, so multiply these avoirdupois pounds by 14.583 to get the weight in troy ounces:

   0.42 avoirdupois pound × 14.583 = 6.12 troy ounces

3. Now to find the silver content in troy ounces, you have to know the fineness of the silver goblet. You look on the bottom and see the

word "sterling" stamped there, so you know the goblet is 92.5 percent pure silver. Now you multiply again, expressing the fineness as a decimal:

6.12 troy ounces × .925 fineness = 5.66 troy ounce fine silver

4. To calculate melt or market value, you must multiply the number of fine troy ounces by the market or spot price. For the current market price, look in your newspaper on the page with commodity quotations, or ask your local stockbroker or silver dealer for the "spot price of silver." He or she tells you spot silver is $5.00. Now you're ready to multiply:

5.66 troy ounces fine silver × $5.00 spot silver price = $28.30 melt or market value

How to Calculate the Melt or Market Value of Coins

The process is identical to finding the melt value of silver scrap, but the fineness is different. U.S. silver dimes, quarters, and halves minted before 1965 are 90 percent silver by weight. U.S. dollars minted before 1936 are also 90 percent silver by weight.

We take a shortcut here because we already know the silver content of coin in troy ounces. We use the trade weights rather than the mint weights to allow for wear:

U.S. Coins

This Face Value . . .	Contains This Much Fine (Pure) Silver
1 silver dollar	= 0.765 troy ounce fine silver
1,000 silver dollars	= 765 troy ounces fine silver
2 silver halves	= 0.715 troy ounce fine silver
4 silver quarters	= 0.715 troy ounce fine silver
10 silver dimes	= 0.715 troy ounce fine silver
$1,000 face value dimes, quarters, or halves	= 715 troy ounces fine silver
2 silver halves, 1965–70	= 0.295 troy ounce fine silver
$1,000 face value 40% halves	= 295 troy ounces fine silver

Example, U.S. 90 percent silver coins:

You have $216.15 face value U.S. silver dimes, quarters, and halves. First, calculate how much silver that represents:

$216.15 × 0.715 ounces per dollar face value = 154.54 ounces silver

Now ask your broker or dealer the spot price of silver. He or she tells you it's $5.00. Calculate the melt value:

154.54 troy ounces × $5.00 per troy ounce spot price = $772.70 melt value

Example, U.S. 40 percent silver halves:

You have $355.50 in U.S. 40 percent half dollars minted between 1965 and 1970. First, calculate how much silver that represents:

$355.50 × 0.295 troy ounce per dollar face value = 104.87 troy ounces fine silver

You already know that the spot price of silver is $5.00, so you multiply the number of ounces times the spot price:

104.87 troy ounces × $5.00 per troy ounce spot price = $524.35 melt value

Canadian Coins

Before 1920 Canadian silver coins were 92.5 percent silver. From 1920 to mid-1967 it was 80 percent silver.

Eighty percent silver:

1 silver dollar, 1936–66	= 0.600 troy ounce fine silver
1,000 silver dollars	= 600 troy ounces
2 silver halves, 1920–67	= 0.585 troy ounce fine silver
4 silver quarters, 1920–67	= 0.585 troy ounce fine silver
10 silver dimes, 1920–67	= 0.585 troy ounce fine silver
$1,000 face value dimes, quarters, or halves	= 585 troy ounces fine silver

Fifty percent silver:

The silver content of Canadian coins was changed in mid-1967 from 80 percent to 50 percent. In mid-1968 silver was removed altogether. No 50 percent halves were ever struck. Some commemorative 80 percent silver dollars have been struck since 1966.

4 silver quarters, 1967–68	= 0.3748 troy ounce fine silver
10 silver dimes, 1967–68	= 0.0375 troy ounce fine silver
$1,000 face value 50% dimes or quarters	= 374.8 troy ounces fine silver

Example, Canadian 80 percent silver coins:

You have $431.10 in Canadian 80 percent silver coins. First, calculate the silver content:

$431.10 × 0.585 troy ounces per dollar face value = 252.19 troy ounces fine silver

Now assuming the spot price of silver is still $5.00, multiply the number of ounces times the spot price:

252.19 troy ounces fine silver × $5.00, spot price = $1,260.95 melt value

SILVER AND NOT SILVER—DOLLARS AND NOT DOLLARS

Strictly speaking, silver collectibles and silver numismatic (collector's) coins are not investments in silver. That doesn't mean they cannot be extremely profitable investments, or that they are not valuable, but simply that the reasons they gain or lose in price have little to do with fluctuations in the value of their silver content.

You may have inherited or acquired some silver object that, because of its rarity or artistic value, is far, far more valuable than its mere silver content. Should you hang on to it or sell it now?

That depends on you. Do you prefer the silver artifact and whatever enjoyment its presence brings? Or would you rather have the cash? If evaluating and cherishing the article require far more expertise than you have or intend to acquire, why not sell it for a fair price now, so you can enjoy the cash and let some genuine connoisseur enjoy the artwork? Don't let greed trap you. Maybe the price of your particular treasure *will* shoot for the moon someday, but will you be around to cash in when it does? Do what *you* want to do, and don't torture yourself about the big price you might get *someday*.

One more word about U.S. silver coins: You're perfectly free to melt them or do anything else you want with them. (For a few years after 1967 Congress made melting them illegal, a prohibition that was almost as universally derided and ignored as its alcoholic namesake.) In fact, because in recent years coins have traded at a discount, dealers have continuously melted them and sold them as bullion to profit from their tiny discount to the bullion price. There are several reasons, however, why coins are more valuable than bullion to the farsighted investor.

First, U.S. 90 percent silver coins are the most widely recognized form of silver, the most liquid form of physical silver, and the most divisible. A bag of dimes, for instance, divides 715 ounces of silver into *ten thousand* pieces, and you can buy, sell, or trade 90 percent silver coins with thousands of dealers or millions of individuals from coast to coast.

Second, nineties cover several investment bases at once. Survivalists recommend that you have a bag of 90 percent coins for every member of the family, in case the monetary system breaks down and you need something to use as money. Those who fear inflation, too, want 90 percent silver coin so they will have something to spend in case the paper money fails. Even though these are fairly remote possibilities, it's true that 90 percent coins are the best protection in those circumstances. Last, it's one of the cheapest ways to buy physical investment silver as well. If you can cover more than one base with no extra cost (or even lower cost!), why not take advantage of it?

Third, 90 percent coins have historically carried large premiums to their silver content. Although appearance of the American Silver Eagle .999 ounce coin took much demand away from 90 percent, we think that will change and the 90 percent coin premium will rise. Dealers have continued to melt 90 percent coin, so the supply is continually shrinking without any possibility of replacement. Very few people recognize that the supply of 90 percent is declining. U.S. 90 percent coins used to be the public's favorite physical silver investment, and as more and more people pour into the silver market, more and more will recognize the advantages of 90 percent coins. We believe that at some point the premium on 90 percent may reappear, and offer you a kicker on your 90 percent silver coin investment that no other form offers. So buy 90 percent silver coins for the physical investment silver you intend to hold personally.

Finally, when you're thinking about silver investments in coins, *forget* the word "dollar." It only confuses you. Yes, we talk about "dollars" of 90 percent silver coins being worth so many "dollars" in paper money, but they're not the same "dollars" at all. They differ as utterly as a Hong Kong "dollar" differs from a U.S. Federal Reserve note "dollar."

Talking about the "price" of silver in "dollars" is ridiculous, because a "dollar" of silver, constitutionally and legally, is just a weight of silver equaling 371.25 grains. Asking the "price" of silver in "dollars" is like asking the "price" of milk in "quarts." The so-called dollar we are forced to use in the United States is actually a *legally irredeemable* paper bank note issued by one of the twelve Federal Reserve regional banks (or its equivalent in bank credit on the computerized books of some commercial banks). So the price of silver you hear quoted is really denominated in these Federal Reserve Unit Accounting Dollars—*FRAUDs* for short. Don't let these different "dollars" confuse you.

Chapter 9

THE SILVER LINING FOR SILVER TRADERS: OPTIONS AND FUTURES

Suppose the Silver Fairy lent you her magic wand and you could create the perfect silver investment vehicle? You would probably wish for the following advantages:

Low cost: The same deep commission discounts and tiny bid-ask spreads enjoyed by giant miners and refiners, government mints, and other industrial users who trade tons of silver every year.

Easy to track: Publicly established and audited prices, reported in daily newspapers.

Easy to trade: As simple to buy and sell through any broker as shares in a well-capitalized stock or large mutual fund. But more critically, easy to sell, with your choice of custom services such as stop loss and price limit orders.

Peace of mind: A proven way to lock in profits, limit losses, and protect yourself from the 10 percent to 50 percent price swings typical of silver bull markets—without eliminating upside profitability. No worries about the safety of money or metal on deposit with your broker or dealer.

Pure play: No dilution of the silver investment. No distortion by variables such as mining company dividend payouts and ore reserve estimates, or the ebb and flow of the latest collectibles or numismatic fad.

Risk control: You can select precisely the amount of leverage, from fully paid bullion to plunking down only a tiny percentage of the cash value (for maximum potential profits).

Interest income: A way to earn interest on your silver while the market is locked in sleepy sideways consolidations that can last weeks or months, even during a long-term bull market.

Flexibility: Additional strategies that mean you can profit even in bear markets.

Then you wake up. Reluctantly, you hand the magic wand back to the Silver Fairy. Alas, you think no such silver investment exists.

Surprise: This investment vehicle is not a dream. It's found in the silver futures and options contracts traded every day on the New York Commodity Exchange (Comex) and the Chicago Board of Trade (CBOT), two of the world's largest, most liquid exchanges. The benefits we listed above for our ideal silver investment are just a few of the host of benefits that futures and options contracts offer. Hardly one investor in ten knows about them, and they're not limited just to the big people. Every single silver investor can tap right in.

A TWO-THOUSAND-YEAR SUCCESS STORY

The practices of today's futures market are grounded in rice trading systems from ancient Japan. The options concept was pioneered by medieval gold- and silversmiths. Trading standardized commodity contracts for delivery at a later date (the modern futures contract) began in Chicago more than a hundred years ago.

Today, futures and their associated options perform many duties. Investors can use them to generate capital gains or premium "interest" from options. Commercial interests can lock in commodity prices and hedge the risks that always threaten profit margins on commodity inventories. Or they can lower investment costs and give investors the chance to become market makers.

Futures and options exchanges are the twentieth century's biggest financial success story. Trading volume swelled to more than 450 million contracts in 1992, easily surpassing the combined dollar volume of all U.S. stock and bond markets. In 1992 more than 12 million of these transactions were precious metals contracts. On a normal trading day, silver orders are executed within seconds, with bid-ask spreads amounting to only a fraction of a cent per ounce.

FUTURES CONTRACTS

A futures contract is a standardized agreement that legally binds two parties—the seller (the short) and the buyer (the long)—to delivery of a commodity in a specific month. Quantity, quality, delivery point, and date are the same for each contract traded. Only the price is left unspecified until the trade is executed on the exchange's floor. It is just as easy to go short (try to profit from falling prices) as it is to go long (try to profit from rising prices).

Although the futures contract is a legally binding agreement for an actual transaction, you can satisfy that obligation at any time before the delivery date with an offsetting transaction. If you are long a contract, you short a contract to offset it, and vice versa. Only a small minority of contracts are settled by a physical delivery of the commodity. The vast majority are offset prior to delivery.

Between the time a position is taken and the time it's liquidated, the price of the contract will fluctuate, resulting in a profit or loss. (Contrary to widespread folklore, there is no risk of waking up to a pile of unwanted soybeans or pork bellies on your front lawn.) To enter a futures contract (short or long), you must deposit the *margin* required. Generally, margin runs 3 percent to 10 percent of the cash value of the contract. Here's where the leverage comes in: Although the margin you must put up is only a fraction of the contract's total value, you profit (or lose!) based on the price of the *entire contract*.

Unlike stock margin, futures margin is not a down payment on a loan. Rather, it is a *good-faith performance bond* by which you guarantee a specific dollar amount of losses. If your position winds up profitable, the margin will be returned to you. If you lose money, the loss will be subtracted from your margin before any refund.

At the end of every trading day futures contracts are *"marked to market"*: The gains and losses in your account are toted up and adjusted. Although you have to add margin to make up losses, you can also withdraw profits when they exceed the margin requirement, or use them to finance new positions.

This margin system affords *very efficient* leverage for investors and hedgers. By adjusting the amount of money you use to back each position, the degree of leverage can be controlled *precisely*. That's why futures are equally attractive to the most conservative or the most aggressive investor.

OPTIONS ON FUTURES

Options on futures are also contracts, but they differ from futures contracts in one monumental way. The option buyer (holder) has the right, but not the *obligation,* to buy or sell a futures contract at a fixed price before the option expires. The seller (writer) assumes the obligation to buy or sell a futures contract at that fixed price before the option expires.

Because options are based on, or *derive from,* underlying silver futures contracts, they are often called "derivatives." For all practical purposes, however, an option on a silver futures contract is an option directly on silver bullion.

Think of options as *insurance.* When you buy a put or a call option, it's like buying an insurance policy: You're trying to protect yourself against a loss or a missed opportunity. The option contract writer collects money for assuming the option buyer's risk, just as an insurance company assumes your risk when it writes a policy.

Options make possible market positions for far less money; far less risk; and, at times, far more leverage than outright futures contracts. Unlike insurance policies (and because options are traded just like futures contracts), option buyers and sellers are free to offset their positions during market hours, taking profits or cutting losses. Option *holders* may exercise the option, resell it in the market, or let it expire if it has no value. An option *writer* can offset his or her obligation at any time before the exercise date by buying an identical contract to close out his or her position.

156

HOW THEY WORK

All options on futures contracts specify four conditions:

1. Put or call. Does the option grant a right to *buy* ("call") or the right to *sell* ("put")? Calls and puts are *separate* option contracts, not opposite sides of the same transaction. Put options become more valuable as the futures price falls; call options gain in value as the price rises.

2. What's behind the option? What backs the option? In the case of silver futures options, it is silver futures contracts. When an option is exercised, this is what the holder receives, not silver bullion.

3. The "strike" price. At what price may the buyer exercise the option? This fixes the "strike" or "exercise" price at which a futures position is received if the option is exercised. Put and call strike prices are listed above and below the current futures price.

4. The expiration date. That's the last day when an option may be exercised. After that it expires.

The price the buyer pays for an option is called the *premium*. Whether or not the holder exercises the option, the writer gets to keep the premium. The decision to exercise is entirely up to the buyer. If the buyer chooses not to exercise by the expiration date, the option expires worthless.

Economic laws of supply and demand determine the premium of the option through competitive bidding on the exchange floor. Although the trading floor of a commodity exchange (sometimes called the "pit") looks like a crowd of maniacs screaming at each other, even while they are buying and selling, five fundamental factors are influencing the premium.

1. Where's the strike price versus the futures? If the current futures contract price is above the strike price for a call (or below the strike price for a put), the option has *intrinsic* value. An option with intrinsic value is *in the money*. An option without intrinsic value is *out of the money*. If the option's strike price equals the futures contract price, it is *at the money*.

157

2. How much time before it expires? The more time that remains in an option, the higher the premium tends to be. More time provides more opportunity for the underlying futures to move and make the option's strike price profitable. An option is a wasting asset. As the option approaches maturity, the time value declines to zero. At expiration, the options value consists only of its in-the-money value.

3. How volatile are the underlying futures? There is a simple but significant relation between option premiums and volatility (the degree of price variability): The greater the volatility, the higher the premium. Higher volatility gives the option a greater likelihood to go in the money by the expiration date. Because that means more risk to the writer, he or she charges a higher premium for the option.

All option premiums do not move the same as underlying futures prices. The closer an option comes to the in-the-money level, the closer it tracks futures prices. The ratio between the change in the option's premium and the underlying futures' price is the *delta factor*. For example, at-the-money options have a delta of 0.50—for every dollar the futures move, the option premium moves 50 cents.

4. What volatility does the public expect? If the public expects the underlying futures to become more volatile, then the risk to the option writer rises—so he or she charges more for the option.

5. Where are interest rates? The current, risk-free, short-term interest rate affects option premiums. Why? Because option writers use income from premiums to invest in the money market.

Warning: Never trade silver options unless your broker has an on-line computer program that instantly values all options based on the above criteria. This gives you a tremendous edge on the market, identifying the perfect option contract for any need.

YOUR STRATEGY TOOL CHEST

Silver futures and options (or options/futures combinations) offer formidable flexibility and range. The accompanying table summarizes the more popular strategies. Remember: Selling (*"writing"*) calls or puts is a means to earn premium "interest" income on silver.

If you think silver prices will:

Rise   *Buy* the futures or calls, and/or write put options with strike prices *below* the market.

Fall   *Sell* the futures, write calls *above* the market, or buy puts *below* the market to protect profits in your core position.

Remain steady *Write* calls against your core long futures position, or write call/put combinations ("straddles") above and below the market.

Here are some special situations where the futures exchanges can become very beneficial tools:

BUY BULLION FROM THE COMMODITY EXCHANGE

If you are going to buy more than 1,000 ounces of physical silver, the cheapest and most secure alternative is to buy it directly from the commodity exchange. You simply go long in the current (spot) month contract and take delivery.

You can either (1) take a *vault receipt* from an exchange-approved warehouse, or (2) take physical delivery (have the silver delivered to your door). U.S. exchange vault receipts are honored internationally, can be easily pledged as collateral, placed in trust, negotiated offshore, or instantly sold back into the market by simply shorting the spot month futures contract.

Warning: You must pay to have physical bullion delivered to you.

Once bullion leaves the exchange-approved warehouse, you must pay again to have it recertified for purity before it can be sold back into the market. This is a slow, expensive process, so think twice before taking physical delivery.

Here's the best news: The total cost to buy up to 5,000 ounces of silver through the spot futures contract should not exceed $150. There are no sales or excise taxes, and no extra 5 percent to 10 percent spreads many banks and private leverage dealers pile on top of their sales commission.

With the futures market you avoid all those add-on expenses and easily save yourself up to 95 percent in transactions costs. Finally, the annual storage fees at exchange-approved vaults are far lower than any comparable alternative.

HOW TO BUY SILVER FOR 3 CENTS ON THE DOLLAR

Sometimes silver call options will be priced so low that you can use them to buy silver at a far lower break-even cost and with far less risk than fully paid physical bullion. Call options grant you the right *but not the obligation* to be long silver at the option's strike price until the option expires.

These opportunities usually emerge when the silver market is consolidating (moving sideways) or when sentiment is overwhelmingly bearish. Options fix both your out-of-pocket expenses and your risks, while their profit potential is unlimited. Still, timing is critical because out-of-the-money options expire worthless.

How do you decide whether to buy call options or physical silver bullion? Your broker should calculate the difference by comparing the annualized break-even costs of the alternatives, including the *opportunity cost* of not receiving interest income while your money's tied up in silver bullion. At the same time, he or she should weigh the market's technical condition.

DOUBLE BULLION PROFITS WITH NO EXTRA RISK

What's the best-kept secret in silver trading? The often spectacular extra profits you can earn simply by owning more distant futures contracts. In the accompanying price tables, notice how the prices of silver contracts rise in the more distant (deferred) expiration months. This difference in price between the spot (cash) price is called the "cost of carry" or "spread." It consists of the storage, insurance, and interest costs of buying cash silver and holding it for delivery into the deferred month. In silver bull markets the spread tends to *increase*—sometimes dramatically—especially when interest rates rise along with the silver price, to the great advantage of investors holding distant contracts.

FUTURES OPTIONS PRICE TABLE
HOW TO READ FUTURES OPTIONS QUOTATIONS

A composite from several sources but typical of newspaper futures quotations.

Silver (Comex): 5,000 troy ounces; cents per troy ounce, Wednesday, Oct. 6, 1993

Strike Price	CALLS—SETTLE			PUTS—SETTLE		
	Nov.	Dec.	Mar.	Nov.	Dec.	Mar.
375	53.8	56.2	66.0	0.1	2.5	9.0
400	29.2	36.2	49.5	0.5	7.5	17.0
425	9.0	20.5	36.0	5.3	16.8	28.0
450	1.2	12.0	27.0	22.5	33.3	44.0
475	0.3	8.0	21.0	46.6	54.3	62.5
500	0.1	5.5	15.5	71.4	76.8	82.0

Est. vol.: 6,500   Tues. 2,246 calls 687 puts
Op. int. Tues.   68,373 calls 23,906 puts

The option values are quoted in cents per troy ounce. To determine the full market value of any option in dollars, multiply the price quoted by 50 (= 5,000 x .01).

1. Strike (or exercise) price of the put or call option.
2. Expiration months (most newspapers show only three months).
3. Volume of options traded in the session quoted.
4. Volume of options traded in yesterday's session.
5. The number of options (each unit represents both the buyer and writer of each open position at the close of the previous session).
6. Closing prices in each option.

Is this just chicken feed? That depends on the size of the rooster. Between September 1979 and February 1980, the one-year deferred contract gained an extra $4.00 an ounce over cash silver—a $20,000 bonus for every 5,000-ounce deferred contract you held. These reasons powerfully imply that the serious investor should hold his or her core silver position in deferred contracts at least one year out, and continue to roll into deferred contracts when listed by the exchange. The potential extra profits *for free*—exactly the same margin and commission costs as the nearby contracts—can easily mean 25 percent to 50 percent in the blink of an eye.

FAIL-SAFE SILVER TRADING GUIDELINES

The futures and options contracts we have introduced in this chapter are the premier silver *trading* vehicles, offering the greatest liquidity and flexibility, lowest commissions, and smallest bid/ask spread of any alternative. But their greatest advantage is also their greatest risk: *leverage*. That leverage can translate even small moves in spot silver prices into a quick 100 percent gain or loss.

Leverage means risk—and risk means that if you use these contracts, *you must strictly obey time-proven rules and guidelines to keep that leverage (and the byproduct emotional pressures) under rigid control.* We asked noted precious metals analyst and trader Steve Belmont and his brokerage team at Fox Investments in Chicago to compile these indispensable trading rules to guide your trading.

1. Know what you really want. Decide what you want to do, and stick with it. Either speculate on short-term trades, or invest for the long term. Successful short-term speculation—selecting trades, managing risk, and maintaining the proper mind-set—requires an outlook exactly opposed to successful long-term investing. Never try to mix them, because that will make it impossible for your broker to help you.

2. Keep it simple and consistent. Most beginners try to watch too many indicators and listen to too many different opinions. The result? They are perpetually confused and overwhelmed into inaction. Professionals rarely use more than two or three simple, commonly available indicators to spot clear-cut opportunities quickly.

3. Watch the big picture. Monitor silver with weekly and monthly charts and indicators rather than daily or hourly series. Weekly and monthly range indicators give fewer, but generally more reliable, buy-and-sell signals. Daily indicators will whipsaw you with false one- or two-day breakouts that disappear on the weekly and monthly charts. Likewise, *ignore popular media commentary on silver,* except at extremes when it forewarns important trend changes. When the silver boom makes the cover of *Time* magazine, call your broker and take profits without delay! When *Newsweek* announces that "silver is dead," buy all you can afford.

4. Always undercommit. Investors commonly try to hold positions larger than their risk capital can justify. This creates extra stress, guaranteeing bad judgment and losses. Professionals intentionally *undertrade,* holding smaller positions than necessary to ensure their own emotional balance. This is popularly called "trading down to your sleeping point." Never carry a trading position so large that it keeps you awake nights. *Never, never* "bet the farm"—unless you want to wind up farmless.

5. Be patient. Even in powerful bull markets, silver undergoes long, sideways consolidations and price retracements. These can amount to 80 percent of all price action within the major trend. Learn to accept this reality. Instead of fretting and complaining, use the circumstances to your advantage.

6. Put the odds in your favor. Making money in silver is a lonely business. You want to do it consistently? Then you must buy when everyone else wants to sell, and sell when everyone else is buying. In a bull market this means buying when silver is resting on important weekly or monthly support after a long correction has terrorized the market. Be careful, however. Countertrend trading—trading against the existing trend—is especially risky even within long corrections. A proverb says, "The trend is your friend." Don't buck it.

7. Trade in twos. Whether you are a speculator or an investor, divide your position into two equal parts: one for short- to intermediate-term trading, the other for longer-term trading (you define the time frames). For example, if you hold only one futures market contract or option, you must be totally out of or totally in the market—risking that a temporary price setback will push you out just as another upward price leg is beginning. By taking partial profits, you can cash out your original investment and still ride the major trend. Because there are so many choices in so many sizes—different futures/options combinations as well as the 1,000-ounce minifutures—even the most modest investors (with only a few thousand bucks) can trade in twos.

8. Use stop-loss orders. Before you enter a trade, decide how much you are willing to risk, and enter a stop-loss order at this level. There are many different stop-loss and price orders available for both futures and options. Ask your broker for a complete list of those currently authorized, and never enter the market without them.

9. Use futures/options combinations. Markets present us with many opportunities to protect a futures position by adding *self-financing* option price "floors." One example: If you are already long a profitable silver futures contract, write call options well above the market and use the premium income simultaneously to *buy* a put option under your futures contract. At times this strategy can limit your total risk to just a few hundred dollars (the difference between the price of the futures contract and the strike price of the put option) while still allowing you up to $5,000 of upside profit potential.

10. Build a professional broker relationship. Discount brokers may be all the rage, but a full-service broker, a genuine professional with years of experience, can help you develop your trading plan, monitor markets and stop-loss orders, calculate options values, fax or mail you current charts, and otherwise fine-tune your silver portfolio. A professional broker brings you skills and resources hard-won through years of daily experience and study. This can save you countless hours of time and trouble, help you avoid ignorant mistakes, and dramatically enhance your likelihood of profit. However, a professional broker is only your helper, not your substitute. Never push your broker into making final decisions for you. Duck as you may, the *buck* stops with you.

GETTING STARTED

Don't feel overwhelmed. Properly organized, a silver futures and option investment program requires very little time. Set aside a few minutes at the same time every week to review markets with your broker, check for significant closes above or below weekly or monthly trend line support or resistance, and consider new option situations (whether to take new positions or protect profits).

You may want to use the futures contract as a long-term buy and hold core position. If so, finance your position with extra margin—say, 15 percent to 30 percent of the contract's total cash value—so you can maintain better control over leverage. Under certain circumstances you can hold these excess funds as interest-earning Treasury bills in your account.

If you are seriously interested in profiting from the unique advantages of futures and options, request a free copy of the latest *Silver 2000 Alert*. This is the only advisory publication dedicated exclusively to silver futures and options trades, including futures/options combinations and deferred contract strategies. You can request a free copy from Silver 2000, P.O. Box 402, Chicago, IL 60690–0402. If you're in a hurry, telephone (312) 341–5845 or fax (312) 341–7556.

TYPES OF ORDERS

Among the many advantages of futures and options over the cash market are the wide variety of orders that may be placed. They include:

Market order. Executed at the best price available as soon as it reaches the trading pit. This is the most popular alternative.

Stop order. A resting order that becomes a market order when the market trades at or beyond the specified price. A "buy stop" is placed above the current market. A "sell stop" is placed below the current market.

Limit order. Sets the absolute maximum (buying) or minimum (selling) price at which the transaction can be made.

Spread order. A combination buy/sell order for an equal number of contracts in different delivery months. It is usually placed as the desired price difference between the two contracts.

Day order. An order good only for the day it is entered.

Open order. An order that is good until canceled (GTC).

Not held. When these words are added to the order, the floor broker is given limited discretion in executing it.

Market on close (MOC). Executed during the very last trading that day, to obtain a price within the closing range.

Chapter 10

THE NEW WORLD OF SILVER STOCKS

Potential silver investors whose appetites have been whetted by the tall tales of the great silver booms—and the profits in silver shares—that peaked in 1968 and 1980 will find that the world of North American mining in the nineties has completely changed. First, we will consider some of these changes (and threats) to the mining industry and then narrow our focus to silver mining stocks.

MINING WITH A GLOBAL FOCUS

Without a doubt, today's big story in the mining industry, and the largest change currently under way is the enlargement of the playing field for North American companies, both large and small. The trend toward a global field of interest, which started a few years ago, has grown dramatically and promises to continue unabated into the foreseeable future. This global outlook began in earnest a few years ago, focusing on South America, particularly Chile. As time passed, a significant gold mine, financed by North American companies, was placed into production in Guyana and several exciting finds were announced in Venezuela, while Mexico, Central America, and the Caribbean all came under increased scrutiny. In addition, announcements by North American companies of projects in such far-flung places as Uzbekistan, Zimbabwe, West Africa, and Turkey are becoming more common. In the past year, Mexico has arguably become the *hottest* spot for North American companies to focus attention and finances. The emphasis on Mexico and, most recently, an emerging interest in Peru carry momentous import for silver. These countries are the world's major sources for the white metal. They are silver "elephant country."

ENTER THE ENVIRONMENTALISTS

Why have North American companies turned their spotlights on foreign investment? The environmental movement has generated an increasingly adverse *political* environment for mineral development in the United States and, to a lesser extent, Canada. What started as a legitimate need to lessen the environmental impact of mining has evolved into a morass of overkill. This swampy tangle has primarily been the work of several well-funded special interest groups (and their subsidiary organizations) that have a specific political agenda. They have attained their goals because they are particularly adept at politicizing regulatory decisions that should have been made on the basis of scientific and technological data, *if at all.*

Although the increased costs arising from protecting the environment are sometimes onerous, they have been accepted by the industry as simply another cost of doing business. Much more serious are the related costs generated by delays. These bottlenecks are spawned in the bureaucratic briar patch of securing the scores of permits and approvals that governments at several levels require before mineral development can even begin.

EXPLORATION

As badly as environmental costs and regulations have hammered mining, however, a far more serious threat to U.S. and Canadian mine development has recently emerged. The very real hazard of politically driven expropriation has appeared, jeopardizing projects after developers have already spent tens or even hundreds of millions of dollars. The danger of expropriation—either de facto, through orchestrated delays—or outright, by simply taking—is the 98-octane fuel powering the shift of capital and corporate focus onto foreign mineral investment. The cutback of mining development in the United States is, to paraphrase Ross Perot, accompanied by the giant sucking sound of North American mineral investment draining off to Latin America, with or without NAFTA.

NEW MINING TAXES

Not content with hamstringing development under the white hat of environmental protection, special interest groups have also succeeded in introducing legislation that will most probably lead to a federal mineral royalty. The royalty will apply only to mineral production taken from public domain lands in the western United States. Although much western U.S. mineral production comes from private land, the cost of doing business for a significant segment of the U.S. industry will climb still more as a result. Any additional tax burden on public land miners can only enhance the value of existing properties on private land—and speed up the flight of U.S. mining capital to safer climes offshore.

THE SPLIT ESTATE

When you consider U.S. mining companies as investments, one important eccentricity of mineral ownership in the American West must be borne in mind, and that is the split estate. This describes a piece of property in which more than one owner has an interest in different rights belonging to that property. Think of property as a bundle of sticks: It contains a bundle of rights. There are surface rights, development rights, water rights, mineral rights, oil and gas rights, easement rights, etc.

If one person owns some of those rights and someone else owns other rights in the same piece of real estate, that's a split estate. A classic example is the utility easement right. Almost all town lots are actually split estates, because in most cases some utility company has a right to a utility easement on that property. Although someone else owns title to the property, the utility company has a legal right within a certain corridor to cross with a power or water line and to enter to maintain the line.

In the American West, the U.S. government has retained the underlying title right to vast areas of land, while title to mineral claims on the same land may have been perfected by other owners. Because of U.S. threats of levying a mineral royalty, investors must understand the difference in title rights. Companies with "patented claims" own both the ground *and* the mineral rights. With an "unpatented claim" the company owns *only* the mineral rights, while title to the property itself may be in government or private hands. You should always prefer companies that operate as little as possible on public land, although companies by no means should be ruled out on that basis alone.

FLYING SOUTH

The changes in the political environment in both the United States and Canada have not been lost on developing Latin American countries. Spurred by Chile's triumphant attraction of investment capital, many countries are aggressively pursuing North American mining capital. While South American legislatures are enacting laws favorable to investors and mining, various government agencies are actively accommodating and attracting mineral development.

And—*surprise*—New Latin American mineral development financed by North American companies is universally designed to meet U.S. EPA standards. In many instances companies are doing this *absent* any legal requirement! The advantage lies in the speed with which permits can usually be obtained—several months instead of several years. Furthermore, environmental extremists have only the remotest chance of stopping Latin American projects on the basis of irrational, unsubstantiated fears or emotional appeals to public opinion. North American mining companies have gotten the message, loud and clear. As one noted European mining analyst recently stated, the only country acting like a banana republic is the United States!

IMPLICATIONS

Investing in silver stocks is vastly different today than it was in the late 1960s or early 1980s. The long silver bear market has taken its toll on silver mining. Because companies have diversified out of silver, few major companies offer a significant—let alone *pure*—silver play. Chances are better to find high exposure to silver price appreciation in the ranks of smaller, less diversified developmental companies.

THE DILUTION PROBLEM

When investing in larger silver-rich diversified companies, it is imperative to ask what other metals the company produces. Silver is usually a by-product of gold or base metal deposits. The problem is dilution of the silver play. The greater the proportion of company revenues that come from metals other than silver, the more the silver play is diluted, and the less silver's rising price will raise the price of the company's shares. Since gold and silver prices generally move in tandem, a diversified gold-silver producer gains little special benefit from silver price appreciation. On the other hand, silver and base metal prices often do *not* move in tandem. This means that climbing silver prices could have a lusty effect on the earnings (and thus the share price) of a diversified silver-base metals producer—*if* base metals don't crash as silver soars.

Despite rising political risk in the United States and Canada, mining will most certainly continue in these countries. The major companies will continue to operate, and many large projects will probably become mines. Some, but definitely not all, of the earnings of these majors will be affected by the probable new royalties on mining on federal lands. The majors will emphasize finding new reserves near already permitted facilities. Outside exploration will be reduced and focused on private lands. Smaller companies whose primary assets are exploration or development projects on federal lands will probably have to change their emphasis to survive. The already unfolding outcome of the environmentalists' harassment of mining is an industry trend toward concentration.

Investors should be prepared to see North American companies with considerable foreign involvement. The Cordilleras, which run like a mountainous spine from Alaska to the tip of South America, constitute the happy hunting ground of silver mining. In 1992, six countries produced nearly two thirds of the total world output of silver. Five of those —Mexico, the United States, Peru, Canada, and Chile—lie astride the Cordilleras, and produced almost 86 percent of those two thirds of world output. Opportunities abound in Latin America for significant silver finds, as well as for other metals. Although political risk currently appears fairly low (and dropping) in many Latin American nations, investors would still do well to follow political and economic developments in host countries, in addition to the usual corporate news. The new global outlook for mineral development has created an excitement in the mining business not matched since the early 1980s. This excitement, plus the emerging precious metals bull market, is bound to give careful, prudent investors a great bang for their buck.

FOCUSING ON SILVER

The overwhelming fact in American silver mining today is that there just aren't any primary silver producers left (except one, which we will look at in a moment). Two major silver producers are still running at a loss. The thirteen-year bear market has decimated the silver mining industry. There are some hopes, and a bunch of shut-down holes in the ground. That also means there aren't any real silver mutual funds. Unfortunately, outside Canadian and U.S. companies, there just aren't any good silver companies for investors.

NORTH AMERICAN SILVER SHARE MARKET

Like gold mining shares, silver-related shares can be divided into majors, juniors, and penny stocks. Unfortunately, your old buddy Uncle Sam got to the junior and penny share markets with his regulatory Bowie knife and performed surgery on their livers. The "surgeon" is fine, but the patients died.

Generally, U.S. and Canadian precious metals mining companies may be size-ranked by their market capitalization ("market cap"). Roughly speaking, market cap is calculated by multiplying share price times the number of shares outstanding. More precise calculations would also make adjustments for outstanding stock options. At the beginning of August 1994, the total market cap of this group was about $34.5 billion. American Barrick Resources Corporation led all precious metals mining companies with a market cap of more than U.S. $6.38 billion. Compare just one Big Board stock, General Motors, with a market cap of almost $38.5 billion to get an idea of how really tiny the market in precious metals mining shares is, let alone silver shares. At that time only 8 of these companies had market caps of more than $1 billion, 24 companies of more than $50 million, and about 45 companies of more than $10 million. Many, but not all, of these companies mine some silver.

Usually, lower market cap companies are less liquid and more speculative. Although the classification is admittedly arbitrary, "senior" or "major" mining companies have market caps greater than about $250 million. The market caps of "junior" companies range from approximately $5 million to $10 million up to $250 million. Although companies designated as "penny" companies by the U.S. Securities and Exchange Commission (SEC Rule 15c2-6) are not defined by this measure, they are likely to have market caps of less than $2 million and to sell for less than $5 a share on a non-NASDAQ market.

Investors who owned silver stocks during the 1968 and 1980 silver booms will find major changes in today's mining markets, whether for silver, gold, or base metals. Because of amalgamations and mergers, there are fewer larger "major" companies today. With few exceptions, these are multinational companies with diversified metal holdings. Thus many companies once considered "silver plays," or companies whose earnings —and therefore share prices, too—appreciate substantially with the silver price, no longer have earnings as strongly tied to silver. Agnico Eagle Mines, Coeur d'Alene Mines Corporation, and Hecla Mining Company are three companies that have diversified away from silver. Sunshine Mining, beset by grave economic problems not totally grounded in depressed silver prices, remains one of the purest silver companies. However, overall industry changes have led to a softer impact of silver prices on the earnings of major companies. An investor is probably more likely to find the best silver plays within the ranks of the more speculative, lower market cap companies in the junior and even penny categories. International Dusty Mac, for example, controls the old California silver fields, on top of its healthy income from natural gas well production.

172

A second change from the "good ol' days" of silver stock investing is the disappearance of most U.S. junior and penny companies. Approximately 85 percent of the top 300 mining companies ranked by market cap are Canadian. This reflects the calculated destruction of U.S. venture capital markets by U.S. securities regulators. Not only were hundreds or thousands of U.S. and Canadian companies rendered powerless shells, but, by estimate, *more than $1 billion* were taken from tens of thousands of shareholders by the destruction of what little liquidity there was in these markets. The surviving junior and penny companies (now largely Canadian) are much more sophisticated and often have more highly trained and professional staffs than in earlier times. Although promotional abuses are still possible, the small companies as a rule are better regulated and have a much better chance at technical success than in the old days.

EXTRAORDINARY PROFIT POSSIBILITIES IN JUNIOR SILVER STOCKS

The fact that former silver giants such as Agnico Eagle, Coeur d'Alene Mines, Hecla, and Sunshine Mining have experienced some difficult times or have diversified in a major way away from silver doesn't mean that these companies aren't going to see a huge run-up in price. In other words, even though these companies are not pure silver mining operations (and, in the case of Sunshine, have had some difficult problems), as silver explodes and the equity market desperately looks for places in which to put investors' money in "silver stocks," they'll turn to these stocks. They should soar in value as a result.

Most investors feel that these companies are just about the only "silver plays." The perception in the market is that there are no other good silver mining companies. But does this all mean that there aren't any good junior silver stocks? Are there no well-managed, well-financed, small mining companies currently taking advantage of the largest silver deposits in North America, Mexico, and Latin America?

The fact is that there are some superb North American mining companies that we predict will take advantage of record low silver prices (in real terms) by (1) tying up the best North American silver reserves available; (2) buying both producing and nonproducing silver properties in Mexico;

173

and (3) buying those same types of properties in Latin American countries, especially Peru.

We understand that there are several North American companies using this precise game plan of buying silver in the ground at today's cheap prices. The stocks of these companies will be extraordinarily profitable to the contrary-opinion silver investors. These types of silver stocks of companies with large silver reserves should move up much more dramatically than silver bullion.

As Doug Casey points out in his 1993 book *Crisis Investing for the Rest of the '90s,* the big money in precious metals stocks will be made by those companies that have most of their investments in the Third World: The future of the mining industry, at least for the foreseeable future, will not be in North America, as has traditionally been the case. Instead, it lies in Third World countries.

You may have a certain understandable reluctance about, in effect, sending your money to exotic locals with questionable reputations. But that's precisely why these are the places to go. It's why, although momentum has been building toward Latin America, in particular since the mid-1980s, prices are still low; investors perceptions sometimes lag by years. Their desperate economic state means that there will be little of the obstructionism that makes mining a nightmare in North America.

Most Third World countries have already learned about the practical effects of nationalizations, high taxes, huge bureaucracies, and socialist policies from firsthand experience. At this point, chastised by grinding poverty, they are less likely to shoot themselves in the foot again, at least for quite a while.

The mining environment in Third World countries, and particularly for silver in Latin America, is extremely positive, largely because of a new free market revolution, which is moving toward low real tax rates, less government regulation, and open markets. Also in Latin America, because investors have been slow to realize how positive the trends are in places such as Mexico, Chile, and Peru, you can still buy mining properties for about 10 percent less than what you would pay for similar properties in the United States or other more developed countries.

In fact, there are extraordinary differences in the prices of actual mineral deposits in Latin America itself. In the case of Chile, a country that for years has been in the midst of economic reform, tending toward less government regulation and lower taxation, mining properties are already trading for a premium over comparable properties in other parts of Latin

America. For example, the Latin American subsidiary of AngloAmerican purchased a copper deposit in Chile for $250 million in 1992. The government of Peru, which is now privatizing all of its mining properties, offered a similar copper deposit for sale, and AngloAmerican, one of the first big companies in Peru, was able to buy this deposit for just $10 million!

It is well known that the world's major mining companies are concentrating on base metals, such as copper, in their explorations and investments in Latin America. Gold properties are also highly sought after, but no one seems to be interested in silver properties. The world's big mining companies have no real interest in buying silver properties, and, of course, that is precisely why silver deposits are a bargain. In other words, Latin America is elephant country for huge silver deposits that are selling for cents on the dollar compared to their real value. So the mining companies that will make the most money in silver will be those that buy these huge silver deposits, develop them, and put them in production themselves, or (as is more likely) enter into a deal with a major company.

As this is written, events are unfolding quickly, excellent silver properties are being analyzed, and the most important profit opportunity in all

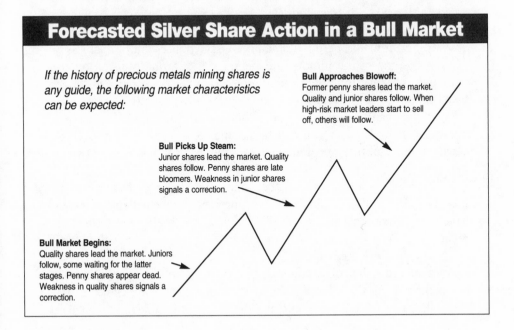

Forecasted Silver Share Action in a Bull Market

If the history of precious metals mining shares is any guide, the following market characteristics can be expected:

Bull Approaches Blowoff:
Former penny shares lead the market. Quality and junior shares follow. When high-risk market leaders start to sell off, others will follow.

Bull Picks Up Steam:
Junior shares lead the market. Quality shares follow. Penny shares are late bloomers. Weakness in junior shares signals a correction.

Bull Market Begins:
Quality shares lead the market. Juniors follow, some waiting for the latter stages. Penny shares appear dead. Weakness in quality shares signals a correction.

of precious metals may well be emerging. For specific junior silver stock recommendations, call Rick Rule, Torrey Pines Securities, 7770 El Camino Real, Carlsbad, CA 92009, tel. 1-800-477-7853; Charles "Berry" Huelsman III, Paulson Investment Co., Inc., 4773 Falls View Drive, West Linn, OR 97068-3520, tel. 503-657-3340; Glenn Dobbs, National Securities Corp., Box 119-B, South Shore Drive, Chelan, WA 98816, tel. 509-687-9564; or Ben Johnson, First Securities Northwest, 111 S.W. 5th, Suite 4180, Portland, OR 97204, tel. 1-800-547-4898.

PENNY STOCKS: AN ENDANGERED SPECIES

How did the SEC gut the penny stock and junior stock markets? Via the designated security or penny stock rule, promulgated by the SEC and implemented in 1991. Under the rule, the stock of any company without a listing on a recognized exchange, or with assets of less than the $2 million threshold requirements, or with a stock price of less than $5 a share, is a designated security.

Many western brokers grumble that this rule, like so many promulgated by the SEC, was encouraged by the major New York brokerage houses. The rule didn't affect them since they didn't deal in these stocks anyway, and it would help put small brokerage houses out of business.

Even if some of the juniors and penny stocks formerly listed on the Spokane Exchange look good, they are so small that they are no longer listed on an exchange and do not qualify for any exemptions under the rule, so they can't really be traded publicly. Most brokerage houses will not trade them. Even if you can find someone who will sell you those stocks, one awful question remains: *To whom will you sell them when that time comes?*

So how can anyone invest in the juniors and pennies? Who can you buy them from? If you can find someone who can sell them, you may have to buy them on a strictly unsolicited basis; the broker cannot recommend them. You may have to sign and mail designated securities forms *before* you can buy them.

Another thing that makes juniors and pennies only marginally attractive is the way they are traded. The spreads are gigantic (a 2-cent bid, 10-cent ask is not uncommon), and the prices are often imaginary because the market is so thin. Suppose silver leaps to $25 and your shares of the Get-Rich-Quick Mine jump to a 25-cent bid. You call the lone remaining broker who buys them and he or she says, "Sure, I'll take 'em off your hands. I'll give you 25 cents for the first 1,000 of your 100,000 shares, 10 cents for the next thousand, and 2 cents for the other 98,000." It's very hard in thin markets to sell any significant number of shares at the published prices.

A FEW SILVER STOCKS

As we have already observed, many companies that were silver giants in earlier days have diversified away from silver or fallen on very hard times. The thirteen-year bear market in silver has taken its toll on primary silver producers. Most primary silver mines in North America have been shut down or placed on care and maintenance.

Thus the greatest obstacle in picking silver stocks is that there just aren't many companies. Those few that still exist are either in great financial difficulty or the percentage of their revenues generated by silver is so low that the silver play is diluted away. To gain the greatest leverage on the price of silver, we are looking for companies that earn almost all their revenues from silver. We aren't looking for companies that produce a lot of silver, but companies that produce nothing but silver. Very, very few companies that brokers and the public traditionally call "silver stocks" earn a substantial percentage of their revenues from silver. For most of these "silver stocks," silver generates less than 10 percent of their revenues.

This just adds to the profit potential for silver stocks. In the first place, "silver bugs" are even more fervid than "gold bugs," because the former understand so well that silver has a much higher upside potential. Second, most precious metals investors buy mining stocks because they are easier to handle than physicals and offer much more leverage. As the price of silver increases, share prices increase faster than silver bullion itself. But there are very few silver shares, and even fewer pure silver plays. So all of the money—potentially *huge* flows of new investment capital—will be focused on just a few shares, which adds explosive fuel to the upside potential. As our friend Doug Casey describes it, "It's like trying to put the Hoover Dam through a garden hose."

PROFESSIONAL HELP

Because markets change daily as events and trends unfold, investing in mining stocks can be a very time-consuming business. Most people can't afford the time to pore over all the professional journals, newspapers, brokerage reports, and private information sources necessary to keep up with the market. Even if you did all that, you would still need contacts in the mining industry to keep you abreast of current developments and to warn you about changing trends.

That's why we publish *Gold Newsletter*. We do the background research necessary to keep you abreast of the market, but also much more than that. After almost twenty-five years in the hard-money and mining community, we've been around long enough to distinguish a genuine profit opportunity from a hole in the ground that just *looks* like a silver play. In addition, we have developed a host of friends, contacts, and information sources that others just don't have. When new silver plays appear, we find out about them long before other publications, and bring you this indispensable information. But whether you subscribe to *Gold Newsletter* or some other publication, if you invest in silver stocks you'll need some constant, dependable source of information about changes in the silver stock market. For a free sample of *Gold Newsletter,* call (800) 877-8847.

WHICH STOCKS TO BUY

The market in silver stocks changes rapidly, but as we write, three companies in particular appeal to us. One is a blue chip among silver mining companies, and the other two are much more speculative juniors. The best possible way to play silver stocks is to buy the relatively few junior silver stocks that are pure silver plays. As this book goes to press, there are two specific junior silver shares that we highly recommend. Because they will be applying new strategies to accumulating and controlling silver resources, we think these juniors offer a ground-floor opportunity to lock up silver resources. Let's look closer at our blue chip and the two juniors.

COEUR D'ALENE MINES
New York Stock Exchange Symbol: CDE

In the world of silver mining, Coeur d'Alene Mines Corporation is a major blue-chip operation with solid management. However, since 1989 CDE has been taking its lumps from silver's declining price, which has forced the temporary closures of several mines. Those closures have shifted the mix of CDE's revenues so that silver has contributed less and less as a percentage of revenues. In 1992 silver made up 38.2 percent of CDE's revenues; in 1993 it was 29.7 percent. Believe it or not, among all the well-known silver producers, that makes CDE the second most leveraged to silver. (There is one company more leveraged to silver, but for other reasons we can't recommend it at this time.)

While low silver prices prevailed, CDE sidelined significant low-cost silver resources. Now that silver's price is climbing and holding on to its gains, these mines can be brought back into operation fairly quickly. *Conceivably* CDE could increase its silver production by 70 percent in eighteen months. However, it will need to see a sustained silver price of $6 an ounce and stable markets before these mines reopen. Once they reopen, it would take one and a half to two years for the new silver production to hit the bottom line and change the revenue mix, but long before that happened the public's expectation of the impact of rising silver prices on CDE's stock will have driven up the price of its shares. If you are interested in playing the silver bull market through silver shares, you have to own Coeur d'Alene.

Coeur d'Alene Mines Corporation, P.O. Box I, Coeur d'Alene, ID 83816-0316; tel. (208) 667-3511 or fax (208) 765-0324.

FIRST SILVER RESERVE
Vancouver Stock Exchange Symbol: FSR.V

This company is new, but don't let that bother you. It has a new strategy that guarantees success if management applies it correctly. First Silver Reserve wants to offer the investor an absolute and total focus on silver by buying silver in the ground at a discount.

The name says it all. There are no listed companies with "silver" in

179

their name that focus solely and strictly on silver. This will be the first. The "silver" in the name is obvious, but why "reserve"? The company's long-term objective is to build a gigantic silver reserve. It will forge this position from three sources: exploration and development, silver from current producers, and physical silver on hand. The company will pay dividends in silver and will hold its surplus cash in the form of physical silver.

First Silver Reserve will buy silver from current producers. Two thirds of the silver produced comes as a byproduct of base metal or gold mining. The company will offer to advance money to lead-zinc, copper, or gold-silver producers in exchange for a share of all silver produced, or all minerals produced. (This avenue may later offer significant leverage to base metal prices.) Silver producers who view silver's potential less optimistically than First Silver Reserve can grab this offer to lock in price for their silver production.

The issue of *market recognition* makes this offer very attractive for some producers. Many companies that produce some silver get no recognition from the market for that production, so their shares trade on the basis of the metal contributing the bulk of their revenues. It's as if in valuing the shares of a company the stock market overlooks the silver production of, for example, gold producers. Because the market allows them no potential for their silver, these gold producers trade on the basis of the gold price alone. For the silver that now is giving them no market bang at all, First Silver Reserve will trade them cash that the market can see.

From other companies' silver production First Silver Reserve will take its payback from other companies' silver production by one of three routes: net smelter return, a fixed amount of silver, or a combination of net smelter return and a percentage of net profits.

First, FSR will provide financing to explore and develop *new* silver projects or to expand existing reserves, and take their repayment either in silver or in cash. This may take the form of a *net smelter return* (NSR), where the miner pays FSR a percentage of the total value of all minerals produced for the life of the mine. FSR will have two choices for receiving this payment: either in cash, with the price of silver fixed as of the date of the contract, or in physical silver. Effectively this gives FSR a very long-term call option on silver. If silver were to drop below the contract price, FSR could take cash. If silver is above the contract price, the company takes silver.

Second, with primary silver producers FSR can put up money *now* in exchange for a fixed number of ounces of silver yearly *for the life of the mine*. That amounts to a long-term forward silver sale to FSR. FSR gives a producer cash now, and gets silver back in the future.

Third, FSR can combine both approaches. When a producer is reluctant to promise future silver because he thinks silver will rise, FSR can take a combination of net smelter return and a percentage of net profits, which should rise along with silver prices. FSR would take payment in cash or silver at its option.

First Silver Reserve won't be an exploration and development or production company. Rather, it wants to finance good projects in North and South America and build a reserve of silver for the coming boom. If you are looking for a pure silver play, this is it, but remember, this is a speculative, risky venture. The key assumption for the investor is that *silver will rise*. Otherwise an investment in FSR makes no sense at all. Only a rising silver price gives FSR its explosive upside potential.

First Silver Reserve, Inc., Suite 500, 626 West Pender Street, Vancouver, B.C. V6B 1V9, Canada; tel. (604) 669-2252 or fax (604) 669-1700.

SILVER STANDARD RESOURCES
Vancouver Stock Exchange Symbol: SSO.V

Silver Standard Resources focuses on exploring for bulk precious metals deposits in the Americas. It also has some involvement in diamond exploration in Canada, a royalty interest from a producing gold project in Nevada, and numerous base and precious metals projects throughout North America. Through a company in which it currently owns an 11 percent interest (Mutual Resources Ltd.), Silver Standard also has a foothold on a number of West African gold projects.

Silver Standard Resources originated with the Silver Standard Mine near Hazelton, British Columbia, in 1946, and once again the company is focusing on silver. SSO is looking for bulk silver-gold deposits in the Americas, along the Cordillera mountain chain. From Alaska to the Lower 48 and all the way through Mexico, Central America, Peru, Bolivia, Ecuador, and Chile, this region has always been silver elephant country. SSO wants to locate and develop silver "elephant" properties in Central and South America.

Remember that SSO stock is a risky venture. It is exploring properties

181

and has not yet determined whether they contain economically recoverable ore reserves.

*Silver Standard Resources, Inc., 900–850 West Hastings Street, Vancouver,
B.C. V6C 1E1, Canada; tel. (604) 689-3846 or fax (604) 689-3847.*

ONE FINAL WORD

I personally have substantial stock positions in all three of the companies
recommended above: Coeur d'Alene, First Silver Reserve, and Silver Standard. I feel that I would be foolish *not* to: As silver rises and rises, twenty-
five or thirty or fifty silver companies will appear for you to invest in; but
the early birds (such as the stocks above) will have a tremendous advantage over everyone else. Remember, however, that markets change rapidly
and constantly. That's why we recommend you subscribe to *Gold Newsletter* (or some other suitable publication) to keep yourself informed on
silver and silver stocks. Without it, you're flying blind.

Chapter 11

How to Pick a Mining Company

Methods of evaluating a mining company are as numerous as analysts and investors, but most investors simplify the process of choosing shares by using a single method: *Investigate nothing.* Their investment decisions usually occur when a broker calls them and makes a recommendation. However, with just a few simple criteria—some *hard questions*—you can avoid 80 percent of those land mine deals that blow up in your face.

Stockbrokers often have trouble separating the customer's interest from their own. If you want to buy silver mining shares, *look for a broker who specializes in precious metals stocks and does his own careful and diligent research.* Because there's no substitute for experience complemented with hard work, you really need the advice of a broker-specialist to invest in precious metals mining shares. You can move to Vancouver and do your own research, or you can pick a good broker. It is practically impossible for a lone individual investor to match a specialist's knowledge and timing.

Unfortunately, people of integrity and knowledge are few and far between. The very few really good broker-specialists spend thousands, even hundreds of thousands, of dollars yearly to research and gather information from hundreds of mining industry contacts. Pick a broker with care, and don't be embarrassed to check him or her out *before* you invest with that person. Some people who *claim* to be experts wouldn't know a gold mine from a hole in the ground if they fell down the open shaft.

One word about hot newsletter tips. There are people of integrity in the newsletter industry who do their best for their readers. There are also unscrupulous scoundrels who load up on some cheap, worthless stock, suddenly "discover" it's a great buy, and then tout it to their readers. The junk stock skyrockets, the scoundrel bails out, and the stock evaporates quicker than you can say "Swiss bank account." Newsletter tips may in fact be great buys, but you still have to check them out yourself. Here's another place where a broker-specialist with integrity can make the difference between lining your pockets and losing your shirt.

We asked our friend Glenn Dobbs, an experienced stockbroker who does specialize in precious metals stocks, to work up a list of hard questions you should ask *before* you invest. From his experience and study, here's what he told us.

THE THREE "P'S" OF MINING STOCKS

There are three cardinal elements in the success of any company, but most especially mining firms: *people, property, and pelf.*

PEOPLE

The people who actually run a mining company day by day are the *most important ingredient in its success.* Well-intentioned, ignorant simpletons can ruin an investment just as quickly as get-rich-quick hucksters. Look for *teams of professional, well-credentialed people in both the technical and managerial areas.* Look for a diversity of talent bringing good business management skills, experience, and financial and technical skills. Good management can make a poor property work. Poor management can turn a good silver mine into a flooded hole in the ground.

PROPERTY

The best management in the world is helpless without a good property to work. How good are the company's properties? Is it a single-property or multiple-property company? Does it have exploration projects? Can the properties be worked year-'round, or do they shut down in the winter? Radical environmentalism has made the *location of properties a crucial concern*. Are the company's properties on government or private land? Are they "patented" or "unpatented" claims? Are they foreign or domestic? What are the political risks of direct or indirect expropriation?

Pelf

Nobody can mine without money. Proper funding is an art that must avoid dilution of shareholders' interests. What about debt? Will it cripple the company and gobble up cash flow? *Cash or cash equivalents in the bank are a good indication of management's ability to raise money.* What is the company's cash position? Where did the cash come from? What about debt? Can the firm service existing debt? How is the debt structured? How will it be repaid? When was the company's last private placement? Will they use private placements in the future or a public offering? *Companies that are able to fund their early projects without undue dilution tend to be able to fund projects on into the future.* In summary, look for companies with balanced, knowledgeable directorships. Insist on companies with prospective properties in areas of proven mining activity with few operating problems and low political risk. Finally, do they have or can they raise enough money to do the job? If *people, property, and pelf* are all present and accounted for, then the company may deserve further attention. Without these three, keep on looking.

Once the candidate passes the three "p's," we still have three other checklists: *production, market measures, and share liquidity.*

PRODUCTION, RESERVES, AND SOME FRONT OFFICE QUESTIONS

Production

We need to research a candidate's production: How big is it? How good is it? How long can it last? How is it sold? How much does it cost to bring to market?

Is the firm an established producer? What is its *annual production* of silver, gold, or other metals? Is it a *primary* silver mine, or is silver a *byproduct?* How much income comes from silver or gold versus base metals? With answers to these queries we move on to the question that generates more lies, more fudging, and more optimism than "Just what *does* your waistline measure?" Namely, the question of reserves.

RESERVES

There's nothing as black and blue from abuse as the word "reserves." The value of reserves is a product of three factors: silver in the dirt, technology to get silver out of the dirt, and the silver price. First, is there silver there? Second, can a mill extract the silver with existing technology? Third, at the present price of silver, does it pay to extract that silver?

Technically "reserves" describes a portion of a deposit (dirt in the ground) that has been measured in varying degrees and determined to be mineable, and for which the economical silver yield under existing technological and market conditions has been estimated. If portions of a mineral deposit are for any reason not mineable, they should be excluded from reserve calculations.

The measure of reserves also gives us a rough idea of what the company is worth, since *when you buy a silver mine you are simply buying silver in the ground.* If the company sits on 1 million ounces of reserves, and silver is at $10 an ounce, then at present prices it's worth about $10 million (ignoring for the sake of a rough estimate the fact that they can't get all of the silver out in the next 10 minutes). If there are 1 million shares outstanding, and the shares trade at $40 an ounce, this is probably not a stock we want to buy, *unless* there's some reason, not widely known, that makes the stock more valuable than it appears. For example, does management have a special knack for taking the proceeds of silver production and finding or developing new *low-cost* reserves?

Higher silver prices make marginal mines economically feasible. As the price of silver rises, good management will shift production from higher-grade ore to lower-grade ore. Miners should always mine the *lowest grade of reserves that is economically feasible* to make the most of reserves and to extend mine life. As marginal reserves are depleted, the company will begin working the next higher grade.

Reserves are expressed in three categories, each determined by the level of confidence in the estimate. Reserves break down into *proven, probable, and possible.* We also want to look at the *life of reserves,* or how long they will last.

PROVEN RESERVES

"Proven" ore reserves are those that have been delineated in three dimensions by excavation or drilling from which the reserves' geological limitations have been determined. Obviously the company has spent a lot of money to reduce doubt to a minimum, so "proven reserves" figures can be used with the *level of maximum confidence.* Beyond proven reserves, everything gets a mite flaky.

PROBABLE RESERVES

"Probable" refers to material for which tonnage and grade are computed partly from specific measurements, partly from sample or production data, and partly from projection for a reasonable distance on geologic evidence. We all know what "probable" means. When you ask your brother-in-law for the money you lent him, he says, "I'll *probably* pay you next week." You may be able to count on it, but don't fill out the deposit slip yet.

POSSIBLE RESERVES

"Possible" is a very imprecise, nontechnical term. It is little used in the real mining industry. Essentially it says that if all trend data were extrapolated out to nothingness, it is possible that the ore body contains a zillion ounces. Here, too, the meaning is clear. "My brother-in-law would *possibly* make a good nuclear physicist (if he had an IQ of 240, a Ph.D. in nuclear physics, and worked more than two months a year.)" From an investor's standpoint, "possible reserves" are pie in the sky—meaningless.

LIFE OF RESERVES

The life of a mine is calculated by dividing the amount of proven reserves by the annual production. For how many more years can a firm operate on a particular property? If present reserves are nearing the bottom of the barrel, does the company have exploration or acquisition prospects?

TONNAGE AND GRADES

Some armchair analysts focus primarily on tonnages and grades. You can calculate the approximate life of the mine by multiplying the number of tons of ore by the rate at which they feed ore through the mill. Multiply the number of tons of ore by the number of grams or ounces per ton, and you can figure the deposit's size and make some reserve calculations. But there's more to it than that. Is the silver locked up metallurgically so that it's impossible or very expensive to extract? Grades and tonnages just aren't enough. Recovery rates are crucial, too, as demonstrated by a bulk test.

RECOVERABILITY

How much silver can actually be recovered from proven reserves with existing technology? How much silver can be recovered economically at current silver prices? Is there some hidden technological difficulty with these reserves that will make them especially expensive to refine? Without answers to these questions, reserve figures are meaningless.

Reserve statements usually are accompanied with a "cutoff" grade— say, 10 million tons grading 3.14 grams per ton (approximately 0.1 ounce), using a cutoff of one gram. The cutoff grade is the minimum value per ton at which the ore body can be economically mined.

WHEN WILL IT COME TO MARKET?

With exploratory companies, prefer issues that have *near-term production prospects.* There are so few undervalued silver mining issues of companies that plan to start producing in 1993 or 1994 that the risk of speculation is high. Well into a silver boom, expect a squeeze on mining equipment and personnel. If silver fever heats up a mining boom, there won't be enough equipment and technical personnel to get all the nonproducing companies into production before 1997. Investigate open-pit, heap-leaching issues. It takes two to three years to put a leaching operation into production versus five to seven years for a hard-rock mine.

CASH COST OF PRODUCTION

These figures can be misleading. Cash cost of production is the cost of producing an ounce of silver, including smelting and refining charges and byproduct credits, before depreciation and depletion expense and financing charges. This is the cost of production before the accountants get to it. However, low cash costs won't help a company overloaded with debt or burdened with an aging mill and inefficient management. Cash cost *can* be helpful to compare one company to others in the industry. Cash cost can help identify high-leverage companies, those with high production costs and low profit margins.

LEVERAGE

Leverage (sometimes called "gearing") is the multiplier by which the stock price increases for every dollar increase in the price of silver. When a company can produce silver for $6.50 and silver is quoted at $7.50, the firm has a $1.00 profit margin. When the price of silver rises to $8.50 (13.3 percent), the $1.00 price increase actually doubles the profit margin: from $1 an ounce to $2 an ounce. Thus the share price should increase considerably faster than the underlying silver price. *This leverage, which makes mining shares rise faster than the price of the metal, is the main attraction of silver shares.* It is not, however, invariably true that shares outperform bullion, especially as a bull market matures. Often the shares will peak in *anticipation of* a top in bullion.

FORWARD SELLING

Will the company benefit from rising silver prices, or has it already sold the silver? *Forward selling* is an agreement to deliver a certain amount of the company's silver production at some specified future date at a specific price. This minimizes the risk of price movements and increases the predictability of income.

But if all the production is sold forward, the company can't benefit from rising prices. The effect of forward sales on profits (and share prices) in a bull market is sometimes mitigated if forward sales contracts (*not* futures) have cash buyout provisions. The presence of forward selling usually indicates fairly sophisticated management.

MARKET MEASURES

Here are some measures that apply to any stocks, but are equally important for silver producers. We want to compare our candidate to the rest of the firms in the industry and to the rest of the stocks in the market.

Market Capitalization

Market capitalization equals the number of shares outstanding multiplied by the current market price of each share. Along with other measures, market cap gives us an idea of the size of the company and the market's assessment of the company beyond merely looking at the individual share price.

Market Price History

Look at where the shares are trading now versus where they have been in the past five years, two years, and one year. Individual stocks tend to undergo cycles of market favor. Stocks trading at the top of long-term ranges may be ending a cycle. However, if the price of silver is booming, that may be boosting the stock's price. *Avoid buying near tops of normal cycle swings and try to buy near the cycle bottoms.*

Earnings

Typically, exploration and developmental companies do not have earnings because all resources are channeled into their properties. Smaller companies commonly have no earnings at all. If earnings are present, what is their source? Did they come from operations, or extraordinary, nonrecurring events such as asset sales? What became of the earnings? Were they retained or plowed back into exploration targets? Does company policy require paying out all or part of earnings as dividends?

Price/Earnings Ratio

The price/earnings ratio (P/E) is the ratio of the stock's market price to its after-tax earnings. Calculate it by dividing the current market price by the last annual earnings. P/E helps to evaluate a company's current market price relative to its earnings, and to compare the price of an individual stock to industry averages. Logically, stocks within an industry should trade at about the same P/E. When earnings drop, the stock's price should drop so that it maintains about the same P/E as the rest of the industry. When earnings rise, the stock's price should rise to stay abreast of the industry. P/E helps determine whether a stock is relatively under- or overpriced. Stocks of companies near the end of their reserves should have lower P/Es to account for lower earnings expected in the future. Companies about to make major acquisitions might show higher P/Es. During bull markets, expect to see P/Es for silver mining shares soar. In bear markets, they drop.

Yields

The formula for "yield" or "dividend yield" is simply to divide the annual dividend by the current market price. Yields, expressed in percentages, are useful for comparing the return on one investment with returns on alternatives.

Dividends

One of the advantages of investing in a company that pays dividends (besides the cash in your pocket) is that dividends are here and now. A bird in the hand . . .

Typically, North American mining companies pay no dividends or minimal dividends. Rather, they prefer to reinvest their earnings in expansion and development of other properties. Investors in North American mining stocks do not expect dividend income but rather capital gains.

Communication

Companies should communicate well with their shareholders and with the investment industry through regular and annual reports. *Visibility* increases demand for the shares and keeps up steady buying pressure.

191

Look for companies that issue a steady stream of news announcements. You should even be able to call the company's investor relations department with your questions. If the company doesn't communicate well on all fronts, there may be something rotten in Idaho. Beware.

SHARE LIQUIDITY

Before we buy into a company, its shares must be *liquid*. Is there a ready market for the shares? Is it big enough to trade? How many shares has the company issued?

COMPANY SIZE

Silver-related shares come in three sizes: *majors (or seniors), juniors, and penny stocks.* As a rule of thumb, *the smaller the company, the less liquid the shares and the greater the risk.*

Companies are divided by *market capitalization* (see above). "Senior" or "major" mining companies have market caps greater than about $250 million. "Juniors" range from $5 million to $10 million up to $250 million. "Penny" companies have market caps of less than $5 million.

Most U.S. *junior* and *penny* companies are "gone with the wind," thanks to your Uncle Sam. Many of these stocks were traded on the Spokane Exchange, which new SEC rules effectively shut down in 1991. Be careful when buying these shares. You must answer the next question before buying.

IS THERE A READY MARKET FOR THE SHARES?

To whom will you sell the shares if they rise? There simply is no active market for the shares of many small companies. If there is a market, brokers may charge spreads so huge that you can't profit. Brokers are not even willing to *sell* the shares of some issues except on an unsolicited basis.

Prefer junior issues listed on the National Association of Security Dealers Automated Quotation System (NASDAQ). Look for companies that have a policy of blue-skying their shares (legally qualifying them for sale) in most of the fifty states of the United States. That maximizes the number of brokers who can sell and speculators who can buy an issue, and makes the issue far more visible.

How Big Is the "Float"?

How many shares are outstanding? It's much harder for the shares of a 20-million-share issue to jump up than those of a 5-million-share issue. It's a simple matter of supply and demand: The smaller the float, the better the profit potential. Cast your *most jaundiced eye* on juniors with floats of more than 6 million shares, or penny mining issues with more than 10 million shares.

Who Is Buying the Shares?

The market for industrial stocks is dominated by institutions, and the senior gold mining share market is no different. Expect silver issues to follow suit. Institutions tend to move in herds, so expect volatile silver (and gold) mining share markets as silver heats up. Institutions prefer established production to future production—silver in the ground to silver in the bush. This means that established, quality silver stocks will offer a lot of action in a silver bull market.

Expect investors to be attracted more by size than by profitability. Conservative investors feel more secure with large silver (or gold) producers than with a more profitable small operation. Size means sizzle and safety, and folks will pay a premium for it.

"FIRST WITH THE MOST"

After the War Between the States, someone once asked General Nathan Bedford Forrest (whom Robert E. Lee thought the most brilliant general of the war) how he always won. He replied, "Get there first with the most."

We'd like to repeat that advice in selecting stocks. *Seek value waiting to be discovered.* Buy an issue *before* promotion is glowing with white-hot hype. If every hard-money newsletter, investment adviser, and broker is recommending a stock, it's probably too late to buy it. Buy *before* the crowd discovers an issue, and sell as its popularity puffs it up to overvaluation.

Whatever you do, avoid a very popular investment method that works like a dart game. Forget trying to pick stocks, says this method, and just throw darts at the quotation page from *The Wall Street Journal.* Buy whichever stocks the darts hit. That may be fine for OPM (other people's money), but not for yours. You can take 80 percent or more of the risk out of your stock purchases by diligent but fairly simple research. The suggestions above don't by any means exhaust all the possibilities, but they're a good start. For almost every investor, the one real key is to find a stockbroker specializing in precious metals shares *who is known for integrity and doing his or her own research.*

Or you could buy a dartboard.

AFTERTHOUGHT ON SELLING

From wearisome experience we know that selling is the hardest part of investing. People fall in love with winning investments and won't sell. Worse, even more fall in love with *losing* investments and won't sell. Just as there's a time to sow and a time to reap, there's a time to sell and a time to cover your back. Inoculate yourself in advance against *bull market fever,* which will keep you from selling when you should. Here are some rules that will make selling easy.

STOP-LOSS ORDERS

At the same time you buy a stock, enter a *good till canceled sell stop order* with your broker. You will have to renew these orders periodically any-way, so review them every month. For stocks worth $25 or less, place your sell stop at *30 percent below your acquisition cost.* For stocks worth more than $25, place sell stops at *15 percent below your acquisition cost.*

Don't go to sleep at the wheel, either. When you check your stocks once a month, *raise* the stop orders as the price of your stocks rise. If you are stopped out, *normally you should not rebuy*.

One problem: As a practical matter you just can't enter stops for OTC and Canadian issues. In that case you'll have to write down the sell stop yourself and check the stock frequently when the price nears your bailing-out point. When the stock touches that point, close your eyes and sell. *Learn to love a small loss.*

This trick will help you keep up with your stocks. Buy a three-ring notebook, and keep notes on every stock. Make up a sheet for every stock you buy, including total acquisition cost and current stop-loss orders. This will take 10 minutes and save you thousands of bucks. *Too much trouble?* Maybe, but a lot less trouble than losing your money.

SELLING TARGETS

It would be nice if we could give you some hard and fast mathematical formula for when to sell, but we can't. Selling half your investment when a stock doubles might be a good idea (for the broker), but it might rob you of far greater profits. Some stocks should be sold long before they double, some long after. Never fall in love with any stock: All stocks are made to be sold.

Another market proverb: *Cut your losses short and let your profits run.* The best rule we can give is, *Keep on checking.* When your stock runs up, keep asking, *Does it look as good now as when I bought it? Is it time to sell?* This is where a reliable stockbroker-specialist makes the difference between real and imaginary profits.

Most of all, we don't want you to fall into the trap of *never selling.* Many unsophisticated investors buy a stock, ride it up to glory, and then ride it back down to shame. Keep on reminding yourself that no matter how much your stock has appreciated, *there's no profit until it has been sold.* Finally, there are far too many precious metals mining shares for any investor to analyze and track, nearly twenty-eight hundred in North America. Don't try to buy more than ten different issues, fifteen at most. That will give you plenty of diversification and plenty to do.

Chapter 12

THE DREAM OF HONEST MONEY AND THE REMONETIZATION OF SILVER

Certain conceptual blocks are built into the thinking of many economists about money, blocks that prevent understanding or even conceiving how a specie money system works. (A specie money system is backed by gold and/or silver.)

Today we have a debt money system, managed through private fractional reserve banks. These banks operate on a "fractional reserve"; they are required to keep only a fraction of their deposits in reserve against possible withdrawals. Banks are subject to "reserve requirements," which, considering the banking system as a whole, amount to only 1.66 percent of total savings, time, and transaction deposits. This means that for every $100.00 the banking system receives in deposits, it can theoretically lend out money by a multiple equal to the mathematical reciprocal of the reserve requirement. The mathematical reciprocal of 1.66 percent is 100/1.66, or 60.39. For every $100.00 that banks receive in deposits, the banking system can generate $6,039.38 in loans. At the same time, every dollar not loaned out, whether to private or government borrowers, is an opportunity lost for the banking system. Therefore, under a fractional reserve requirement, the banking system has an inherent bias—an imperative, if you will—to increase debt.[1]

Notice that the *actual* income generated by the bank—the value of the money-creating monopoly to the bank—is not by any means limited to the interest generated on the loans it makes. Rather, the income generated by banking is *both the interest generated by loans and the total capital created through loans!*

When we say that central banks and fractional reserve banks have an inevitable tendency to increase debt, and increase it *permanently,* we're not just hyperventilating. For example, take the Bank of England, founded in 1694. That early banking environment, as yet naive regarding the consequences of its actions, operated with considerably more abandon than today.

Throughout the seventeenth century, the English government struggled with its financing. More than once, Stuart kings closed the mint or treasury and confiscated private deposits on account there. By 1688, when William III and Mary ousted the last Stuart king, the royal finances were a train wreck. Because of the history of debasements, expropriations, and other official weaseling and confiscation, the Crown had to pay meaty interest premiums to secure loans. In 1694, the Scotsman William Paterson for the third time put forward a proposition to found a joint stock banking company to lend the Crown money. Because war with France had "financially embarrassed" William, Parliament approved the Ways and Means Act of 1694. This act granted a charter for a joint stock banking corporation, the Bank of England. The subscribed capital was fixed at 1.2 million pounds sterling, to be immediately lent to the king in return for a number of privileges, including that of issuing notes payable on demand ("bank notes") up to the amount of the loan to the Crown, and upon that security. The bank could also deal in bills of exchange and gold and silver and make loans upon security.

The merchants of London were not slow to recognize a paper gold mine when they saw it. The bank's capital was subscribed *in ten days,* and the king soon secured his first loan of 1 million pounds at 8 percent, a considerable improvement of interest rate. (The Bank of England opened up in Mercers' Hall, then moved to Grocers' Hall, where it remained until it moved to Threadneedle Street forty years later, hence its nickname, The Old Lady of Threadneedle Street.) Certain inherent absurdities in the fractional reserve system surfaced quickly; the bank experienced its first run in 1696, two years after its founding.

The original loan was to be a *perpetuity,* an *eternal* loan upon which no principal is ever paid, although the interest keeps on ticking forever. By 1743, the bank not only had a *legally enforced* monopoly on joint stock banking (granted in 1697), but also had lent the government more than 9 million pounds, an amount equal at that time to 2.19 million ounces of gold.[2]

Another name for this *perpetuity* is *national debt.* Surprise: The national debt is *intended* to be permanent. Because it forms the security ("backing") for the notes of the central bank, paying off the national debt means that the money supply must shrink: *deflation,* with all its depressionary economic implications. Once the bank notes or credit of the central bank becomes a substantial portion of the national money supply, it is nearly impossible to reduce the national debt without deflating the money supply and thereby choking off economic activity. It is to the benefit of the holders of the debt that it never be paid off. It exists as a sort of advance claim on the production of the nation—*forever.*

In the United States today, private fractional reserve banks operate under a *cartel* through a central banking system ("the Federal Reserve") and enjoy a *legally enforced monopoly.* This system so thoroughly pervades the globe, and has wielded its iron rod so long, that hardly a person is now alive who has even seen any other kind of banking system. Frankly, it *is* hard to imagine what a specie money system would look like today, after so many decades of debt money. However, if we are correct and the era of central banks, fractional reserve banking, and debt money is dying, we need to plan for the transition to its free market replacement, a stable monetary system centered around specie—gold and silver. Nothing less than a completely new specie banking system will suffice.

A CHANGE IN THINKING

Fundamental to this transition is a *change of numeraire in the public's thinking*. The numeraire is simply the currency in which any transaction is denominated. In Japan, the assumed numeraire is the yen, in the United States the dollar, in Germany the mark, in England the pound sterling. But all of these currencies are simply the fiat money of their respective governments. Because the folk of these nations use these currencies daily, they think in terms of them. When they perform a calculation involving gold or silver, they still think in terms of *fiat* yen or dollars. The market must begin to calculate its transactions in terms of gold and silver—to think in gold and silver. Because money is, by one definition, that economic good with the *lowest transaction costs,* institutions must arise that lower gold and silver transaction costs in the marketplace.

Except from 1934 to 1977, when gold clauses were specifically outlawed, the right to contract out of legal tender money has always existed for Americans. During and after the War Between the States, the courts universally held that you couldn't be forced to accept legal tender paper money if the contract specified payment in gold or silver. If, however, you make a contract for unspecified "dollars," then you can be forced to accept anything that the law has termed a "dollar"—for example, a Susan B. Anthony token coin—or has declared to be legal tender *for a* "dollar." Congress has created a class of things that can be substituted for real dollars if the type and quality of "dollar" is not specified. That's the reason the government had to outlaw gold contracts from 1934 to 1977: to close the loophole. Since gold clause contracts were "legalized" again in 1977, the loophole is open again.

If a contract doesn't *specify* the form of payment but only provides for payment in "dollars," then any form of "dollar" substitute will do, and that means you have to accept legal tender *fiat* money. In the law, a "dollar" equals a "dollar," regardless of its form.

Americans have been robbed of a specie money system by guile more than by legislation. How did the government do it? In terms an economist would use, by increasing the information and transaction costs. Duplicitous legal tender laws were passed that appeared to say one thing but actually said another. The laws were stated so that laypeople would naturally assume that they applied to them in all circumstances when in fact they did not.

In the first place, since Article I, Section 10 of the U.S. Constitution reserved the power to declare legal tender to the states (but restricted that declaration to gold and silver coin), the U.S. government could make a legal tender only in its own jurisdiction—the District of Columbia, possessions, territories, forts, magazines, arsenals, and places where the states have specifically ceded jurisdiction to the federal government.

Second, where before the legal tender laws it required an act to get into the paper money system (you had to agree to take banknotes), now it requires an act (putting a specific clause in a contract) to stay out of the paper money system. The information cost has risen.

Third, the government raised specie money transaction costs by limiting the supply of metallic money. As a practical matter, it was difficult to get specie money for business. In 1934 the government stopped minting gold coins. It made contracting in gold or silver coins illegal, or, to be more exact, unenforceable. The law decreed you couldn't enforce a contract specifying payment in a particular coin or currency (talk about raising the transaction cost!). In 1935, the government stopped minting silver dollars. Still, you could have avoided the legal tender system from 1934 until the mid-1960s by taking your paper silver certificates to the bank or the government and exchanging them for silver dollars. But not many folks did. Why?

Markets abhor nonstandardization precisely because it raises transaction and information costs. The more abstract the market, the more it abhors nonstandardization. Money is the most abstract good in the entire economy. Business is just more *difficult* with more than one form of money. Not impossible, just more difficult. When gold clauses were outlawed, paper money and bank credit were easier to deal in than silver, so the market standardized on Federal Reserve notes and bank credit denominated in Federal Reserve notes.

By the natural tendency of the market to standardize on some money that offers zero transaction cost, the very idea of contracting out of the legal tender money system was squelched. The government didn't have to do it; the market did it.

In fact, it has been legal to contract in gold or silver since 1977, but nobody does. Since 1986, we've had American Eagle coins of silver and gold. The old gold and silver coins are still available, or you could contract in foreign gold or silver coin. Still, nobody contracts in gold or silver, because the Federal Reserve note remains the *numeraire* in the economy, the standard of value monetary unit. Another and considerably less shiny reason is that *most Americans profit, and expect to profit, from inflation.* They don't want an honest money system.

To get there from here—to replace the present *fiat* system—with a specie monetary system—several conditions must be fulfilled. First, the *fiat* system must become too expensive in terms of risk and transaction costs. It must break down, the signs of which (as we discuss below) are now emerging. Second, we must found institutions that lower the transaction and information costs of dealing in silver or gold money. Third, we have to begin to think in terms of silver and gold. Fourth, we have to contract out of the legal tender system.

Next time you walk into your local convenience store, look on the door. There's probably a notice there: "We do not accept $100 bills." They have put you on notice that they are contracting out of the legal tender system, at least in $100 denominations. They can do it.

Why not put a different notice on the door of your business, or in your contracts: "We only accept gold and silver in payment—we may accept other forms of payment by special arrangement." You've put your customers on notice. With a hand-held calculator or even an abacus you can figure the value of any gold or silver coin in a couple of seconds. A quick phone call to any brokerage house will tell you the current metal price in Federal Reserve notes. Since you would be cutting out the middleman for acquiring gold and silver coins, you could afford to give your customers a better price on whatever they buy. Both of you get a better deal.

Then the market will take over. Only legal tender laws make Gresham's law work. By contracting out of the legal tender system, you can reverse Gresham's law. If Americans aren't forced to accept bad money, then good money will drive bad money out of circulation.

All by yourself, you will have accomplished what the almighty U.S. government itself, with all its Ph.D. economists, planners, and policy wonks could not do: *You will have reestablished gold and silver money.*

COLLAPSE OF DEBT MONEY

The marketplace has already definitively rejected central bank debt money. The 1993 collapse of the European exchange rate mechanism was effectively a free market vote of no confidence in the monetary and economic policies of the countries that participated in that exchange rate cartel. Speculators recognized that the high interest rate/low growth policy of those countries that had historically lacked monetary "integrity" (if such a word can be used to describe central bank management of any fiat currency) would collapse in the face of growing unemployment and economic distress—political pressure.

The "dirty speculators" take the blame from central banks and politicians, but those speculators are the elite shock troops of economic freedom. Their attack through the currency markets warns the rest of the players that government monetary fraud is coming, and prevents government from using money as an instrument of social, fiscal, and economic policy. In the crude words of a southern proverb, It don't do no good to set a trap if the bears already know where it's at. The discounting and information spreading efficiency of global free currency markets has robbed governments of effective, long-term control over their own national currencies, and with it, control over their own economies.

PRIVATE REMONETIZATION AND SPECIE BANKING

Gradually, as these national currencies become weaker and weaker, they will become less and less suitable for daily economic transactions and business planning. Gradually, we believe, free markets will replace fiat national currencies with the only genuinely effective international monies, gold and silver. When the precious metals are wholly freed from government price manipulation, they will once again claim their supremacy in the marketplace.

In fact, for the past twenty years and more, the public has already been *privately remonetizing* gold and silver, although both metals still fall far short of a complete alternative to debt money. For many years, U.S. firms and Swiss banks have offered gold and silver certificate or storage programs. Generally, buying or selling through these programs costs only a little more than a simple foreign exchange transaction: You simply exchange any paper money of the world for gold or silver, and vice versa. From a bookkeeping standpoint, these transactions are no more complicated than a foreign exchange transaction or simple bank deposit accounting. Gold loans have grown in frequency among gold mining companies. Silver "leasing," another form of borrowing, is also popular among industrial silver users.

SPECIE BANKING: HOW IT WILL LOOK

One firm we know is already preparing for private remonetization of silver and gold. To avoid the pitfalls of fractional reserve banking, the following criteria must be stringently met:

- guaranteed 100 percent reserve backing for all deposits at all times, unless the customer specifically contracts otherwise;
- audited, guaranteed storage, with periodic published reports.

Some may object that this system robs banks (and the economy) of the ability to create money and capital and allocate capital to economic needs, but that is simply not true. Historically, the Bank of Hamburg operated in exactly this fashion from its inception in 1619 until Napoleon ordered its liquidation, when every ounce of silver the bank owed customers was still in its vaults, plus an overage. Specie banks can and will do everything fractional reserve banks now do: make loans, transfer funds (checking accounts), store money, and issue banknotes. There is in fact no technical reason why specie money and specie banking could not replace the present system *tomorrow,* other than its present lack of availability and the market's ignorance.

MOBILIZING GOLD AND SILVER CAPITAL

The new specie banks can offer loans by syndication among the depositors. Depositors who want only to leave their specie on deposit would be free to do so, at some nominal storage charge. Those depositors who want their money loaned out and who accept the increased risk can contract with the bank to perform that service for them, *understanding, however, that their deposits may not be withdrawn while the loan is outstanding without some penalty.* This is wholly different from fractional reserve banking, where the bank treats the deposits of all and sundry as its own, and uses them as fractional reserves for whatever loans it pleases the bank to make. A specie bank would at least rid us of the pious fraud behind which fractional reserve banks now hide, namely, that the bank has "reserves" when in fact the bank has only loans and the speedy flight of ever-whizzing electrons whirling around in the bank's computer. At least with a specie bank, all the banking cards would be on the table.

The ability of the specie bank to make gold and silver loans would mobilize gold and silver capital that remains otherwise paralyzed. The objection that "gold and silver don't earn interest" would effectively be eliminated, and the mobilization of precious metals capital would be a giant step toward eventual remonetization.

THE GIRO OR CHECKING ACCOUNT

The specie bank will mobilize gold and silver capital for daily use by performing the *giro* function. The giro account originated in Italian banks in the late Middle Ages. Translated literally, it means "circular banking," and simply transfers sums from one person to another on the bank's books. The term "giro account" is still used in European banking to describe a non-interest-bearing account subject to immediate withdrawal or transfer to other accounts within the bank without necessarily using a check. Their use corresponds approximately to checking accounts in the United States.[3]

In the giro account, the specie bank would simply transfer silver or gold balances on its books from one account to another on the order of the depositor. Specie bank checking accounts would perform this same function for the settlement of debts to persons outside the bank.

SPECIE BANKNOTES

Given their history, we are almost loath to mention the issue of banknotes by specie banks. However, provided a 100 percent reserve of precious metals is maintained against these notes, there is no reason not to take advantage of their convenience, and secure banknotes are a ready means of effectively increasing the circulation of gold and silver.

THE MYTH OF SCARCITY: "THERE'S NOT ENOUGH GOLD AND SILVER TO GO AROUND"

As incredible as it seems, many economists argue against gold and silver money on the basis that it is too scarce. But this is exactly the problem with debt money: It's too plentiful, and too easy to create. Government debt sure isn't too scarce. In fact, scarcity is one of the classical characteristics and prime prerequisites of a practical money. The only scarcity that present debt money enjoys is the artificial scarcity contrived by legal monopoly, or the force of guns in the marketplace. That's some basis for money in a free country, isn't it?

Scarcity, however, presumes another question: At what price? Because of political demonetization, the prices of gold and silver are far below their historical purchasing power levels. For example, according to the U.S. Government Bureau of Mines, the 1913 average annual price of silver at 60 cents an ounce was the equivalent of $8.22 in 1987 dollars. Stated another way, a dollar of silver (0.7734 troy ounce), for its silver value in 1913, was worth $3.81 in silver value, but this doesn't by any means tell the whole tale. The legal tender value of the same silver dollar would buy as much as $13.70 in 1987 dollars.

As the monetary demand for gold and silver increases, their price in terms of other goods and services ("purchasing power") will increase as well. At some vastly higher level than today's gold and silver prices, a stable ratio between precious metals money and all other goods and services will emerge. At some price, there is plenty of gold and silver money to satisfy the market.

THE CHIMERA OF STABLE PRICES

The chimera of "stability" and "stable prices" is most often held out as the chief ground for leaving control of the supply of money in the hands of governments and central banks. This is, however, a demonstrably impossible dream that attempts to contradict all the facts of free market economics.

In the first place, it's a revolt against nature. Economies and, more precisely, markets by their very nature are not stable, not static, but dynamic, living organisms. Their very purpose is to adjust to the changes in conditions of weather and efficiency and technology and harvests so that there will be enough of everything to meet the needs of humanity. The purpose of markets is to adjust production to physical changes as well as the changes in desires of those myriads of honest laborers who by the sweat of their brows earn a right to vote in the market with their hard-earned dollars and marks and pounds and yen and francs and zlotys.

The virtual collapse of communism worldwide should by now have laid to rest in all honest minds the impossible—indeed, wicked—idea that any group of people can control the economic destiny of the vast masses of humanity—living, individual human beings each with a worth and dignity of his or her own—who make up the economies of the world. Only those who hate the idea of human freedom and human responsibility, only those who despise the notion of all those teeming millions going about their own business, living their own lives, and laying their fortunes on the line to please others and feed themselves—indeed, only those who at the very deepest level hate humanity and themselves can possibly cling to the notion that governments can make better economic decisions than the very people who are the economy.

It is simply *not important* that prices be stable. In fact, for economies and markets to work at all, *prices must be unstable*—free to adjust to changing economic conditions, free to respond to changing flows of supply and demand.

It's not even important that the price of money be stable. The history of centuries proves as a practical matter that prices are not stable in any event—not even the prices of gold and silver money, as Professor Roy Jastram and others have so exhaustively shown. The history of the floating exchange rates of the past twenty years proves that, as difficult as they may render trade and rational business planning, it is not even indispensable that the prices of currencies be stable internationally. Markets have even adjusted to floating exchange rates. Certainly, no such instability ever existed under a silver standard, a gold standard, or a bimetallic standard as that which fiat money has provided the world.

Whatever ivory-tower economic theoreticians may maintain to the contrary, humankind has to date found no philosopher-kings capable of managing a money divorced from the essential reality that a metallic money system enforces. At the end of a more than one-hundred-year worldwide regime of nonmarket control of money, the experiment is an utter, unalloyed, undeniable, scandalous failure. It is a failure that reeks as foully as the rotten corpse of communism—to which it supplied the central pillar. Central banking has failed—past all questioning—to bring stability to economies or to money or to prices. It has succeeded only in breeding instability in its own money, and in silver and gold money as well.

What, then, is required in a money? The answer is so self-evident we blush to name it. First, it must be a stable standard of value widely known and knowable, a store of value reliable over time, and a medium of exchange accepted worldwide. Most of all, *it must not be subject to political manipulation, as fiat currencies are.* Otherwise, those who take part in the economies of the world—those who with genuine, if unconscious, humanitarian zeal produce the goods and services that the rest of mankind need to survive—face a game in which the rules continually change. Every time the players get near the goalposts, the referees keep moving them back to prevent a touchdown. What is important is that the economic players of the world, all those who work in just expectation and reasonable hope of a reward for their honorable efforts, have the framework of stable money within which to build their economic futures.

It's not even important that there be only *one* money; two will do just as well, as proven by the history of centuries in which gold and silver worked in harmony with each other and humankind. And whatever the shortcomings of gold and silver money, whatever small and transient risks they threaten, they have proven infinitely more stable than politicized bank credit, fractional reserves, central banks, and fiat currencies, which have been responsible for the uncontrolled and uncontrollable fevers of economic booms and busts that have racked the body of free enterprise around the world in the past two centuries.

For reasons buried in human nature that transcend our knowing, humankind values the mirror of eternity that shines in gold and silver. By reason of their scarcity and this mysterious worth in themselves, gold and silver are perfectly suited to fulfill the functions of money.

First, the demand for silver and gold that gives rise to their value is so universally spread among the diverse peoples of the world that no one body or person can reasonably be expected to control it, absent the guns and truncheons of government intervention.

Second, the increase of the stock of gold and silver enjoys, thus far in the six-thousand-year experience of humanity, about the same rate as the

207

natural growth rate of economies. Even at the very worst, the experience of gold and silver inflations (such as that after the discovery of the New World) have been healthful, not harmful to the economies of the world because they were real and not imaginary increases in the available wealth of the world.

Third, the value that gold and silver carry in themselves is in quality, unlike the value of the debt-based money that now afflicts humanity. Their value does not depend on the questionable and ephemeral credit-worthiness of individual borrowers or the imponderable mutabilities of governments and central bankers, but on the individual decisions of billions of market participants.

Surely at the end of a century of fiat money torture, it is time for a final separation of economic and monetary control from government, a separation as unyielding and fundamental as the separation of church and state. The control of money supply is far too critical, too crucial to the welfare of every human being on this planet, to be left to the vagaries, whims, and power lust of politicians, academicians, or financial elites, who by their very nature can only pursue their own selfish interests. Leaving control of the money supply to the markets, even the present unpredictable markets for precious metals, may not be the perfect solution, but it's the best alternative. At the very least, a metallic money system distributes the awesome power of money among the greatest number of hands possible under present circumstances.

The finance minister of Louis XIV once confronted a conference of French businesspeople to ask them what the government could do to help them. Monsieur LeGendre, a plainspoken businessman fed up with government interference, replied, *"Laissez nous faire!"*—(Leave us alone!). To all the monetary meddlers in the world so busily paving our road to economic hell with all their good intentions we say, "Leave us alone."

At the height of the great American monetary controversy of the past century, silverite William Jennings Bryan earned a place in history with a speech that climaxed, "You shall not crucify mankind upon a cross of gold!" With the experience of the past hundred years on our backs, we say better a cross of gold or silver than the cross of fiat money that has borne in its train more sorrow, more hardship, more poverty, more death, more shattered dreams and hopes than all the gold and silver money systems the world has ever seen.

On the eve of the third millennium, the monetary cry of the centuries is undeniably: Leave us alone. Let us be done with monetary schemes that promise prosperity and stability and yield only misery. Let the monetary planners and schemers be done with trying to repeal the law of monetary gravity. Give us back our freedom. *Give us back our honest silver money.*

Chapter 13

THE BIG PICTURE: BRINGING IT ALL TOGETHER

We need to get out of the forest, up on the mountaintop, and look at the very long-term horizon to give us a framework for our conclusions about investing in silver. Economics has become so *empirical* that it has lost its claim to membership among the humanities or the liberal arts. Economists have openly sought to reduce economics to an empirical science. It is even possible in some universities today to get a Ph.D. in economics without ever taking a course in economic history.

However, as economist Ludwig von Mises rightly insisted, economics is *not* a quantifiable science but a study of human psychology—human action, if you will. It is *not* quantifiable in the sense that chemistry or physics is quantifiable, because it deals with human beings who do not act as mere functions of mathematical statistics but of human emotions and desires. These are social, individual, mostly nonquantifiable, and often preeminently nonrational.

It is precisely the experience and understanding of this human element that make trading, especially silver trading, an art rather than a science. The commodity broker or stockbroker who went to work in 1981 knows only that silver always goes down. He or she has never lived through a bull market so cannot imagine it. Any broker who has not lived through both bull and bear markets can endanger your financial health, because that person lacks the indispensable long-term perspective to understand the market. Therefore we insist that, although both technical and fundamental market analyses are essential to understanding the silver market, they are useless without taking into account the human psychology that in the end drives markets.

Our framework for understanding silver in the long term—and by long term we mean both in the past six millennia and the past two hundred years—is monetary, for monetary factors drive the silver market. These are inherently human and, in the past two hundred years, increasingly political factors. The two-hundred-year trend in money has been away from the view of money that humankind had accepted throughout its entire history—that money must have some intrinsic value, or be so commonly desired as to have the equivalent of intrinsic value, and toward money as the *fiat* of the state; away from money as an instrument of integrity in human dealings, and toward money as purely an instrument of political power. This trend has marched hand in hand with the rise of the omnipotent, messianic state in the West.

It is no exaggeration to say that the fiat money system has been the prerequisite condition for the existence and maintenance of the messianic state. *Control of money is the jugular vein of totalitarianism.* There is, after all, a limit—even in modern docile Western societies—to the amount that states can take from their citizens via the *open* route of taxation. That puts a natural limit on spending (and therefore political power), whether for wars or for welfare. Because the limit of taxation controls the limits of spending, it also ultimately controls the actions of governments. By controlling the essence of money, the state effectively frees itself from this limitation—indeed, frees its actions from all limitations—and approaches the godlike condition it has so openly claimed in the twentieth century.

Certainly this is no new idea, and does not arise from monetary crackpots. As long ago as 1946, Beardsley Ruml, then chairman of the Federal Reserve Bank of New York (the most powerful regional Federal Reserve bank), could write in an article cogently titled, "Taxes for Revenue Are Obsolete":

> The necessity for a government to tax in order to maintain both its independence and its solvency is true for state and local governments, but it is not true for a national government. Two changes of the greatest

consequence have occurred in the last twenty-five years which have sub-stantially altered the position of the national state with respect to the financing of its current requirements. The first of these changes is the gaining of vast new experience in the management of central banks. The second change is the elimination, for domestic purposes [and since 1971, for international purposes as well] *of the convertibility of the currency into gold* [emphasis added].

FREE OF THE MONEY MARKET

Final freedom from the domestic money market exists for every sovereign national state where there exists an institution that functions in the manner of a modern central bank and whose currency is not convertible into some other commodity. The United States is a national state that has a central banking system, the Federal Reserve System, and whose currency, for domestic purposes, is not convertible into any commodity. It follows that our federal government has final freedom from the money market in meeting its financial requirements. Accordingly, the inevitable social and economic consequences of any and all taxes have now become the prime consideration in the imposition of taxes.

WHAT TAXES ARE REALLY FOR

Federal taxes can be made to serve four principal purposes of a social and economic character. These purposes are:

1. as an instrument of fiscal policy to help stabilize the purchasing power of the dollar;
2. to express public policy in the distribution of wealth and of income, as in the case of progressive income and estate taxes;
3. to express public policy in subsidizing or in penalizing various industries and economic groups;
4. to isolate and assess directly the costs of certain national benefits such as highways and Social Security.[1]

212

APPLYING THIS IDEA THROUGH HISTORY

The cynical notion that the essence of money lay within the power of the state to create or destroy has been contested from ancient times up to our day. Whenever this idea has been put into effect, its consequences have been uniformly disastrous. It helped destroy the Roman Empire. It destroyed Byzantium. It crippled the economic development of Europe in the Middle Ages. It has crippled and tortured modern economies for the past two hundred years.

Before the widespread use of credit and paper money, the fiat money system was limited to clipping and debasing the coin in circulation. As the use of credit grew (beginning about the time of the Renaissance) and banks of issue began to spring up (the Swedish Riksbank about 1655, the Bank of England in 1694), their potential for mischief grew as well. In the eighteenth century alone, the Mississippi Bubble under John Law in France (1720), the South Sea Bubble in England (1720), the history of the American Colonies (1680s–1776), the American inflation during the American Revolution under the Continental Congress (1776–89), and the disastrous inflation under the French Revolution (1792–98), all proved that bank credit and fiat money, whether originating from governments or banks of issue, had grown to such size that they could not only threaten but also *annihilate* entire national economies.

Although Colonial and Revolutionary experience no doubt induced the American Founding Fathers to insert a prohibition of fiat money into the Constitution of 1789 (Article I, Section 10, "No State shall . . . coin Money; emit Bills of Credit; make any Thing but gold and silver Coin a Tender in Payment of Debts. . . ."), the ink on the document hadn't even dried when schemes for a central bank were already afoot.

Indeed, one might argue that the primary motor of American economic history until the War Between the States was the fight against fiat money —against a central bank (First Bank and Second Bank of the United States), the state banks, and banks of issue—for a sound metallic currency. From the war's beginning, both North and South were financed by fiat money, legitimated only by the promise to pay money, either gold or silver, *eventually*. But the war itself, with its unprecedented demand for money and the Northern victory, legitimizing as it did acts of questionable constitutionality passed during the emergency, left the friends of paper

213

money and bank credit victorious. The U.S. Supreme Court was shuffled and placed its after-the-fact blessing on fiat money.

The later disastrous and unnecessary political demonetization of silver removed at one stroke an enormous metallic component of the world's money supply. It was but one more milestone in the centuries-long trend toward money as a *creature of the state*. The resulting worldwide gold standard, as we have elsewhere observed, was in fact no gold standard at all. It would have been an impossibility resulting in an unthinkable deflation had not the quantity of money been supplemented by banknotes and bank credit. (In fact, it did result in a deflation and depression that plagued the last quarter of the nineteenth century.) As the years passed, bank credit and notes gradually pushed metallic money aside, not so much from consumer preference but because metallic money was so much more valuable to the bankers as part of their reserves.

The creation of the U.S. Federal Reserve system in 1913 completed the worldwide subjection of national economies to central banking. If any reader questions just how supreme the victory of fiat money is over all other forms, ask yourself this question: How many people do you know who do *not* have and use a checking account or credit cards almost exclusively? We repeat: Bank credit money, created and controlled by government-mandated central banks, has completely supplanted every other form of money in daily use. We add "in daily use" because gold, and to a lesser extent silver, continue as the "monies of last resort" around the world, hanging on despite a vicious 350-year campaign against them.

Below we will examine some of the many reasons why we think silver (and, of course, gold) will rise in the coming years. Before those specifics, however, let's take one last view from the mountaintop and get our bearings.

DECENTRALIZATION HAS ARRIVED

We believe that the secular trend toward the messianic state and other massive, centralized institutions of control such as central banks is dying. Replacing that trend in the development of human relations is a trend toward decentralization, returning to individuals independence, freedom, and power over their own lives.

The change of trend will be neither pretty nor easy. Joseph Stalin observed, "Obsolete classes do not voluntarily abandon the stage of history. . . . Dying classes take to arms and resort to every means to save their existence as a ruling class." There will be rumors of wars, actual wars, political confusion, and social and economic upheavals. The realignment of social and economic institutions will utterly change the way we do business and think of the world. Established interests will fight it every step of the way, but—as events in East Germany and other erstwhile totalitarian states prove—they cannot prevail. The walls of the world are crumbling.

We suspect, but cannot prove, that as this transition to individual freedom intensifies, *there will be an increase of monetary demand arising from (1) a wish for safety, and (2) a desire for a means of exchange autonomous from the state or any debtor.* As the entire world, but primarily the West, becomes increasingly uneasy about the stability of its institutions, the desire to protect the lifeline of the basic necessities—such as money —and the demand for dependable money will increase. In other words, increasing Western pessimism about the future will send people running to silver and gold for safety.

The inherent economic instabilities, deficiencies, and contradictions in our present system of debt money—generated by central banks and fractional reserve banks and dependent for its life on continuing borrowing—seem to be heaping up to a denouement, a crisis that may, and we hope will, gradually but finally abolish the debt money system and replace it with an intrinsically valuable metallic money, along with all the natural stability such a system implies once the transition is completed.

Only within the framework of these century-long trends can we understand the near- and long-term prospects for silver and gold. Now let's look at specific factors that will inexorably force the prices of gold and silver to rise.

REASONS WHY SILVER WILL RISE

Every way we turn, the factors raising silver's price hit us in the face. We have discussed these in earlier chapters, but a summary is in order.

THE U.S. FEDERAL DEFICIT

Government spending has become structurally institutionalized. Handouts are the beams and posts and stringers that hold up the skeleton of our government. As a practical matter, that spending is unchangeable short of a cataclysm that makes it impossible. Like lung cancer, spending will continue to expand until it destroys its host. The reelection of every representative to Congress, every senator, every president, every governor, every state legislator, every mayor, every alderman, every ward heeler depends on continuing it. The constituencies of those dependent on government—from welfare corporations to welfare recipients—form the voting blocs that win elections. Since the New Deal, government spending has been the indispensable cement of successful candidacies.

There is no constituency for cutting the deficit or the budget, or at best it is scattered and ill organized. There is a clearly defined, powerful, and readily mobilized constituency to prevent every spending cut. The Clinton tax-cut legerdemain was merely one more ineffective slapstick effort to "cut the budget" or "cut the deficit." It did neither. *It was a plan to cut the rate of growth of spending.* Eventually, someday, maybe down the road, somebody will cut the size of the deficit—three years after raising taxes and spending more money. Compared to similar plans of the past thirty or forty years, the Clinton plan is remarkable for only one reason: It betrays an even more reckless, cruel, and callous disregard of the American people and their economy than its predecessors.

Can anyone really believe that raising taxes—*removing capital from the hands of producers in the market*—will help the economy? Worse yet, it comes on top of *chronic recession!* What will the government do with the money? Why, it will spend it, or, in Clintonese, it will *invest* it. The whole scheme boils down to this: *We can spend ourselves into prosperity.* Yet higher taxes will only choke off business activity, and the money spent will simply be consumed. This is the same lunacy that has been steadily pulverizing the American economy and its capital base for the past sixty years. Doesn't anybody in Washington ever catch on?

The answer is plainly *no.* Government has no limit to the amount of money it can spend ("taxation for revenue is dead") except the willingness of the public to accept the money created through the central bank. The upper limits of open taxation are already emerging and will become much more well drawn as the deficit interest burden expands and compounds, threatening to consume all the government's revenue.

Therefore, government deficits will never be reduced (except photogenically) *until the whole system of deficit spending and debt money system hits the wall.* Government policymakers are likely candidates for a flat face. They are not pragmatists but ideologues to whom the consequences of their actions matter not at all as long as they serve their ideological goal: socialism.

Debt Is Money

The present U.S. and world monetary system is a "debt money" or "bank credit money" system. Money is *created* in one of two ways: private or government borrowing. Here's how it works.

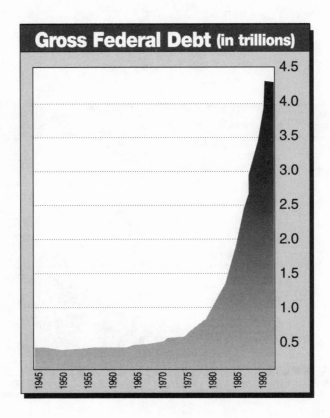

John Doe wants to borrow $10,000 to finance his gas station. Down at Last National Bank, the banker says to him, "John, you've always been a good borrower and a loyal customer. We'll be glad to lend you $10,000." The banker calls upstairs to the computer room and says to the bookkeeper, "Enter a $10,000 loan for John Doe."

The banker executes the loan documents, John Doe signs them, and he's on his way with a new $10,000 in his checking account. Upstairs, the bookkeeper keys in an entry that shows that the bank's *assets* in the form of a loan to John Doe have increased by $10,000, the amount of the loan. A second entry shows that the bank's *liabilities,* in the form of the balance in John Doe's checking account balance, have also increased by $10,000. Because on the balance sheet, liabilities are netted out against assets, the bank's books stay balanced, and everybody is happy.

What happened? The bank just *created $10,000 in money out of thin air,* backed by John Doe's promise to pay $10,000. The bank just increased the nation's money supply by $10,000. The mysterious ritual of "inflation" has just taken place. *You* can't create money, and *we* can't create money, but the *bank has been granted a legal monopoly to create money.*

Here's the second way to create money. The U.S. government is run-

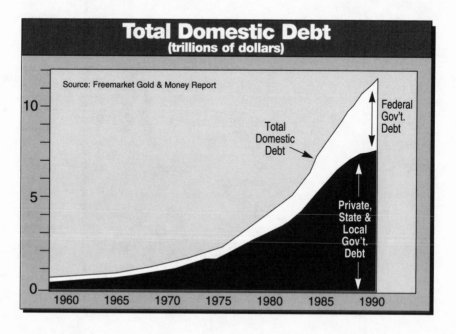

218

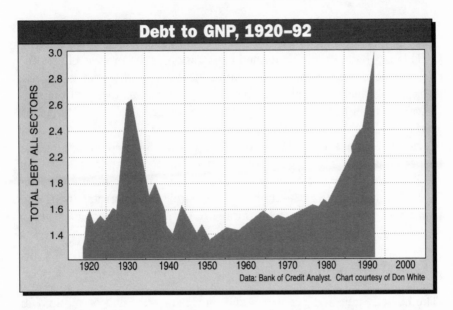

Debt to GNP, 1920–92

Data: Bank of Credit Analyst. Chart courtesy of Don White

ning a little tight this month. It needs $1 billion bucks to keep those OSHA inspectors on the road so employers won't kill off all their employees. The Treasury Department calls up the Federal Reserve. The Federal Reserve banker says, "Treasury, you've always been a good borrower and a loyal customer. We'll be glad to loan you $1 billion." The Federal Reserve banker calls upstairs to the computer room, and says to the bookkeeper, "Enter $1 billion loan for the U.S. Treasury."

The Federal Reserve banker executes the loan documents, Treasury Department signs them, and the government is on its way with a new $1 billion balance in its checking account. Upstairs, the bookkeeper keys in an entry that shows the Federal Reserve bank's *assets,* in the form of a loan to the government, have increased by $1 billion, the amount of the loan. A second entry shows that the bank's *liabilities,* in the form of the balance in the Treasury's checking account balance, have also increased by $1 billion. Once again, the books are balanced and everybody is happy.

What happened? The Federal Reserve just *created $1 billion out of thin air,* backed by the government's promise to pay $1 billion. The bank just increased the nation's money supply by $1 billion. The alchemical miracle of "inflation" has just occurred, turning debt into money. Legally, *you* can't create money, and *we* can't create money, but the *Federal Reserve*

219

banks—*private corporations*—*have been granted a legal monopoly to create money*.

This is an admittedly simplified explanation of the process of creating debt money, but it explains the nature of the system. There is nothing whatsoever that gives value to this money except the ability of the borrower to repay it. *It is pure debt money: the liability of those who created it, pyramided on the liability of the borrower*. Every dollar of debt money in circulation carries a burden of interest that must be paid. If new money is not constantly borrowed into existence, the aggregate interest cannot be paid, and some borrowers will go bankrupt. The system must expand or it will die. What is truly unbelievable is that all Americans living and dead have been soaked by this confidence game for the past eighty years!

The Debt Matters

The United States has been on a debt binge since the end of World War II. Government, business, and consumer debt have all soared, on the theory that as long as you can make the payments, everything's okay. The debt doesn't matter, economists, politicians, and government experts tell us.

But everything is *not* okay. Because every dollar that comes into circulation must be *borrowed into existence*, the burden of debt becomes bigger every year. The debt money system must keep on expanding, *or the economy dies*. When the debt backing the money is liquidated, *the money supply must shrink*. Purchasing power contracts. This is deflation. If the United States government paid down its debt, the deflationary impact would overwhelm and annihilate the American economy.

Some analysts say that low growth (a.k.a. chronic recession) and low inflation (a.k.a. banks scared to lend and no creditworthy borrowers) weren't so bad in the 1950s, so they're not so bad now. After all, government debt in the 1950s, after World War II, was much higher as a percentage of the GNP than it is now. Right; *but in the 1950s every company, consumer, and government in America was not hocked up to their earlobes in debt, either*. Back then there was still plenty of liquidity in the system, and plenty of room for borrowers to increase their debt. Today there's no liquidity, asset values are declining, corporations are hacking back operations, and everyone is already carrying as much debt as he or she can carry. Where will the liquidity come from to fuel the next boom?

As the asset values slowly wither away, as the U.S. stock market becomes less and less credible with historical measures of value shrunken to 1929 proportions, as banks refuse to lend, as America and Japan and Europe struggle with "weak recoveries" (a.k.a. chronic recession), can anyone honestly say that *the debt doesn't matter?*

The debt *does* matter. It stifles growth, prevents expansion, and eventually must be liquidated in bankruptcy. Look at the chart "DEBT to GNP, 1920–92." Just how much more explanation is needed? Total debt in all sectors exceeds the swollen debt levels of 1929–30. *And on top of everything else, America will be saddled with national health care to soak up half of corporate profits.* What mighty bird do investors and the government think will swoop down from the sky to save us from all this—the Money Fairy?

MONETARY MEDDLING GUARANTEES DISASTER

Whether the *external* face of monetary meddling is inflation or deflation doesn't really matter, because the inevitable *economic* result of either is the same: *depression*. Governments cause economic depression both through inflation (increasing the money supply) and deflation (decreasing the money supply). Rising prices and the boom-for-some face of inflation help to mask and postpone the depression, but eventually it always arrives, like the unwelcome drunk who crashes the party.

How can we expect deflation when the government and the central bank are inflating (adding to the money supply)? Consider these points:

- *Deflation* is a decrease in the money supply.
- *Inflation* is an increase in the money supply.
- The *nominal* increase or decrease in the money supply is not what affects the economy. What affects the economy is the increase or decrease in purchasing power.
- Inflation's artificial increase in the money supply actually reduces the purchasing power of each monetary unit.
- Inflation *always* causes depression. Why?

Inflation misallocates resources (encourages malinvestment). The interest rate, which is only the price of money, tells producers whether con-

221

sumers want to increase their future purchases. Artificially abundant money creates artificially low interest rates, which trick producers into investing in plant and equipment to produce things consumers don't really want in the future. Low interest rates and cheap money send the wrong signals about consumer preferences to producers. When at last the future arrives and the malinvestment surfaces, the bad investments and bad debts must be liquidated. This amounts to a deflation of the asset base: a depression.

INFLATION CAUSES DEFLATION

In direct proportion to the rate of inflation, fiat money (inflation money) actually *deflates* the purchasing power of the entire money supply *even while the nominal amount of the money supply is increasing.* This is what Andrew Dickson White, author of *Fiat Money Inflation in France,* called the Law of Accelerating Issue and Depreciation. Because the public expects that the currency will continue depreciating, the faster the government or central bank issues money, the faster it depreciates. We call it "von Havenstein's trap."

During the 1920–23 hyperinflation, Reichsbank president Dr. Rudolf von Havenstein was asked why he kept on issuing so much money. He replied that the country was suffering from a *dearth of purchasing power and circulating media,* and, of course, he was right. The faster he issued money, the faster it depreciated, and the faster the actual money supply (in terms of purchasing power in circulation) decreased.

Therefore, *the underlying economic condition of every inflation is depression.* This may be masked by periodic or sectoral booms. The inflation rate rises or falls over time; some sectors win, others lose, and it takes time for the inflation to work its way through the economy. However, because of the inflation-engendered malinvestment and the decrease in the actual purchasing power of the money supply, deflation and depression are building all the time.

Eventually, overvalued assets and bad debts, both pumped up by the inflation of private and government borrowing, must be liquidated. This liquidation must last in time proportionate to the length and severity of the preceding inflation. Our inflation has been under way since 1933 or 1950, depending on your definition. Draw your own conclusions about the length and severity of the deflation.

BUT WHAT ABOUT INFLATION?

The apparent contradiction is that you can have a *nominal* monetary inflation while a deflationary depression rages. Look at Germany in 1920–23. The stock market roared up, but only in nominal, not in real terms. Over the hyperinflation's course, stock market investors lost because businesses were losing.

The German hyperinflation brought almost all business activity to a halt. This can be attributed in large part to the dearth of purchasing power, for no matter how big the number of paper currency units in circulation, they had almost no purchasing power. Eventually there was not enough purchasing power in circulation even to run the economy. When this happens, the economy falls back to the most primitive level: barter.

In a system such as ours, where money is backed by debt, debt liquidation is deflationary. If liquidated by hyperinflation, then the debt's full purchasing power value is not paid off. If liquidated by deflation—bankruptcy—the creditor still watches the value of his or her assets evaporate. Debt is what backs our money supply. Every dollar of debt that's written off, bankrupted, not borrowed into existence, or not rolled over is another dollar the money supply must shrink.

Our conclusion: The underlying deflation has bitten, and won't let go until the money supply thunders. The purchasing power of the money supply cannot be expanded by inflationary increases because (1) banks are afraid to lend; (2) there are few creditworthy borrowers; (3) under a debt money system, money can only be borrowed into existence, and without borrowing the money supply decreases; and (4) the underlying asset deflation is so mighty that it overwhelms small doses of new money.

In large doses, inflation only worsens the underlying deflationary economic conditions. Why? In the lower ranges of inflation, new fiat money raises interest rates and, in our illiquid and overindebted economy, higher interest rates stimulate only bankruptcies. In the upper ranges, hyperinflation *accelerates* the shrinking of total purchasing power, exacerbating the dearth of money.

At present, American interest rates are bumping along at multiyear lows, but the investors of the world are no longer the suckers they were in the '50s, '60s, and '70s. They are so wise to inflation that any hint of its return sends interest rates up. Further, the chief tool a central bank must use to "control inflation" is *higher interest rates*. Higher interest rates cost the federal government billions. Under present economic conditions, higher American interest rates would spell Waterloo for the economy.

GOVERNMENT DEFICIT: HIT BY THE TRAFFIC COMING AND GOING

The government deficit sharpens the problem. Why? As the currency's purchasing power decreases, loanable capital (in real terms) decreases along with it. This is a deathblow to an economy in which all producers are chronic borrowers. In the face of this shrinking capital supply, government borrowing must nevertheless increase because interest on the deficit must be served. If the central bank simply monetizes the government debt (inflates more), then the situation becomes *hyperbolically* worse, because as inflation rises, interest rates rise (after a certain point in the inflation rate—initial doses of money lower interest rates when inflation is in the lower ranges). Rising interest rates then *increase* the amount of money the government must borrow to service its debt, crowding private borrowers out of an already overcrowded capital market.

The point is this: Nominal monetary inflation can occur simultaneously in an economy with deflationary depression conditions. In fact, inflation will always bring on a deflationary depression because eventually it shrinks total money supply by shrinking its purchasing power. As silver investors we don't care whether there's inflation or deflation, because the underlying condition of either is *deflationary,* which favors silver even more than inflation. Our fundamental case for silver, which depends on rising demand, limited supply, and rising monetary demand, remains bullish.

INFLATION OR DEFLATION: DOES IT MAKE A DIFFERENCE?

Financially, low interest rates *favor* silver, since they lower the opportunity cost of holding silver. It may be that inflation will not reemerge. The long credit inflation of the past forty years began unwinding in some sectors in 1980. The billions of dollars channeled by inflation into uneconomical investments must now be written down (deflated) to their true market worth.

Deflation does not frighten gold and silver investors. The historical record surprisingly shows that *gold and silver perform better in deflations than in inflations.*[2] In the U.S. deflation of 1814–30, prices dropped 50 percent while in purchasing power silver rose 89 percent. In the deflation from 1864 to 1897, silver's purchasing power increased 29 percent. During the last big inflation, 1951–79, gold's purchasing power increased 240 percent *while silver's purchasing power shot up 380 percent, outperforming gold.*[3]

INFLATION

What about inflation? It is certainly possible under Clinton because of his ideological bias toward government spending. Unhappily, Clinton reminds everyone of Carter, and we all know what happened to money under Carter. What's worse, Chairman Alan Greenspan is not Iron Paul Volcker. But as we outlined above, nominal monetary inflation does not contradict the underlying economic deflation and depression that every inflation brings. In fact, every inflation is inherently deflationary, in real terms.

If inflation comes, in the public mind that means gold and silver must rise. This certainly can't hurt silver. Further, inflation feeds the generalized social perceptions of decay and malaise that feed, in turn, monetary demand for silver, even as a weak dollar hurts the whole world economically.

SUPPLY AND DEMAND FUNDAMENTALS

Fabrication demand for silver is rising faster than supply. Silver supply has been in deficit for the past four years, and in 1993 the short fall more than doubled. No ready economical substitute for silver exists in most applications. Some silver is irrecoverably lost and thus taken off the market every year. *Long lead times* are required before mine production can be increased.

Long lead times will also be required to reduce silver usage further. The 1970s and 1980s were decades of squeezing silver out of industrial applications. To achieve greater economies of silver usage now will re-

quire relatively more expensive research efforts, yielding diminishing returns.

There appears to be a lot of silver in the world, until you look closer.
In fact, very little is available at prices under $20. In the words of Charles
River Associates, "The common perception in the market that silver stocks
are very large and thus readily available is wrong. The stocks are large
but are not all readily available."[4]

FABRICATION DEMAND

Worldwide use of silver rises step by step with rising world economic
development. As economic freedom continues to spread in China and
India, pent-up consumer and investment demand will explode, as we
have seen in Japan, Korea, and the new Asian Tigers. With or without
inflation in the West, the growth of these economies will cause both
components of silver demand, monetary and consumer, to surge. What
will happen to silver demand when 1.2 billion Chinese want to take
photos of their families? Rising standards of living will feed enormous
demand for infrastructure, consumer goods, jewelry, photography, and
medical care. In all of these industrial uses, silver is essential and irreplaceable.

Our analysis omits rising consumer demand in the newly freed Eastern
Bloc countries of Europe and the former Soviet Union. Not only is the
political situation in these countries unstable, but also socialist bureau-
crats and holdover Communist politicians have maintained a stranglehold
on political and economic power. However, as these barriers to growth
are eliminated over the next decade, the world will see an economic
rebuilding boom that will dwarf the Marshall Plan in Europe after World
War II. That economic growth will inevitably add more fuel to fabrication
and monetary demand for silver.

THE WILD CARD: MONETARY DEMAND

At the same time that fabrication demand is surging, rising incomes mean
savings for these thrifty Easterners. Traditionally, the people of these areas
regard gold and silver as primary savings vehicles. In some areas, such as
India, silver is viewed by the bulk of the population as the savings vehicle

of choice. In others, gold may be preferred, but silver investment demand will no doubt benefit from the substitution effect we have discussed. Investment demand for silver will ride gold's coattails not only in the East but around the world as well.

THE TECHNICAL OUTLOOK

Technical factors indicate that gold began a new bull market in 1985 or 1993. At this point it seems unquestionable that in 1993, silver—"poor man's gold"—broke out of its thirteen-year bear market prison. Elliott Wave analysis alone (see Appendix 1) points to a once-in-a-generation investment opportunity.

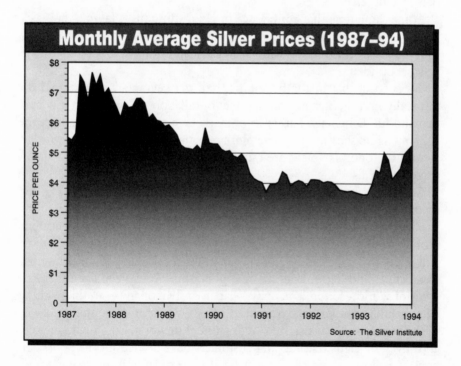

Monthly Average Silver Prices (1987–94)

Source: The Silver Institute

PESSIMISM AND LOSS OF CONFIDENCE IN THE WEST

Whole societies can massively and suddenly lose confidence in themselves. This hopeless pessimism has been seen many times in the past. Europe facing the Black Death in 1348 simply gave up hope and waited to die. The Aztec Empire facing Cortez fought at first, but then quickly accepted Spanish rule as its fate.

We believe that there is a secular trend in the West, a growing loss of confidence in existing economic, government, and social institutions. With the Soviet Union no longer a threat, the West must face militant Islam. Domestic civil unrest, intractable foreign wars, and chronic recession are all contributing to a general lack of confidence in the future and an increased desire for safety, which translate into an increased monetary demand for silver.

At the same time that confidence in old institutions is failing, there is a positive trend: Power is being decentralized and lodged in individuals. This increases impatience with decrepit institutions and accelerates the loss of confidence.

We suspect that in the beginning, bull markets in silver and gold do not really find their cause in the threat of inflation, or even in supply and demand fundamentals. Rather, bull markets in the precious metals begin the way fights start in bars. The more experienced clientele begin to edge toward the door as voices are raised. They're looking for the exits at the first whiff of fisticuffs.

Gold and silver bull markets begin in the guts of investors, in a deep-seated public suspicion that *something* is wrong. They watch the administration thrash around and realize that its ineptness and persistent economic stagnation portend very bad things. They realize that Clinton will apply the same old Keynesian nostrums that federal administrations, Democratic and Republican, have applied since Roosevelt. The other engines of world economic activity—Japan and Germany—are likewise in deep trouble. The more experienced among Western investors, watching the fight brewing, have started edging out of the room. The prices of gold and silver are signs that the first customers have headed for the door. For now, it is a quiet run. Because it has begun quietly, most analysts and investors don't believe in the new bull market in silver. But it's here. It's growing.

Finally, silver bull markets begin when investors recognize that *some-*

thing is up. That something is silver. The supply and demand statistics are available to everyone. They can't be kept a secret, any more than silver's exploding price. As more and more investors recognize the bull market in silver, a buying panic will ensue, and the strength of silver will astonish every onlooker.

SILVER DOESN'T NEED INFLATION

During the 1960s and 1970s, pressure was building under the government-controlled prices of both silver and gold. To hide the effects of their inflationary monetary policies, governments had to keep the lid on precious metals prices. The explosion in 1980 was the top blowing off the boiler. The market won.

But it's taken a long time to work off the excess supplies of silver that blowoff brought onto the market. The booming 1980s helped dampen interest in both silver and gold, but the world's frame of reference has changed. By now, no one tries to maintain the myth that gold is not money. Every newspaper in the world quotes the gold price, and the whole world watches the gold market. The final collapse of the European monetary system in the face of market pressure against its artificial exchange rates nailed shut the coffin lid on fiat currencies. The market has won, but the financial institutions of the world have not yet worked out the implications of that victory. Eventually both gold *and* silver will reestablish their millennia-long roles as the world's primary monies.

In the meantime, industrial demand for silver has a potential that simply astonishes us. What is more astonishing, *the world is paying no attention!* The financial community, even the hard-money community, seems to have given up on silver after its thirteen years in the wilderness. But the fundamental elements are all in place. Inflation or deflation, boom or bust, *silver's day has arrived.*

Chapter 14

THE CASE FOR SILVER, AND WHAT YOU NEED TO DO NOW

SILVER AS MONEY

For nearly six thousand years silver has been the most common money of everyday commerce, the reliable foundation of families, nations, and empires.

Even though in modern times governments have tried to demonetize silver, the metal is now making a monetary comeback. In the past several years, seventy-four different nations have produced legal tender silver coins. *World coinage use grew by an astonishing 14 percent in 1993,* partly due to Mexico's historic reintroduction of silver into circulating coinage. It is estimated that world silver demand for new coins will increase by 100 percent or more by 1997.

Perhaps the biggest story of the rest of the 1990s will be the private and official remonetization of silver. The world's central banks have long sold off their silver reserves, making private investor stocks and new silver mine production the only sources for minted coins. As the powerful trend toward new silver coin production grows, this factor alone should drive the price of silver dramatically higher.

A DRAMATIC NEW SURGE IN SILVER DEMAND

For most of the years between 1950 and 1978, the supply and demand situation in silver resulted in an annual deficit. Twenty of those years saw that deficit averaged at 53.2 million ounces. From 1967 to 1970 there was a four-year combined surplus of 511.3 million ounces, a brief aberration due to official government silver sales. In 1971, the typical annual deficits resumed, totaling a staggering 435.7 million ounces in the eight years following.

In 1976, as investors began to recognize the cumulative effects of the annual silver deficits, the real rush into silver began in earnest. The world was running out of silver, and suddenly everyone became aware of this astonishing fact. These building deficits caused the price of silver to multiply more than thirty-nine times, from a low of $1.32 in 1971 to a high of $52.50 in 1980.

Many investors expected the price of silver to soar to $75 or higher, but the ball game was over. Little recognized by the market, the annual silver deficits had disappeared, and there was a massive change in the supply/demand dynamic. In 1980 the silver surplus-over-demand climbed to an astonishing 207.2 million ounces, and we had reached the beginning of what would become the third-largest commodity bear market in American history. Silver dropped from more than $50 in 1980 to $3.50 in 1993, a 93 percent wipeout.

However, again completely unnoticed by the marketplace, the surplus quietly dropped from its 1980 high of 207.2 million ounces to just 3.2 million ounces by 1989. Amazingly the marketplace took no notice.

Compelling evidence supporting this new trend came in 1991, when the annual silver deficit more than doubled, to 83.2 million ounces, and again when it climbed to 91.7 million ounces in 1992. But still no one seemed to notice, and the price of silver continued to drift lower. Ironically, in 1993, the price of silver reached its low of $3.50.

Although the Silver Institute had predicted an incredible 1993 deficit of 143 million ounces, the market ignored it. When the final figures for

1993 came in, they revealed that the deficit had actually climbed even higher than the estimate, to an astonishing 207.5 million ounces!

Ironically, this was almost precisely the level of the *surplus* of 1980.

Current Silver Institute estimates predict that once the final figures are in, the silver deficit will have soared yet again in 1994, to 248.4 million ounces. I expect that that bullish trend will continue, and by the end of the 1990s deficits could reach 400 million ounces to 500 million ounces per year.

It is now safe to say that a major sea change in favor of silver has occurred, and this trend will continue driving silver prices higher and higher through the rest of the 1990s.

FOUR MEGATRENDS FAVORABLE TO SILVER

In the 1980s four megatrends began to accelerate that would become the major forces for the rest of the 1990s and into the twenty-first century.

1. The fall of the Soviet Union and the rejection of communism. Now that the Soviet Union has fallen and the entire philosophy of social-ism and communism has been repudiated, there is no longer an "evil empire" to suppress the Third World by subsidizing centrally planned economies. The new forces of freedom and free markets around the world *guarantee* higher economic growth rates and therefore guarantee a higher demand for silver.

2. The world free market revolution. Even before the collapse of the Soviet Union, nations all over the world—including economic giants such as China and smaller nations such as Chile—were wholeheartedly joining what I call the "global free market revolution."

For most of the world, the twentieth century was dominated by cen-trally planned economies, dictatorships, and various forms of collectiv-ism, from socialism to fascism to communism. In the 1980s this began to change slowly. Now we can see that the free market revolution is in full force, spreading the philosophy of low tax rates, free markets, and less government regulation around the world.

Although the breakup of the Soviet Union was a powerful contribution to this new economic age, the free market revolution is really driven by the final realization that socialist interventionist economies simply do not work. Ironically, the top intellectuals, businessmen, and government officials all over the world are becoming "free market revolutionaries." As with high economic growth rates spread around the world, the demand in all forms of industrial fabrication, including silver jewelry, will continue to climb dramatically.

3. The shift of economic power from the West to the East. Asia, a sleeping giant, has awakened. Economic growth rates in Asia range from 7 percent to 20 percent annually, compared to the more mature Western economies puttering along at 1 percent to 3 percent. This is extraordinarily bullish for silver, for several reasons. Asians have always thought of silver as money and have a huge appetite for silver jewelry and coinage. The monetary demand (i.e., savings in silver) will grow at least at the same rates as the economies grow, and likely a good bit more.

The demand for precious metals in general, and silver in particular, per unit of gross national product (GNP) in Asian countries can range as much as *fifty times* higher than in the United States and Europe. With Asian populations, savings rates and economic growth rates exploding upward, and with the wealth of literally *billions* of people soaring, the demand for silver will ride this economic crest in spectacular fashion.

A new era for Asia means a new era for silver.

4. The technological revolution. The revolution in modern technology has reached exponential growth rates and will change our lives in nearly every fundamental way by the end of the decade. Silver, the world's most useful metal, is a fundamental part of this dramatic revolution in new technology.

The Silver Institute estimates that a new technological application for silver is discovered every day and a half. For example, fax machines all use silver. The amazingly rapid worldwide spread of this technology in recent years is just one example of how new uses for silver will rapidly expand the demand. Between now and the end of the 1990s, silver will clearly have established itself as *the* metal of the future.

Since the world's four most powerful megatrends are all solidly in favor of higher silver prices, it is hard to see how a long-term investor in silver can go wrong.

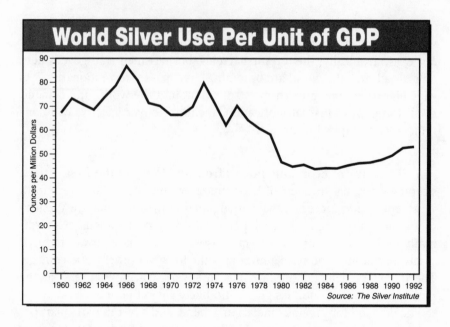

World Silver Use Per Unit of GDP

Source: The Silver Institute

SILVER IS CHEAP

History will attest that the world's most successful investors buy investments when they are grossly undervalued. At today's prices, silver is, without a doubt, the buy of a lifetime. Adjusted for inflation in 1971 dollars, *silver is at its most affordable level since the 1950s.*

If you could go back in a time machine to the early 1970s and buy silver at $1.29 an ounce, knowing that by 1980 it would fly to more than $50 an ounce, there is no question that you would be an eager buyer. The good news is that you don't need a time machine, because today the price of silver in constant 1971 dollars is approximately $1.29. In other words, silver is so undervalued that you are being given a *second opportunity* to buy at 1971 prices.

Any way you analyze it, silver is a superb buy based on real value. Although the metal has collapsed 93 percent in value during the third-deepest bear market in modern history, it still hasn't moved up dramatically from its historically low level. The recent gains have confirmed a new uptrend without wiping out much of the potential profit.

The name of the game in successful investing is "Buy low and sell high." Because of the complete collapse of silver prices since 1980, silver looks like a coiled spring ready to explode.

Perhaps the best measurement of the relative undervaluation of silver is the gold-to-silver ratio, the ratio of the price of gold to the price of silver. In 1991, the gold-to-silver ratio traded as high as 103 to 1. That was a brief historical aberration. Since then, the technical trend has turned dramatically in favor of silver, and as this book is written the ratio is approximately 70 to 1 and *heading much lower*.

Why is this gold-to-silver ratio so important? Because thousands of years of history tell us that a gold-to-silver ratio of 70 to 1 is *dramatically higher* than it should be. Throughout most of human history the ratio has fluctuated between 8 to 1 and 16 to 1. The more common averages have been ratios of 10 to 1 to 12 to 1.

Historians have speculated often on why these ratios persisted for so long, in such a narrow range, but one basic reason is because estimates hold that there are only eleven times as much silver in the mantle of our planet as there is gold. Also, the estimate of total world silver production since 4000 B.C. is 37.45 billion ounces, while it is estimated that the

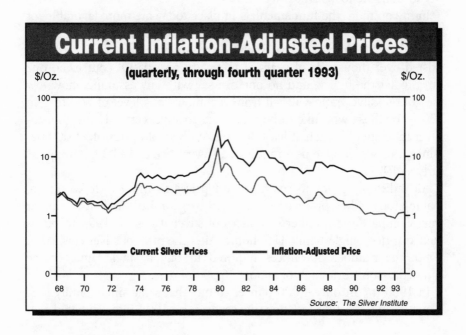

Current Inflation-Adjusted Prices

(quarterly, through fourth quarter 1993)

$/Oz. $/Oz.

Current Silver Prices   Inflation-Adjusted Price

Source: The Silver Institute

235

present world gold stock in all forms is 3.2 billion ounces to 3.5 billion ounces. Thus, we again see a natural ratio—this time comparing supply instead of price—ranging from approximately 10 to 1 to 12 to 1.

This estimation of the historical production of gold and silver, however, does not account for the fact that large amounts of silver are lost or consumed in industrial uses such as photography. The Silver Institute estimates that total world silver stocks of only 19 billion ounces *still exist,* compared to the estimated above-ground gold stocks in all forms of 3.2 billion ounces to 3.5 billion ounces, which yield a gold-to-silver ratio of 5.95 to 1 to 5.44 to 1. Only twice in more than eight hundred years of recorded history did the ratio reach 100 to 1. One of those times was in 1991, and the ratio has been sliding ever since. *I believe that the gold-to-silver ratio will drop to approximately 15 to 1 between now and the late 1990s.*

I also believe that the price of gold will reach, and perhaps exceed, $1,500 per ounce, giving us the potential for a silver price of $100 per ounce. That may seem extreme to some precious metals analysts, but at the peak of the market in 1980, gold topped out at $850, with silver at $50, yielding a gold-to-silver ratio of 17 to 1. If gold climbs to $1,500 by the late 1990s—and I believe it will—that same ratio we saw in 1980 would translate to a silver price of $88.

In my opinion, the fundamentals in place today are more favorable for silver than for gold. It is conceivable that the gold-to-silver ratio could go lower than 15 to 1, perhaps reaching the average ratio of 12 to 1 that existed over thousands of years of monetary history. Of course, no one can predict the future, and no one can say with any assurance how low the gold-to-silver ratio will fall from the anomalous level of 100 to 1 in 1991. For those who like to be more conservative, certainly the gold-to-silver ratio should reach at least 30 to 1. With a gold price of $1,000 per ounce, this would give us an indicated silver price of $33.33, perhaps as early as 1997.

All indicators point to soaring silver prices as the decade wears on, making today's low prices an exceptional bargain. Let's look at it another way: Compare the number of ounces of silver it cost in 1993 to buy a median-price, single-family U.S. home. After the price of silver crashed in 1980, the number of ounces required to buy a single-family home climbed to a historic high of almost 26,000 ounces.

In 1980 it cost only 4,000 ounces to buy that same single-family U.S. home. Using a mildly inflationary scenario, by 1998 it is estimated that the average single-family home will cost $134,137. But with silver prices on the rise, it is likely that once again you will be able to buy that home for 5,000 ounces of silver, which indicates a silver price of $26.83.

In short, by every analysis, today's silver prices represent a historic value. Or to put it another way, silver is cheap—and the smartest investors buy when an investment is cheap. It sounds silly to point out such an obvious investment truth. But history shows that only a very elite group of investors has ever been able to apply this simple wisdom to the markets.

NEW TECHNOLOGICAL DEVELOPMENTS IN PHOTOGRAPHY WILL *HELP* THE PRICE OF SILVER

In all the years I have followed silver during silver bull markets, the silver bears repeatedly refer to a great myth: New technological developments in photography will eventually replace silver-based film. As a silver bull holding for the long term, be prepared to hear this same myth repeated time and again. The simple fact is that new developments in photography will *help* the price of silver, not hurt it. At the Silver Institute's annual meeting in 1993, Paul Ward, laboratory manager of the imaging division for photography at Eastman Kodak, said, *"Silver will never be replaced as the material of choice for high-quality photographic imaging."*

In fact, Ward pointed out that electronic imaging will actually increase the use of silver in photography. Kodak and other major producers of photographic products have so many silver halide-based innovations in the pipeline that we can expect a dramatic increase in silver use for photography.

Another future boost to silver prices comes from Polaroid, the world's leader in instant photography. They have introduced a new product line that will dramatically increase the use of silver-halide film. In the 1950s and 1960s, Polaroid cameras were all the rage and were commonplace in the American household,. But by the 1970s and 1980s, the popularity of 35mm point-and-shoot cameras decreased the demand for instant photography.

Now another major change has come about. By 1989, Polaroid instant camera sales reached 1.4 million units, and by 1991 they had grown to 2 million units, the first increase since 1978. The innovative new Polaroid

Captiva instant camera has met with overwhelming success, and it now appears that the future of instant photography is assured. Remember, all of the silver used in instant photography film is permanently consumed.

Finally, the free market revolution in emerging nations and the high economic growth rates associated with this trend toward market capitalism are opening up massive new demands for silver halide film. Billions of individuals in Asia will soon have the wealth to buy cameras, and that will mean new demand in the hundreds of millions of ounces for silver film by the end of the 1990s. Soon the market will recognize that new technological developments in photography will be very bullish for silver, not bearish.

THE SOARING DEMAND FOR SILVER JEWELRY

Over the past several decades, gold was the preferred precious metal for jewelry. That trend has shifted as one of the biggest factors now driving the price of silver is the incredible new growth for silver use for jewelry and silverware.

In 1980, the worldwide use of silver for jewelry and silverware was 49 million ounces. Demand for silver jewelry and silverware remained fairly stable, at about 50 million ounces a year, until 1986, when the total demand for silver jewelry and silverware started to skyrocket. By 1993, 221.6 million ounces of silver were used in jewelry and silverware manufacturing in countries where detailed statistics were available. Between 1985 and 1993 demand increased by an astonishing 443 percent, and the trend continues to accelerate.

Due primarily to higher economic growth rates in Third World countries, particularly in Asia, silver consumption in the form of jewelry and silverware increased 82.3 percent from 1992 to 1993 alone. The most dramatic story comes from India, where the combination of strong economic growth and reduced government import regulations saw the demand for jewelry and silverware climb from 30.5 million ounces in 1992 to 86.8 million ounces in 1993—a gain of nearly 185 percent!

Silver jewelry and silverware demand rose 37 percent worldwide in 1993. In fact, for the first time since detailed records have been kept, jewelry and silverware surpassed photography as the single largest category of demand, representing 33 percent of total world silver usage.

238

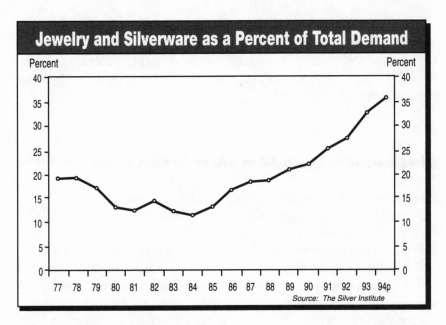

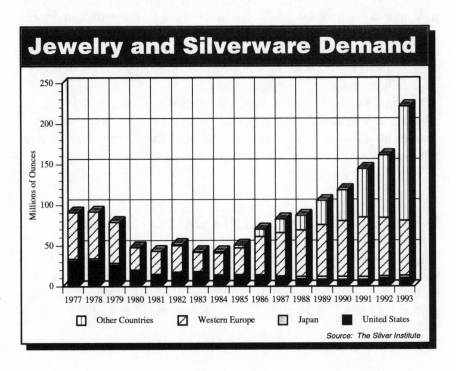

The stronger economic growth rates of Europe and North America are estimated to increase the use of photography by 4.3 percent in 1994, but the demand for silver jewelry and silverware is estimated to surge again, from 221.6 million ounces to 260 million ounces, a very healthy increase of approximately 18 percent.

SILVER MINE PRODUCTION FALLS SHARPLY

After a historic bear market collapse of silver prices from $50 to $3.50, one would expect a corresponding drop in silver mine production. And such has indeed been the case. In 1993, primary silver mine production decreased worldwide by 8.9 percent, falling dramatically from a total of 114.9 million ounces in 1987 to 74.7 million ounces in 1993. There is little prospect that this negative silver mine production trend will reverse anytime soon.

Examples of dramatic drops and primary silver mine production from 1987 to 1993 from the world's four largest silver producers are as follows: In Mexico, a fall from 29.3 million ounces in 1987 to 24.4 million ounces in 1993; in Peru, a dramatic drop from 17.2 million ounces to 7.1 million ounces; a huge drop in Canada from 13.3 million ounces to 5.4 million ounces; and a decrease in the United States from 23.9 million ounces to 18.5 million ounces.

This trend will not reverse itself until the price of silver is dramatically higher and the world's major mining companies start paying attention once again to silver. However, even when such commitments to new mines are made, it takes years for them to come into production.

THE WILD CARD: INVESTMENT DEMAND FOR SILVER

One reason why the prospects for silver are so exciting is because the market is absolutely *tiny* compared to other investment markets. The *daily* trading volume for commodities and currencies is $1 trillion. The total investment coinage demand for silver was less than $200 million *in all of 1993!*

In 1992, when silver prices reached historic lows, investment demand

240

had deteriorated to only 30 million ounces. This compares to investment demand in 1979 of more than 300 million ounces. Although the price of silver has clearly bottomed, there is yet to be a significant increase in silver investment demand.

In 1993–94 we saw a new trend toward large institutional investors becoming interested in silver bullion, futures, and options. This trend is at least partially reflected in the futures markets statistics: Trading volume on the New York Comex rose more than 28 percent in 1993, with the equivalent of an astonishing 25.3 *billion* ounces changing hands over the course of the year. This was the highest level of trading activity since 1984.

There also has been a resurgence of strong physical domestic demand from investors in the Middle East, India, Europe, and the United States. But these are the very early stages of an epic, multiyear bull market in silver and is just a prelude to soaring interest as the price rises and attracts attention from both investors and speculators. This is all the more important since there is already a deficit in 1994 of 248.4 million ounces and an estimated deficit projected for 1995 that could exceed 300 million ounces.

When billions of investment dollars start flowing into the tiny silver market, prices will quickly soar to $10 to $12 per ounce, on the way to much higher levels. Even if there was little investment demand for silver, the extremely favorable supply/demand statistics would be enough to double or possibly triple the silver price within the next three to five years.

That's exciting. But the truly fantastic upside potential in silver will be realized when investors flood the market.

It will take a price of $10 per ounce to bring out 541 million ounces of silver from above ground silver stocks worldwide. That is just $5.4 billion at $10 silver, a drop in the bucket compared to world bond, equity, commodity, and currency markets. But even at a price of $20 per ounce, only 12 percent of the available above-ground stocks of silver would be available to the marketplace.

In fact, the tiny silver market compared to potential investor demand is like a small door for a large crowd. When silver investment and monetary demand begin to grow, this large and determined crowd trying to force its way through the silver market's tiny door will mean that the price of silver will have to rise dramatically to let them all through. But when this determined crowd panics toward the silver door, they will knock it off its hinges and blast out part of the wall, just as they did in 1980, when silver soared to $50 in the wildest investment ride of this century.

It is going to happen again, and this time more dramatically than in 1980. All you have to do is have the courage and conviction to stay with the long-term trend and wait for the silver buying panic of the late 1990s.

CHINA

The biggest surprise in the silver market of the late 1990s will be Chinese demand. When gold began to soar from its bottom in 1993, one of the major reasons was the huge increase in Chinese demand. With an estimated 1.2 billion to 1.7 billion people, and economic growth exploding at rates ranging from 15.0 percent to 19.5 percent, China remains the big story for the gold market. Inflation in rural China is soaring at 30 percent. Since 1978, Chinese per capita Gross Domestic Product has multiplied 400 percent and is accelerating at a rapid pace. Huge amounts of wealth are being created in China, where the people boast a savings rate of 30 percent of their annual income.

China is fast becoming a global superpower. And while everyone seems to be paying attention to the dramatic growth in gold demand in China, the traditional money in the nation has always been *silver,* not gold. Late in 1994, I received reports from China indicating that peasants were using silver not only for savings but also for their larger monetary transactions. For very tiny transactions they use, of all things, Marlboro cigarettes. It is still hard to find Chinese silver import statistics, and it is likely that the silver that was hidden and buried after the Communist revolution is now providing the peasants with money and a means of savings. However, as more than 1 billion Chinese peasants benefit from the rapid economic growth in China, the historical use for silver as money and a store of savings will mean the importation of huge amounts of new silver into the nation.

But the real story behind the dramatic increase in demand for silver in China are the huge quantities of silver that will be required to meet consumer and industrial demand during the country's rapid economic growth during the rest of the 1990s. From fax machines to telephones to refrigerators to televisions and automobiles, the historic growth in Chinese wealth will require *huge* quantities of silver. Based solely on its population of 1.2 billion, the Chinese, at the present level of American silver use, would need about 0.5 ounce of silver per person per year, which translates to nearly *610 million ounces per year!*

WHY SILVER, THE "POOR MAN'S GOLD," IS LIKELY TO OUTPERFORM GOLD

For years silver has been called the "poor man's gold." The gold-to-silver ratio in this century has ranged from 16 to 1 to over 100 to 1, so silver has always been somewhat cheap in price (if not value) compared to gold. Thus the phrase "poor man's gold." But does the fact that silver is somewhat inexpensive compared with gold really mean anything for future silver prices?

First, as we discussed earlier, the gold-to-silver ratio has now technically turned dramatically in favor of silver, leading investors to realize that silver is undervalued. This alone is likely to cause the price of silver to increase at a more rapid rate than gold. But there is more to the story. As we have seen in stock bull markets, low-priced stocks tend to increase at a more rapid rate percentagewise compared with blue-chip stocks. Similar to low-priced stocks, silver usually makes greater percentage moves, in both bull and bear markets, than gold. So in a precious metals bull market, silver is seen as the "cheaper" of the two metals and is the one that attracts higher investor demand.

So in a practical sense, the term "poor man's gold" simply means that many investors, particularly small investors, would rather own a thousand 1-ounce silver coins than approximately fifteen 1-ounce gold coins. In other words, when the final blowoff stage of this bull market occurs and great hordes of small investors are stampeding into the "poor man's gold," silver prices will explode to unrealistic levels. And that is the time when we should be selling to the mob.

SILVER, THE DISAPPEARING METAL

From 1950 to 1994 on average there has been a huge and increasing deficit of silver supplies compared to silver demand.

243

This silver supply gap has been met by a massive drawdown of above-ground silver stocks. For example, in the ten years from 1959 to 1968, the U.S. Treasury stock of silver dropped from an enormous hoard of 2.2 *billion* ounces (65,310 tons) to an extremely small stockpile of 209 *million* ounces. This trend has continued. Now the U.S. silver hoard is tiny and has been completely earmarked for use in silver coinage. *By 1996 it is possible that the entire U.S. silver stockpile will be depleted.*

The same phenomenon that has happened in the United States has also occurred around the world. For all practical purposes, no central bank in the world now has any significant silver monetary reserves. This is bullish for silver for two reasons:

First, since these huge government stocks have already been depleted, the annual supply gap in silver (which, as we have seen, is increasing dramatically) can be filled only by attracting above-ground silver from private hands. The vast majority of the silver will not be available for sale until the price reaches dramatically higher levels.

Second, the fact that every nation in the world has sold virtually all of its official reserves of silver means that governments are powerless to control the price of silver, as they can do, at least in the short term, with gold by dumping the yellow metal. So, unlike the gold market, the risk of official government sales of silver is virtually nonexistent.

ECONOMIC AND MONETARY TRENDS

We will see much higher silver prices whether we have inflation or deflation. Even if we have a massive deflation, which I doubt, it would be quickly followed by a period of hyperinflation just as powerful and far-reaching. The more likely outcome is continued depreciation of currencies on a worldwide scale without hyperinflation *or* a massive deflation. This trend of "mild inflation" will cause a continual depreciation of currencies compared to the real money of gold and silver.

All of these economic and monetary trends make a powerful and undeniable case for dramatically higher silver prices during the rest of this decade. You can be among the elite few who will profit from the coming boom in silver prices. But to do so you must act quickly and decisively.

WHAT YOU SHOULD DO NOW

Here is a summary of my specific advice for entering the silver markets now.

Silver Bullion

The first priority for any silver investor should be to have a position in silver bullion and silver bullion coins. For bullion, I suggest the purchase of 100-ounce, .999 fine silver bars. For silver bullion coins, I recommend bags of .900 fine, circulated U.S. silver dimes, quarters, and halves. These "junk" bags are sold in increments of $1,000 face value and can be purchased at a tiny premium above their silver value. In addition, I highly recommend 1-ounce modern silver bullion coins. Among the least expensive are the pure silver *Libertads* produced each year by Mexico and which can also be purchased at a relatively small premium over their silver value.

Silver Numismatic and Seminumismatic Coins

I also strongly recommend the purchase of foreign and U.S. seminumismatic silver coinage such as the silver "dollars" of foreign countries such as Mexico. I especially recommend numismatic, or rare, silver coins such as high-grade Morgan, trade, and Liberty seated U.S. silver dollars, independently certified in MS-65 or higher grade. These top-quality rare coins are a classic, leveraged play on the price of silver. If silver goes up 50 percent, these coins are very likely to go up 100 percent. To check prices, call Jefferson Coin and Bullion at 1-800-593-2584.

Silver Options and Futures

It is true that you can make a lot of money playing the silver options and futures markets. But it is also true that you can lose more money than you actually invest. I would urge most investors *not* to participate in the risky options and futures markets. One exception is if you are a professional trader who thoroughly understands the complicated and risky nature of these markets. The other exception would be if you have a money manager who has an excellent, *long-term* track record in trading silver options and futures.

Again, by and large, I do not recommend this method for most people who are looking to participate in the silver market.

SILVER STOCKS

After you have established a comfortable position in silver bullion and rare silver numismatic coins, I would highly recommend that you buy the pure silver junior mining stocks we have recommended in this book. I especially recommend junior silver mining shares as a highly leveraged silver investment that doesn't have the extreme risk associated with the options and futures markets.

You can buy the silver stocks recommended in this book, but you must remember that there will be new developments in the world of pure silver stocks, and our recommendations will certainly change from time to time. You must keep updated *on a monthly basis* of the latest developments in these stocks: which to take profits on, which new companies to buy, which stocks should be held for the long term, and more.

For twenty-five years, I have been keeping investors up to date on the latest developments in precious metals through *Gold Newsletter*. Through our well-placed contacts and experience in the market, we are often able to give our readers market intelligence that they just won't find anywhere else. For subscription information, call 1-800-877-8847.

THE SILVER TIDE

There is a tide in the affairs of men,
Which, taken at the flood, leads on to fortune;
Omitted, all the voyage of their life
Is bound in shallows and in miseries.

—WILLIAM SHAKESPEARE

At no time in recent memory has it been as vitally important for investors to step back and take a hard, objective look at the big picture in the silver market as it is now. Forget about inevitable short-term fluctuations in a bull market. Forget about where silver will be next week or next month. An investment in silver is an investment in the future.

However, you must act now. Tides rise and fall. The silver tide is on the rise, and I hope I have convinced you of the powerful case for investing in silver. But if you are to be a big winner in silver through the rest of the 1990s, you must take the specific actions I have recommended to participate in the bull market.

I have been through three major bull markets before, in which I have made millions of dollars. You now have this same incredible opportunity. I have made the commitment to ride the powerful tide toward historic new prices for silver in the 1990s. And I hope you will join me on this immensely profitable journey.

Appendix 1

Resources

COIN CERTIFICATION SERVICES

The Ancient Coin Certification Service (A.C.C.S.), P.O. Box 5004, Chatsworth, CA 91313-5004; tel. (818) 993-7363 or fax (818) 993-6119. The expertise of author and numismatist David Sear.

Numismatic Guaranty Corporation (NGC), P.O. Box 1776, Parsipanny, NJ 07054; tel. (201) 984-6222.

Professional Coin Grading Service (PCGS), P.O. Box 9458, Newport Beach, CA 92658; tel. (800) 447-8848. You can call for a referral to the PCGS dealer nearest you.

TECHNICAL ANALYSIS

The Elliott Wave Theorist, P.O. Box 1618, Gainesville, GA 30505; tel. (404) 536-0309. Subscriptions are $233 per year; two-month trial, $55. Telephone hot line, $377/per year.

SILVER STOCKBROKERS

The following specialize in precious metals mining stocks:

Glenn Dobbs, National Securities, Box 119-B South Shore Drive, Chelan, WA 98816; tel. (800) 826-2633 or (509) 587-9564.

Charles "Berry" Huelsman III, Paulson Investment Co., Inc., 4773 Falls View Drive West, Linn, OR 97068-3520; tel. (800) 433-6115 or (503) 657-3340.

Ben Johnson, First Securities Northwest, 111 S.W. 5th, Suite 4180, Portland, OR 97204; tel. (800) 547-4898.

Rick Rule, Torrey Pines Securities, 7770 El Camino Real, Carlsbad, CA 92009; tel. (800) 477-7853.

SILVER OPTIONS, FUTURES, AND MANAGED ACCOUNTS

Fox Investments, 141 West Jackson Boulevard, Suite 1800A, Chicago, IL 60604; tel. (800) 621-0265 or (312) 341-7300. Attention: Susan Rutsen, Steve Belmont, or Bob Meier. This brokerage team has thirty-seven years' combined experience in buying silver from exchanges and customizing silver futures and options strategies for all types of investors. Client support includes two newsletters, special silver alerts, and a toll-free hot line.

NEWSLETTERS

Freemarket Gold and Money Report (James Turk), P.O. Box 4634, Greenwich, CT 06830; 20 letters per year; $180. Clear, thorough, original economic analysis concentrating on gold, silver, and other money. This newsletter ranks first class anywhere in the world. Gives specific trades with specific entry and exit points and stops.

Gold Newsletter, 2400 Jefferson Highway, Suite 600, Jefferson, LA 70121; tel. (800) 877-8847; $79 for one year, $49 for six months, payable to Jefferson Financial, Inc. For twenty-three years *Gold Newsletter* has served the hard-money markets. Examines both long- and short-term market swings through the eyes of Publisher and Editor-in-Chief James Blanchard and his multitude of precious-metals contacts around the globe. Indispensable.

Mineral Industry Surveys, U.S. Department of the Interior Bureau of Mines, 810 7th Street, NW, Washington, DC 80241. Statistics on silver production.

The Moneychanger, P.O. Box 341753, Memphis, TN 38184-1753; tel. (901) 853-6136; $95 per year; monthly. Franklin Sanders' newsletter, which states its goal: "Our purpose is to help Christians prosper with their morals intact in an age of moral and monetary chaos." Eclectic; covers world events, gold and silver, alternative health, and more. Write for sample.

Silver 2000, P.O. Box 268031, Chicago, IL 60626. For samples tel. (312) 341-5845 or fax (312) 341-7556.

The Silver Institute Letter, The Silver Institute, 1112 16th Street, NW, Suite

240, Washington, DC 20036; tel. (202) 835-0185. Current developments in the silver market and silver usage.

Statistics from the Bureau of Mines, U.S. Department of the Interior, Bureau of Mines, 810 7th Street, NW, Washington, DC 80241. Write for listing of publications available.

Steve Puetz (pronounced "Pitts"), 1105 Sunset Court West, Lafayette, ID 47906. Six months for $90; newsletter only. Six months for $300; newsletter and telephone consultations. Puetz was one of the few analysts who called the 1987 stock market crash. General economic analysis with thought-provoking reader interchange. Especially helpful with statistics and their interpretation; invaluable thinker.

Tony Henfrey's Gold Letter, P.O. Box 26796, Hout Bay 7800, South Africa. One of the oldest precious metals advisory services, featuring extensive, and very long-term technical analysis of silver and other key markets.

SILVER MINING ANALYSTS AND CONSULTANTS

William R. Green, 905 W. Riverside, Suite 311, Spokane, WA 99201; tel. (509) 838-6050. Mr. Green is a licensed professional mining engineer and Ph.D. geologist with more than thirty years' experience in the mining industry. He is a consulting independent analyst of mining securities for stockbrokers, money managers, and individual investors.

PHYSICAL SILVER PURCHASES

Jefferson Coin and Bullion, 2400 Jefferson Highway, Jefferson, LA 70121; tel. (800) 877-8847 or (504) 837-3033.

SILVER STORAGE AND CERTIFICATE PROGRAMS

Jefferson Coin and Bullion, 2400 Jefferson Highway, Jefferson, LA 70121; tel. (800) 877-8847 or (504) 837-3033.

Monex Deposit Company, 4910 Birch Street, Newport Beach, CA 92660; tel. (800) 854-3361 or (714) 752-1400.

Wilmington Trust Company Precious Metals Services, Rodney Square N., 1100 N. Market Street, Wilmington, DE 19890-0001; tel. (800) 223-1080 or (302) 651-8033.

Appendix 2

Model Legal-Tender Act for State Legislatures*

AN ACT relating to legal tender. BE IT ENACTED BY THE LEGISLATURE OF THE STATE OF _____:

SECTION 1. The Legislature of the State of _____ finds and declares that the State is experiencing an economic crisis of severe magnitude caused in large part by the unconstitutional substitution of Federal Reserve notes for silver and gold coin as legal tender in this State. The Legislature also finds and declares that immediate exercise of the power of the State of _____ reserved under Article I, Section 10, Clause 1 of the United States Constitution, and by the Tenth Amendment thereto, is necessary to protect the safety, health, and welfare of the people of this state, by

---

* *Reprinted from Dr. Edwin Vieira, Jr.,* Constitutional Authority of the States and the President to Intervene on Behalf of Sound Money, *with permission of Committee for Monetary Research and Education, P.O. Box 1630, Greenwich, CT 06836.*

guaranteeing to them a constitutional and economically sound monetary system.

SECTION 2. For the purposes of this Act,

(a) The term "State" shall include the State of _____ and all executive and administrative departments and agencies, courts, instrumentalities, and political subdivisions thereof, and all elected and appointed officials, employees, and agents thereof acting in their official capacities; and

(b) the term "silver and gold coin" shall include

(1) the silver and gold coins of the United States coined or minted, or such silver and gold coins of any foreign nation adopted as money of the United States, by authority of Congress pursuant to Article I, Section 8, Clause 5 of the United States Constitution; and

(2) all new certificates of the United States issued by authority of Congress pursuant to Article I, Section 8, Clause 5 of the United States Constitution, which certificates are in law and in fact redeemable on demand in silver and gold coin at their face values; but

(3) in no case whatsoever any note, obligation, security, bill of credit, or other form or species of paper currency or other instrument or document intended to circulate as money emitted or issued

(A) by the United States or any department, agency, or officer thereof, or

(B) by the Federal Reserve System or any board, committee, member bank, instrumentality, official, or agent thereof.

SECTION 3. On and after the effective date of this Act, this State shall not recognize, employ, or compel any person or entity to recognize or employ any thing other than silver and gold coin as a legal tender in payment of any debt arising out of

(a) taxation by the State, where the applicable authority for the tax shall mandate the calculation and payment thereof in silver and gold coin;

(b) expropriation of private property pursuant to exercise of the power of eminent domain by the State or by any entity privileged by the laws thereof to exercise such power;

(c) judgments, decrees, or orders of any court or administrative agency of this State in civil or criminal actions or proceedings, except where and only to the extent that the court or agency granting such award shall find, on the basis of clear and convincing evidence, that payment of silver and gold coin shall not constitute just compensation for the damages suffered by the prevailing party, and therefore shall mandate

(1) specific performance of a contract or agreement by other than the payment of money,

(2) specific restitution of identifiable property other than money, or

(3) other like relief; and

(d) contracts or agreements for the payment of wages, salaries, fees, or other monetary compensation to any person, corporation, or other entity who or which shall provide goods or services to the State in aid of performance of its governmental functions.

SECTION 4. The unit and measure for determining what shall constitute legal tender in payment of any debt specified in Section 3 hereof shall be the standard silver dollar, containing 371.25 grains (troy) fine silver, as coined or minted by authority of Congress from time to time pursuant to Article I, Section 8, Clause 5 of the United States Constitution.

SECTION 5. The value of any silver and gold coin as a legal tender in payment of any debt specified in Section 3 hereof shall be denominated in "dollars" ($), such denomination to be calculated as follows:

(a) the value of any silver coin shall be calculated by dividing the weight of fine silver in grains (troy) that the said coin shall contain by 371.25 grains, and expressing the quotient in "dollars";

(b) the value of any gold coin shall be calculated by multiplying the weight of fine gold in grains (troy) that the said coin shall contain by the proportion of weight between silver and gold as determined by the Treasurer of the State of _____ as provided herein, dividing the product of such multiplication by 371.25 grains, and expressing the quotient in "dollars"; and

(c) at the beginning of each business day, the Treasurer of the State of _____ shall determine the average proportion by weight by which gold exchanges against silver in the major precious-metals market or markets in the State of _____, and

(1) shall immediately make available such determination to any person upon request, without charge; and

(2) shall permanently certify and record such determination.

SECTION 6. On and after the effective date of this Act, the State shall denominate all public accounts, and record the value of all public assets and liabilities, in standard silver dollars.

SECTION 7. If any provision of this act or its application to any person or circumstance is held invalid, the remaining provisions of the Act or their applications to other persons or circumstances shall not be affected.

Appendix 3

Recent Silver Charts

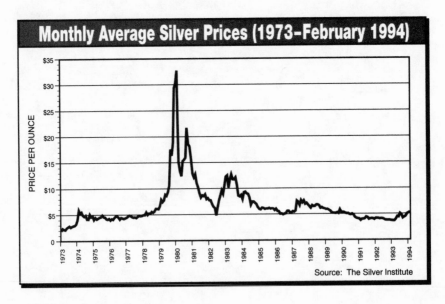

Monthly Average Silver Prices (1973–February 1994)

Source: The Silver Institute

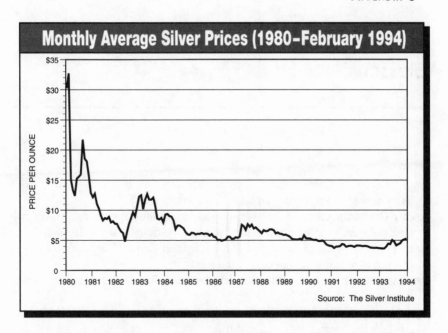

Monthly Average Silver Prices (1980–February 1994)

Source: The Silver Institute

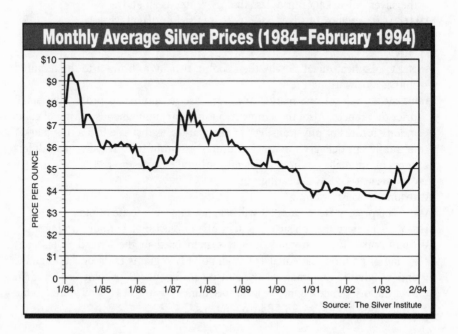

Monthly Average Silver Prices (1984–February 1994)

Source: The Silver Institute

Glossary

ABOUT GOOD A numismatic coin grade indicating the most heavily worn, with lettering and legends worn smooth. Abbreviated AG-3.

ABOUT UNCIRCULATED A numismatic coin grade indicating a coin with small traces of wear visible on the highest parts of the design. Abbreviated AU.

ACID TEST Test for silver or gold content by applying acid or combinations of acids to determine the fineness of the metal.

ACTUALS A physical commodity ready for immediate delivery, as opposed to futures contracts.

Ag Chemical symbol for silver. From the Latin word for silver, *argentum,* from an Indo-European root word that means "brilliant" or "shining."

ALLOY *Verb:* to mix a base metal into silver, usually to harden it. *Noun:* a mixture of silver with some base metal or metals; also, the metal used to alloy the silver. Silver of a purity less than .999 fine is an alloy.

AMALGAM An alloy of silver with mercury used in dental work.

AMALGAMATION A process for extracting silver from ore by dissolving in mercury.

ANNEAL To heat metal slowly, then cool it, usually to bring it to the required softness for working.

ARBITRAGE Sale in one market and purchase in another to profit from small price differences. Also, the simultaneous or near simultaneous buying of commodity futures or physical silver in one market against sale in another market or a different delivery month (for futures) to profit from usually small differences or anomalies in price. Generally arbitrage carries no risk.

ARGENTIFEROUS Silver-bearing ore.

ARGYRIA Silver poisoning.

ASK The price at which a seller will sell. *See* offer. Opposite of bid.

ASSAY To determine the silver content of an object by laboratory testing.

AVOIRDUPOIS The customary weight system used in the United States consisting of pounds that equal 16 ounces of 437.5 grains each, or 7,000 grains and weighs 453.6 grams. Troy ounces are about 10 percent *heavier* than avoirdupois ounces. One avoirdupois ounce = 0.91145 troy ounce. One avoirdupois pound = 14.583 troy ounces.

BACKWARDATION   The reversal of the normal price differential between nearby and forward commodity futures contracts. Normally the forward contracts (those more distant in time) carry a premium to the nearby month. Usually caused by a squeeze or shortage of silver for immediate delivery. Opposite of contango.

BAG   The normal trading lot for U.S. and Canadian silver coins consisting of $1,000 face value in coins. Bags may be quoted at full price (e.g., $3,700 in paper money for a $1,000 bag) or in "times face value" (e.g., 3.7 times face value).

BAG MARKS   Small rubs or abrasions on uncirculated silver coins that occur while they are in mint bags.

BANK CREDIT MONEY   Money (such as ours) based on credit extended by private or central banks. *See* fiat money.

BANKNOTES   Bank obligations to pay a certain amount of money, which circulate as money substitutes. Formerly banknotes were payable in gold or silver coins, now only in other banknotes.

BASE METALS   All nonprecious metals (i.e., all metals but gold, silver, and platinum).

BEAR   One who looks for silver prices to decline. A bear market is a market trending significantly downward over a long time. To be bearish on the market means to expect lower prices. A pessimist.

BID   Price a buyer will pay to purchase a commodity or futures contract. Opposite of ask.

BILLON   A silver alloy used in coinage that contains less than 50 percent silver and more than 50 percent base metal. Typically billon is 20 percent silver or less. Pronounced BILL-en.

BIMETALLISM   A monetary standard under which the monetary unit of account is defined in both gold and silver and under which both are full legal tenders.

BIT   American name for the Spanish *real,* equal to 12.5 cents. The Spanish pieces of eight were coins of eight *reales* or bits. Two bits equal 25 cents, four bits equal 50 cents, etc.

BRITANNIA SILVER   A standard for silverware in Britain consisting of 95.83 percent pure silver.

BULL   One who looks for silver prices to rise. A bull market is a market trending significantly upward over a long time. To be bullish on the market means to expect higher prices. An optimist.

BULLION   Uncoined silver, usually 99.5 percent pure or purer.

BULLION VALUE   The current market value of the silver contained in a silver coin or object. *See* melt value.

CARRY   *See* contango.

CASH COST OF PRODUCTION   The cost to a silver mine of producing an ounce of silver, including smelting and refining charges and byproduct credits, before depreciation, depletion expense, and financing charges.

Cash Market The market in which physical silver is actually bought and sold. Also called the spot market because the full cash price must be paid "on the spot."

Central Bank A government-mandated (but usually privately owned) monopoly that controls a national economy by controlling the supply of imaginary (fiat) money and the interest rate.

Certified Coin A coin that has been certified as to authenticity and grade by a coin certification service. Also called a slabbed coin because it is ultrasonically sealed in a plastic slab.

Clipping Cutting off the edges of silver coins, a common method of debasement before the introduction of reeding on the edges of coins in about the middle of the seventeenth century.

Cob Rough silver coins minted in Spanish America before the introduction of "milling" or minting machinery. Made by sawing a slice of silver off a bar and hand-stamping it with crude dies.

Coin Silver A silver standard consisting of 90 percent pure silver and 10 percent base metal alloy. The standard used for U.S. silver coinage, 1834–1965.

Commercials Dealers in the silver futures market who make the market.

Contango That portion of the price of a silver futures contract in a forward month that exceeds the price of the spot or nearby month, generally reflecting the prevailing rate of interest.

Credit Money *See* debt money.

Crime of '73 Silver protagonists' (Silverites') name for the demonetization of silver by the U.S. Congress in 1873.

Debase To reduce the bullion content of a silver coin while retaining its face or legal tender value.

Debt Money Money that derives its value from an underlying debt obligation. Technically, all the currency and money used in the United States today other than token coinage or, in rare instances, gold and silver coins, is debt money. Debt money includes all bank balances, and may be "backed" by private or government debt. The value of debt money depends wholly on the creditworthiness of the underlying debtor. Same as credit money.

Deflation Technically, a decrease of the money supply or the amount of money in circulation in an economy. Loosely and popularly used to mean a decrease in prices. In modern usage, "money" means the amount of all bank credit and currency. Opposite of inflation. Under deflation the purchasing power of the currency unit steadily increases.

Demonetize To declare by law that a type of money no longer has legal tender status.

DERIVATIVE Financial contracts that derive value not from themselves but from some underlying asset, such as stocks, bonds, currencies, or commodities. Derivatives include forward contracts, futures contracts, and options.

DEVALUATION To redefine legally a monetary unit in terms that lower its value in gold, silver, or foreign exchange.

DOLLAR (1) The money of account of the United States, forever and immutably fixed by Congress (under the authority of the U.S. Constitution at Article I, Section 8, "To coin money, regulate the value thereof . . . and fix the Standard of Weights and Measures") as the standard money of the United States in the Coinage Act of April 2, 1792 (U.S. Statutes at Large, Volume I, page 246) equal to 371.25 grains of fine silver (0.7734 troy ounce). Also, a U.S. coin containing 371.25 grains of fine silver. To speak of "dollars of silver" is to speak of certain measures of silver, like "quarts of milk."

EISENHOWER SILVER DOLLAR Forty percent silver dollar coins issued by the U.S. mint at San Francisco, 1971–76. Contains 0.31625 troy ounce of fine silver.

ELASTICITY The responsiveness of supply or demand for a good price. Goods that respond strongly to changes in price are *price elastic*. Goods which do not respond strongly to changes in price are *price inelastic*.

ELECTRUM A naturally occurring mixture of gold and silver, from which coins were made in ancient times.

EPITHERMAL DEPOSITION Characteristic of silver's frequency of occurrence in the earth's crust that concentrates the richest silver finds near the surface of the earth. Epithermal deposition generally means that the deeper a mine goes, the poorer the silver ore will be.

FACE VALUE The monetary denomination stamped or printed on a coin or note that declares its value in terms of the legally established monetary unit.

FIAT MONEY Money that has no value in itself or as a commodity but that is decreed by law to be legal tender. From the Latin *fiat*, "let there be." Money is created out of thin air. Pronounced FEE-aht.

FINE OUNCE One troy ounce of pure silver, 480 grains or 1.0917 avoirdupois ounces or 31.1034 grams.

FINENESS The purity of an object containing precious metals. Usually expressed in parts per thousand. Sterling silver is 925/1000, .925, or 92.5 percent fine silver.

FINE SILVER Pure silver, usually 99.9 percent or 99.99 percent pure.

FLOAT The number of a company's shares outstanding. The bigger the float, the slower the price can rise, other things being equal.

FORTIES U.S. silver half dollars minted 1965 through 1970 that are 40 percent pure silver by weight and contain 0.295 troy ounce of fine silver per dollar face value or 295 troy ounces per $1,000 face value bag.

FORWARD SELLING An agreement by a silver producer to deliver a certain amount of production at a specified date in the future at a specific price.

FREE COINAGE   A law allowing owners of silver bullion to deposit their bullion with the mint and receive back the full weight of the bullion in silver coin.

FREE SILVER MOVEMENT   Political movement of the latter nineteenth century advocating the free coinage of silver dollars. *See* Silverites.

FUNDAMENTAL ANALYSIS   Market analysis that examines primarily physical supply and demand factors for silver and relies on the presumption that these factors alone move markets.

GERMAN SILVER   Alloy containing little or no silver.

GOOD DELIVERY BARS   Silver bars weighing 1,000 ounces, plus or minus 6 percent, with a fineness of 9990/9999 and which are accepted for delivery on the commodity futures exchanges.

GOLD–SILVER RATIO   The ratio of the price of gold to the price of silver, calculated by dividing gold's current price by silver's current price.

GO LONG   To buy silver. To be long is to own silver.

GO SHORT   To sell silver. To be short is to have sold silver.

GRAIN   The smallest unit of avoirdupois and troy weight, the same in both systems, equal to 0.0648 gram.

GRESHAM'S LAW   A principle of economics that says bad money drives good money out of circulation. It also applies *relatively*—that is, cheaper money drives more expensive money out of circulation. In a monetary system that uses both gold and silver, when the *legal* value differs from the actual *market* value of the two metals, the cheaper will drive the more expensive out of circulation.

HALLMARK   A stamp or mark on silver objects indicating fineness, maker, year of manufacture, place of manufacture, etc.

HEDGE   To protect oneself from price rises or drops by selling or buying an offsetting amount of silver or silver futures contracts. Examples: If you own 5,000 ounces of physical silver, you can hedge it by selling a 5,000 silver futures contract. If you are short a 5,000-ounce contract on the futures exchange, you can hedge it by buying 5,000 ounces of physical silver.

INFLATION   Technically, any increase of the amount of money in circulation in an economy. If the money supply increases faster than the supply of goods and services increase, then prices will rise. Loosely and popularly used to mean any increase in prices. In modern usage, "money" means the amount of all bank credit and currency. Opposite of deflation. Under inflation the purchasing power of the currency unit steadily declines.

INTRINSIC VALUE   The commodity value of a silver coin. Also used to compare silver money to debt or fiat money, since silver money has a value *in itself,* whereas the value of debt money depends on the creditworthiness of the underlying debt instrument and fiat money depends on the force of the state.

IRREDEEMABLE   The adjective defining the legal *inability* to exchange paper currency for a fixed amount of precious metals coins or bullion.

JUNK COINS   U.S. 90 percent silver dimes, quarters, or halves minted from 1854 to 1965. Junk coins contain 715 troy ounces per $1,000 face value bag or 0.715 troy ounce per dollar face value.

LEGAL TENDER   Whatever the law declares that creditors must accept in payment of debts *for which payment is not otherwise specified.* At present in the United States it is possible to *contract* out of the legal tender system if a contract or agreement specifies payment in a certain medium. If no medium of payment is specified, the creditor must accept legal tender in full satisfaction of the debt.

LEVERAGE   A financial arrangement in which the amount of money invested produces a return or loss *greater than* 1 to 1. A 10 percent margin payment when you buy a 5,000-ounce futures contract increases leverage tenfold. For every 20 percent that silver's price rises, your investment doubles or increases ten times as much. If you made a 5 percent margin payment, every 20 percent increase in silver's price would increase *fourfold,* or twenty times. Leverage is the mathematical reciprocal of the margin—that is, a 1/10 (10 percent) margin results in a tenfold (10/1) leverage, and 1/20 (5 percent) results in a twentyfold (20/1) leverage. Leverage *multiplies losses in exactly the same way it multiplies gains.*

LONG   To own silver, silver futures contracts, or silver call options. To "go long" is to buy silver in some form. To "be long" is to own silver in some form. A long position is a bullish position.

MARGIN   The percent of an investment's value that you must deposit with the broker when you buy the investment on partial credit. Synonymous with "down payment" or "deposit," except the margin must be increased or decreased with changes in the value of the investment. Usually 2 to 5 percent of the value of the entire contract. *See variation margin.*

MARGINAL MONETARY DEMAND   The demand for silver *at the margin* of the market—that is, the last unit demanded.

MARGIN CALL   A call from your broker informing you that the market value of your investment has dropped below its original value and you must deposit additional money (variation margin) to maintain the required balance. If you don't "meet the margin call" (i.e., pay up), the broker will sell out your position.

MARKET CAP or MARKET CAPITALIZATION   Roughly the number of a company's shares outstanding times the share price.

MELT or MARKET VALUE   The bullion value at current silver prices of any object containing silver. Same as bullion value.

METALLIC STANDARD   A money system that defines the monetary unit in terms of an amount of precious metal.

MONETARY DEMAND   As used in this book, demand for silver *as silver,* including monetary, investment, and inflation hedge demand for silver.

MONETARY UNIT   The legally defined unit of the standard money of a nation by which all other monetary units are defined. In the United States the "money of account" and "monetary unit" are legally the dollar, consisting of a weight of 371.25 grains (0.7734 troy ounce) of fine silver.

MONEY   In classical economics any commodity that serves as a standard of value, a medium of exchange, and a store of value. Now loosely used to define anything adopted by a government as money and generally used as a medium of exchange.

MORGAN DOLLARS   U.S. silver dollar coins minted from 1878 to 1904 and in 1921, after the designer, George T. Morgan.

NINETIES   U.S. silver dimes, quarters, and halves minted between 1853 and 1965 and that are 90 percent pure silver by weight. Traded in lots of $1,000 face value called bags containing 715 troy ounces of fine silver.

NOMINAL VALUE   *See* face value.

NUMERAIRE   The currency in which a transaction is denominated.

NUMISMATICS   The study and collection of money, medals, and currency. Numismatic coins are collectors' or rare coins.

OFFER   *See* ask.

OLIGODYNAMIC EFFECT   Describes silver's bactericidal activity, in which a little goes a very long way.

PAPER SILVER   Any silver investment that exists only on paper and/or of which the investor does not take actual physical delivery.

PATENTED CLAIM   A land claim that entitles the owner to both title rights and mineral rights. *See* unpatented claim.

PEACE DOLLARS   U.S. silver dollar coins issued from 1921 to 1935 to commemorate the end of World War I.

PERPETUITY   An unending security or bond upon which no principal is ever paid although the interest continues to be paid.

PIECES OF EIGHT   *Piezas de ocho.* Spanish or Spanish-American silver coins containing about 0.8 troy ounce of silver.

PIXEL   Picture cell, the smallest unit of an electronic or photographic image.

PREMIUM   (1) Price of a put or call option; (2) amount by which the actual cost of a silver item exceeds its bullion or melt value, usually expressed as a percentage.

PROBABLE RESERVES   A portion of a silver deposit for which tonnage and grade are computed partly from specific measurements, partly from sample or production data, and partly from projection for a reasonable distance on geologic evidence.

PROVEN RESERVES   A portion of a silver deposit that has been delineated in three dimensions by excavation or drilling from which the reserves' geological limitations have been determined.

PURITY   The proportion of silver in an object. *See* fineness.

RATIO   *See* gold-silver ratio.

REDEEMABLE   The adjective defining the legal right to exchange paper currency for precious metals coins or bullion.

REEDING   The tiny lines impressed on the edges of silver coins to prevent clipping.

RESERVES   A portion of a silver deposit that has been measured in varying degrees and determined to be mineable, and for which the economical silver yield under existing technological and market conditions has been estimated. *See* proven reserves and probable reserves.

SCOTCH STANDARD   Standard of silver fineness equal to 91.7 percent pure silver, the same percentage fineness as 22-karat gold.

SEIGNIORAGE   The charge made by government for minting coins. The profit from the difference between the *bullion value* and the *face value* of coin. Generally, the profit made by government when the face value of its currency is greater than the cost of producing it.

SHORT   An investor who has sold stocks or commodities that he or she does not actually own is said to be short. To "go short" is to sell without owning, also seen as to "short silver" or "short the market."

SHORT SALE   Selling silver you don't physically own. Loosely, selling silver.

SILVERITES   Late nineteenth-century advocates of the free and unlimited coinage of silver in the United States. *See* free silver movement.

SILVERPLATE   Flatware, holloware, or jewelry of base metal overlaid with a thin layer of silver.

SILVER POINT   The boiling point of silver, 2,212 degrees celsius.

SLABBED COIN   A certified coin—that is, a coin that has been certified as to authenticity and grade by a coin certification service and ultrasonically sealed in a plastic slab.

SPECIE or SPECIE MONEY   Coined money or coins containing gold or silver.

SPECULATE   To buy or sell a stock or commodity involving a substantial risk in the chance (or hope) of making a profit.

SPECULATOR   An investor who buys or sells a stock or commodity with substantial risk in the hope (or chance) of making a profit.

SPOT MARKET   The market in which physical silver is actually bought and sold. The full cash price must be paid "on the spot." Also called the cash market.

SPOT PRICE   The price of silver in the cash market. Sometimes indicates the price of futures contracts for the nearest month trading, the "spot month."

SPREAD   The difference between the price dealers or brokers will pay for silver in any form (their "bid" price) and the price at which they will sell (their "ask" price).

SPREAD TRADING   Buying one commodity futures contract and selling another contract for another delivery month at the same time. Investors also trade the spread between futures and physicals or futures and options. Normally the spread increases in futures contracts as they go out in time. That spread is called the "contango." When a shortage of physical silver ready for immediate delivery happens (a squeeze), the spread can reverse itself (a backwardation), and the nearby or spot month will become more expensive than the distant months.

SQUEEZE   Shortage of silver for immediate delivery on the futures exchange. When a squeeze occurs, the spread (the difference in price between futures contracts of different months) can reverse itself (a backwardation), and the nearby or spot month will become more expensive than the distant months. Squeezes are bad medicine for commercials, the big traders and dealers who make the market. Also called a "short squeeze" because it is the "shorts" in the market who are squeezed.

STERLING   A fineness of silver objects equal to 92.5 percent purity.

STOP-LOSS ORDER   An open order to buy or sell entered in the market that is automatically triggered when a certain price is reached. Used to limit risk and loss.

SUBSIDIARY COIN   A silver coin with a silver value lower than its legal face value. From 1857 through 1965, U.S. dimes, quarters, and halves were subsidiary coins—that is, they contained less silver than their face value indicated. The "dollar" of silver is legally defined as 371.25 grains of fine silver (0.7734 troy ounce), but $1 worth of dimes, quarters, or halves contain only 347.22 grains (0.72338 troy ounce) of fine silver—that is, about 93.5 percent of a dollar.

SUBSTITUTION EFFECT   An economic phenomenon that occurs when consumers substitute a similar, cheaper good for a more expensive good. This effect increases as the price of the primary good increases. When the price of BMWs rise, more people buy Cadillacs. When the price of gold rises, more people buy silver.

SYCEE   Chinese silver ingots shaped like a boat or shoe, used before the introduction of silver coinage in about 1907.

TALE   Count. To accept coins "by tale" is to accept them by count instead of by weight.

TECHNICAL ANALYSIS   Market analysis of price, volume, and other data, based on the assumption that the price of a commodity contains all the information the market possesses about the commodity, as opposed to fundamental analysis, which closely examines physical factors of supply and demand.

TROY WEIGHT   The weight system used to measure precious metals, named for its origin in Troyes, France. The system consists of grains (identical to those of the avoirdupois system), pennyweights (dwt.) of 24 grains each, ounces (20 dwt. or 480 grains), and pounds (12 ounces or 5,760 grains). The troy pound weight is almost never used. One troy ounce equals 1.097 avoirdupois ounces, and 14.583 troy ounces equal 1 avoirdupois pound. *See* avoirdupois.

UNPATENTED CLAIM A land claim that entitles the owner to mineral rights but not title rights. *See* patented claim.

VARIATION MARGIN Additional margin that must be deposited when the value of a silver futures contract declines. *See* margin.

WAR NICKELS U.S. 5-cent pieces minted between 1942 and 1945 and identified by the large P, S, or D mintmark over the dome of Monticello on the reverse. Contain about 1.1 troy ounces of silver per $1 face value.

WAREHOUSE RECEIPT A receipt for silver stored in an approved commodity exchange warehouse, usually banks.

Endnotes

CHAPTER 1—SILVER: THE USEFUL METAL

1. "Silver-Based Water Purification System" (Washington, DC: The Silver Institute, 1993).
2. *World Silver Survey 1993* (Washington, DC: The Silver Institute, 1993), p. 32.
3. *The Silver Institute Letter* (April–May 1992), p. 2.
4. Peter Krause, "Silver-Based Photography, Today and Tomorrow," *World Silver Survey 1992* (Washington, DC: The Silver Institute, 1992), p. 93.
5. Ibid., p. 92.
6. *World Silver Survey 1992,* The Silver Institute, p. 83.
7. Krause, op. cit., pp. 85, 86.

CHAPTER 2—SILVER SUPPLY AND DEMAND

1. *World Silver Survey 1993* (Washington, DC: The Silver Institute, 1993), p. 111.
2. Charles River Associates, *Stocks of Silver Around the World* (Washington, DC: The Silver Institute, 1992), p. 76.
3. Ibid., p. 1.
4. Ibid., p. 7.
5. Ibid., pp. 7, 12.
6. Ibid., p. 1.
7. Ibid., p. 31.
8. Ibid., p. 1.
9. Ibid.
10. *World Silver Survey 1993,* pp. 12, 13.
11. Ibid.
12. Charles River Associates, *Stocks of Silver,* p. 142.

CHAPTER 3—DEMAND EXPLODES IN ASIA

1. *The Economist,* (July 31, 1993), p. 13.
2. *Silver Institute Letter,* (April–May 1992).
3. Charles River Associates, *Stocks of Silver Around the World* (1992), p. 148. Chantilal Sonawala estimates that 3.2 trillion ounces (100,000 tons) of silver remain in India. In the April–May *1992 Silver Institute Letter,* Timothy Green estimates 3.84 billion ounces (117,884 tons).
4. Timothy Green, "India: Silver 1991," *World Silver Survey 1992* (Washington, DC: The Silver Institute, 1992), p. 99.
5. Chester Krause, Clifford Mishler, and Colin Bruce, *Standard Catalog of World Coins* (Iola, WI: Krause Publications, 1985), p. 287 ff.
6. Charles River Associates, *Stocks of Silver,* p. 85.

7. "Hong Kong's Boats Land Best Catches in the 'China Trade,' " *The Wall Street Journal* (January 16, 1981), p. 1.

CHAPTER 4—THE GOLD–SILVER RATIO

1. Charles River Associates, *Stocks of Silver Around the World* (Washington, DC: The Silver Institute, 1992), p. 27.
2. Ibid., p. 2.

CHAPTER 8—COLLECTIBLES, NUMISMATICS, AND THE MATHEMATICS OF SILVER

1. Seymour B. Wyler, *The Book of Old Silver: English, American, Foreign* (New York: Crown Publishers, 1937).
2. Alexander del Mar, *Money and Civilization* (Hawthorne, CA: Omni Publications, 1975; originally published 1886).
3. For a complete treatment of American, English, and foreign hallmarks, see Wyler, *The Book of Old Silver*.
4. Coinage Act of April 2, 1792, Sec. 13. U.S. Statutes at Large, I, 246.
5. Chester Krause, Clifford Mishler, and Colin Bruce, *Standard Catalog of World Coins* (Iola, WI: Krause Publications, 1985), p. 1283 ff.

CHAPTER 12—THE DREAM OF HONEST MONEY AND THE REMONETIZATION OF SILVER

1. Data from the St. Louis Federal Reserve Bank. Figures based on U.S. published bank reserves as of May 1993 and figured as follows: In May 1993, total required reserves for all banks and savings and loans amounted to $55.1 billion. M3 money supply equals M2 money supply plus large-denomination time deposits. In May 1993, M3 was $4.171 trillion. Because M3 includes components that are not bank deposits— $336.5 billion in M2 money market funds, $202.8 billion in M3 money market funds, and $304 billion in M2 currency—these must be subtracted from M3. Net bank deposits for May 1993 amounted to $3.3277 trillion. Total required reserves were $55.1 billion, so the effective reserve requirement was $55.1/$3,327.7, or 1.656 percent. The multiplier is the reciprocal of the reserve requirement, so the multiplier for an effective 1.656 percent reserve requirement is 100/1.656 = 60.3984.
2. G. J. Santoni, *"A Private Central Bank: Some Olde English Lessons,"* review of the Federal Reserve Bank of St. Louis, Vol. 66, No. 4 (April 1984), p. 12 ff.
3. Elgin Groseclose, *Money and Man: A Survey of Monetary Experience* (Norman: University of Oklahoma Press, 1976, 1977), p. 102.

CHAPTER 13—THE BIG PICTURE: BRINGING IT ALL TOGETHER

1. From *American Affairs,* Vol. VII, No. 1 (January 1946), p. 35. The article was originally a paper read before the American Bar Association during the last year of World War II.
2. See Roy W. Jastram, *Silver: The Restless Metal* (New York: John Wiley & Sons, 1981) and *The Golden Constant* (New York: John Wiley & Sons, 1977).
3. Jastram, *Silver: The Restless Metal,* p. 130.
4. Charles River Associates, *Stocks of Silver Around the World* (Washington, DC: The Silver Institute, 1992), p. 167.

Bibliography

AMERICAN INSTITUTE FOR ECONOMIC RESEARCH. *The Pocket Money Book: A Monetary Chronology of the United States.* Great Barrington, MA: AIER, 1989.

BURNS, ARTHUR ROBERT. *Money and Monetary Policy in Early Times.* New York: Augustus M. Kelley, 1965; originally published in 1927.

CASEY, DOUG. *Crisis Investing for the Rest of the '90s.* New York: Birch Lane Press, 1993.

CHAMBERLAIN, C. C., AND REINFELD, FRED. *Coin Dictionary and Guide.* New York: Sterling Publishing Company, 1960.

CHARLES RIVER ASSOCIATES. *Stocks of Silver Around the World.* Washington, D.C.: The Silver Institute, 1992.

COFFIN, GEORGE MATHEWES. *Silver from 1849 to 1892.* New York: Greenwood Press, Publishers, 1969; originally published in 1892 by McGill & Wallace.

COOGAN, GERTRUDE M. *Money Creators.* Hawthorne, CA: Omni Publications, 1982; originally published in 1935.

DEL MAR, ALEXANDER. *Ancient Britain Revisited.* Hawthorne, CA: The Christian Book Club of America, 1973; originally published in 1899.

———. *Barbara Villiers: or, A History of Monetary Crimes.* Hawthorne, CA: Omni Publications, 1983; originally published in 1899.

———. *A History of Monetary Systems.* New York: Augustus M. Kelley, 1969; originally published in London by Effingham Wilson, 1895.

———. *The History of Money in America from the Earliest Times to the Establishment of the Constitution.* Hawthorne, CA: Omni Publications, 1966, 1979; originally published in 1899.

———. *A History of the Precious Metals from the Earliest Times to the Present.* New York: Augustus M. Kelley, 1969; originally published in 1880, second edition in New York by the Cambridge Encyclopedia Company, 1902.

———. *Money and Civilization.* Hawthorne, CA: Omni Publications, 1975; originally published in 1886.

———. *The Science of Money.* Hawthorne, CA: Omni Publications, 1967; originally published in 1885.

EMERY, SARAH E. V. *Seven Financial Conspiracies Which Have Enslaved the American People.* Elburn, IL: Educational and Research Library, n.d.; originally published in 1887.

EVEREST, ALLAN SEYMOUR. *Morgenthau, the New Deal, and Silver: A Story of Pressure Politics.* New York: Columbia University Press, 1950.

FARMER, E. J. *The Conspiracy Against Silver; or, A Plea for Bi-Metallism in the United States.* New York: Greenwood Press, 1969; originally published by Hiles and Caggshall, 1886.

FAY, STEPHEN. *Beyond Greed.* New York: Viking Press, 1982.

FERGUSON, ADAM. *When Money Dies: The Nightmare of the Weimar Collapse.* London: William Kimber, 1975.

FLEETWOOD, WILLIAM, BISHOP OF ELY. *Chronicon-Preciosum, or, An Account of English Gold & Silver Money, The Price of Corn and other Commodities and of Stipends, Salaries, Wages,*

Jointures, Portions, Day-Labour, etc. in England for Six Hundred Years Last Past. New York: August M. Kelley, 1969, reprint; originally published in London by T. Osborne, 1707, 1745.

GOUGE, WILLIAM M. *A Short History of Paper-Money and Banking in the United States and an Inquiry into the Principles of the System.* Gouge was an adviser to President Andrew Jackson. This was his 1833 report to President Jackson but is still very sound and valuable for our time. Completely reprinted in Samuelson's *Economic History of the United States.*

GRANT, MICHAEL. *Roman Imperial Money.* London: Thomas Nelson & Sons, 1954.

GROSECLOSE, ELGIN. *Money and Man: A Survey of Monetary Experience,* 4th ed. Norman: University of Oklahoma Press, 1976; originally published under the title *Money: The Human Conflict* in 1934.

———. *The Silken Metal, Silver: Past, Present, Prospective.* Washington, DC: Institute for Monetary Research, 1975.

———. *Silver as Money: The Monetary Services of Silver.* Washington, DC: Institute for Monetary Research, 1965.

HEPBURN, ALONZO BARTON. *History of Coinage and Currency in the United States and the Perennial Contest for Sound Money.* New York: Greenwood Press, 1968; originally published by the Macmillan Company, 1903.

HILL, GEORGE FRANCIS. *Ancient Greek and Roman Coins.* Chicago: Argonaut, 1964.

———. *Historical Roman Coins.* London: Constable & Company, 1909.

HUGHES, ROBERT WILLIAM. *The American Dollar; and the Anglo-German Combination to Make Gold Dearer.* Richmond, VA: West, Johnston & Company, 1885.

JASTRAM, ROY W. *The Golden Constant: The English and American Experience, 1560–1976.* New York: John Wiley & Sons, 1977.

———. *Silver: The Restless Metal.* New York: John Wiley & Sons, 1981.

JENKINSON, CHARLES, FIRST EARL OF LIVERPOOL. *A Treatise on the Coins of the Realm in a Letter to the King.* New York: Augustus M. Kelley, Publishers, 1968; originally published in 1805; second edition in London by Effingham Wilson, 1880.

KRAUSE, CHESTER L., AND MISHLER, CLIFFORD. *Guidebook of Franklin Mint Issues.* Iola, WI: Krause Publications, 1982.

———. *Standard Catalog of World Coins.* Iola, WI: Krause Publications, 1984.

LEITCH, GORDON, JR., *From Dollar to Counterfeit: The Path of American Government Dishonesty.* Scappoose, OR: Bicentennial Era Enterprises, 1981.

———. *The Monetary Errors and Deceptions of the Supreme Court.* Scappoose, OR: Bicentennial Era Enterprises, 1978.

LEONG, YAU SING, *Silver: An Analysis of Factors Affecting Its Price.* Washington, DC: The Brookings Institution, 1934.

MILNE, JOSEPH GRAFTON. *Greek and Roman Coins and the Study of History.* Westport, CT: Greenwood Press, 1971; originally published London: Methuen & Company, 1939.

MOHIDE, THOMAS PATRICK. *The International Silver Trade.* Cambridge, Eng.: Woodhead Publishing, 1992.

———. *Silver.* Toronto: Ontario Ministry of Natural Resources, 1985.

NORTH, GARY. *Honest Money.* Fort Worth, TX: Dominion Press, and Nashville, TN: Thomas Nelson, copublishers, 1986.

ORESME, NICHOLAS BISHOP. *De Moneta.* Originally published in France in about 1360. Ours is a photocopy of an English translation of unknown origin.

SCHUETTINGER, ROBERT L., AND BUTLER, EAMONN F. *Forty Centuries of Wage and Price Controls.* Washington, D.C.: The Heritage Foundation, 1979.

SHAPIRO, MAX. *The Penniless Billionaires.* New York: Truman Talley Books—Times Books, 1980.

SHENFIELD, ARTHUR A. *The British Monetary Experience, 1797–1821.* Greenwich, CT: Committee for Monetary Research and Education, 1981.

THE SILVER INSTITUTE. *World Silver Survey, 1950–1990.* Washington, DC: The Silver Institute, 1990.

———. *World Silver Survey, 1991.* Washington, DC: The Silver Institute, 1991.

———. *World Silver Survey, 1992.* Washington, DC: The Silver Institute, 1992.

———. *World Silver Survey, 1993.* Washington, DC: The Silver Institute, 1993.

SMITH, JEROME F., AND SMITH, BARBARA KELLEY. *Silver Profits in the 80's: The Coming Boom in Silver, Gold and Platinum.* New York: Books in Focus, 1982.

STREETER, W. J. *The Silver Mania: An Exposé of the Causes of High Price Volatility of Silver.* Dordrecht: D. Reidel Publishing Company, 1984.

VIEIRA, EDWIN, JR. *Constitutional Authority of the States and the President to Intervene on Behalf of Sound Money with a Model Legal-Tender Act for State Legislatures.* Greenwich, CT: Committee for Monetary Research and Education, 1983.

———. *Pieces of Eight: The Monetary Powers and Disabilities of the United States Constitution: A Study in Constitutional Law.* Fort Lee, NJ: Sound Dollar Committee, 1983.

WEST, LOUIS C., AND JOHNSON, ALLAN CHESTER. *Currency in Roman and Byzantine Egypt.* Princeton, NJ: Princeton University Press, 1944.

WYLER, SEYMOUR B. *The Book of Old Silver.* New York: Crown Publishers, 1937.

YEOMAN, R. S. *A Guide Book of United States Coins.* Racine, WI: Western Publishing Company, 1980.

Index

Get the Latest News on Silver . . .

FREE

Call today for a FREE copy of *Gold Newsletter*

For decades, *Gold Newsletter* has let investors know when, where, and how to invest in precious metals. It has helped tens of thousands earn hundreds of millions.

And now in this powerful new bull market it can do the same for you.

GOLD NEWSLETTER:
The 24-Year Champion of Precious Metals Investors

Gold Newsletter was founded in 1971 as the official publication of the National Committee to Legalize Gold (NCLG). We were young and inspired back then, and we fought a successful campaign to repeal the ban on gold ownership. Since then, we've gone on to show tens of thousands of subscribers how to maximize their profits in gold, silver, platinum, and palladium.

Gold Newsletter is the only publication in the world with global, comprehensive coverage of ALL the precious metals. Each 16-page issue is packed with information that any serious silver and gold investor must have to profit in today's volatile markets.

In addition to complete analyses of the bullion markets, *Gold News-*

letter also covers world mining shares in depth. We feature the recommendations of leading experts, including regular articles by contributing editor Bob Bishop—recognized as the world's top mining share analyst. From North America to South America, from Africa to Australia and wherever there are new discoveries and opportunities, you'll find out about them in *Gold Newsletter*.

This one-of-a-kind publication also provides the latest fundamentals on precious metals, with authoritative supply/demand statistics and eyewitness reports from silver and gold markets in every corner of the world. You also get complete technical analyses, including reports from leading experts such as Bob Prechter, and information charts and graphs.

> "Whether it's mining shares, economic trends, political developments, or even monetary upheavals, if gold is part of the story, you'll find no more timely and authoritative a source for news than *Gold Newsletter*. It's the monthly bible for serious precious metals investors.
>
> —Lawrence W. Reed,
> Economist and President
> *The Mackinac Center for Public Policy*

(continued on next page)

Get a FREE copy . . .
or a full year's subscription for HALF PRICE!

As a reader of *Silver Bonanza* you qualify for a free sample issue of *Gold Newsletter,* or a full year's subscription at half price for just $49.50 for 12 issues (regularly $99.00).

I feel that this is one of the best investments available today. With your subscription to *Gold Newsletter,* you'll get quality information and advice you simply can't find anywhere else at any price.

Plus, you'll receive "An Investor's Guide to Gold Mutual Funds," a comprehensive guide written by industry expert Dennis Slothower. This massive, 48-page report includes a complete listing and review of gold and silver mutual funds. Plus, a powerful system for pinpointing which fund to buy and WHEN to buy it, a performance ranking of all funds since 1976, a strategy to potentially multiply your mutual fund returns while slashing your risk by up to half, and much, much more.

This is a great time to invest in silver, and a great opportunity to keep updated on the silver market through *Gold Newsletter.* I urge you to call now to get your free, no obligation copy of *Gold Newsletter,* or to sign up for a year at half price.

—James U. Blanchard III

CALL
1-800-877-8847